GERTRUDE BELL

Contemporary Issues in the Middle East

GERTRUDE BELL

THE ARABIAN DIARIES, 1913–1914

Edited by Rosemary O'Brien

With Photographs by Gertrude Bell

Syracuse University Press

*Frontispiece: Gertrude Bell at Quebbed Duris funerary monument in Lebanon,
during her first trip to the desert in 1900. Courtesy of the University of
Newcastle upon Tyne.*

LIBRARY OF CONGRESS CATALOGING-IN-PUBLICATION DATA

Bell, Gertrude Lowthian, 1868–1926

    [Diaries. Selections]

    Gertrude Bell : the Arabian diaries, 1913–1914 / edited by Rosemary
O'Brien.

        p. cm.

    Includes bibliographical references and index.

    ISBN 0-8156-0672-9 (alk. paper)

    1. Saudi Arabia—Description and travel.   2. Saudi Arabia—Social
life and customs.   3. Bell, Gertrude Lowthian, 1868–1926—Journeys—
Saudia Arabia.   4. Bell, Gertrude Lowthian, 1868–1926—Diaries.

    I. O'Brien, Rosemary.   II. Title.

DS208 .B35 2000

953.8'04—dc21   00-032986

To James L. O'Brien

Rosemary O'Brien is an editor and retired freelance journalist. She lives in Princeton, New Jersey.

Contents

Illustrations

Preface

I discovered Gertrude Bell's *Letters* while preparing for a trip to the Middle East in the 1980s. I knew at once that I wanted to write about this intrepid British woman who had traveled the Eastern deserts almost a century earlier. The opportunity to edit her previously unpublished Arabian diaries of 1913–1914 has made that wish a reality.

Diaries and reports such as Bell's provided the British Empire with the raw material that enabled it to govern large parts of the globe with little manpower. These documents were important in another way, enabling people who did not hold office to affect policy by virtue of their expertise. Clearly, Gertrude Bell sought fame and influence in this way. Note, for example, her diary comments about the decline of the Rashid family and the rise of Ibn Saud, her careful observations about water sources (valuable during the Great War), and her recording of which tribes guarded the Hejaz railway and their degree of friendliness toward Great Britain. This last element might earn for certain sheikhs subsidies of British gold in exchange for recognizing the hegemony of Great Britain, a matter of concern in areas of the Turkish Arabian desert adjacent to the subcontinent of India.

It was Gertrude Bell's custom to record her journeys in small notebooks and to sift through them afterward when drafting private reports, articles, or books. On the Arabian trip, however, she kept parallel records: Two notebooks were eventually filled with daily entries, which, cited as "Diaries," appear without revisions as appendixes to this volume. A third notebook contains a brilliant reshaping of the daily entry material, written for Charles Hotham Montague (Dick) Doughty-Wylie, a British army officer with whom Gertrude Bell was in love. Designated the "Doughty-Wylie Diaries" (or "D-W Diaries") they are the center-piece of my book.

The documents are housed in the Robinson Library at the University of Newcastle upon Tyne, the gift of Gertrude Bell's half sister Elsa Richmond. Although I have had the pleasure of reading the originals, my volume is based on a transcript of the diaries previously copied verbatim at the library. They appear here through the kind generosity of the library and the university.

Woven throughout my introduction to the material are excerpts from letters that Bell and Doughty-Wylie exchanged between 1913 and 1915. Some are related directly to her Arabian trip of 1913–1914; others were written in the aftermath of Bell's expedition. I use them for two reasons: to shed light on the intense inward feelings of two remarkable people, each possessing a rare appetite for adventure and romance, and to show how the collapse of an Edwardian world at war tore the fabric of their relationship.

Doughty-Wylie's letters (along with Bell's letters returned by him from Malta in April 1915) were in Gertrude Bell's possession at her death. Because he had no heirs, his letters reside in the Robinson Library as part of the Gertrude Bell Archive. They were given (with the originals) to the library in transcript form, composed by an unknown hand.

Where it seemed necessary, the D-W Diaries have been corrected in the interest of clarity, but the governing intention has been to present everything as written, including gaps in the narrative, misspellings, and so on. For example, on occasion Gertrude Bell used different versions of the same word, as in the surname of the Saudi leader Ibn Sa'ud, which appears also as Ibn Saud. Bell referred to her destination in north Arabia as Hayyil, but Hayil and Ha'il were used by others quoted in this book. Today it is called Hail, a modern city instead of the walled market town Gertrude knew. There seemed no reason to change these spellings as they reflect the usage of their day.

Bell did not employ Arabic transliterations for Damascus (Dimashq), Amman (Rabbas), or Jerusalem (El Kuds esh Sharif). Therefore, those and other transliterations, based on the *Times Atlas of the World,* tenth edition, are bracketed in the D-W Diaries only on their first appearance, for the sake of accuracy. It will also be noticed that the term *Arabs* was used by Gertrude Bell's caravan crew whenever they encountered or observed other people, even though they were Arabs themselves.

Readers will soon become used to Gertrude Bell's graceful and humorous literary style, and perhaps acquire an appreciation for the unusual circumstances in which she was writing, that is, hastily and at dusk, or in the dark of her tent at nightfall, after a long day in the *shedad* (a camel saddle used by women).

In addition to being a gifted writer, Gertrude Bell was an enthusiastic photographer, often developing her own film. She carried the latest in equipment, using a 4 x 4 Kodak in Arabia, with or without a telephoto lens, and she also employed a panoramic camera (Godfrey 1998). Her photos are used here to create a dialogue between text and picture in order to sharpen and clarify her observations and to show readers a world that has all but vanished under the impact of modern life.

Acknowledgments

I am deeply grateful to the Robinson Library of the University of Newcastle upon Tyne for permission to publish Gertrude Bell's Arabian diaries and certain personal letters between Bell and Charles Doughty-Wylie. Dr. Lesley Gordon, curator of the library's Special Collections, was unstinting in aiding my research, as were her colleagues Dr. Thomas Graham, the library's director, and J. G. Crow of the Department of Archaeology, who provided the photographs.

In Princeton I have benefited from the comments of Oleg Grabar, professor emeritus of Islamic art and culture, and Glen W. Bowersock, professor of ancient history, both of the School of Historical Studies of the Institute for Advanced Study. I am grateful to Dr. Terry Grabar for help with research. I thank various members of the staffs at the libraries of the Institute for Advanced Study and Princeton University for their assistance.

I owe a special debt to Dr. Letitia Ufford for suggestions and support. Patricia Hyatt of the Princeton Research Forum was a helpful reader, as were Kirby Hall, Claire Jacobus, and Marianne Grey. I thank Layla Asali for the glossary.

The staff at Syracuse University Press provided continuing assistance, especially the gracious and helpful editor Mary Selden Evans. As a copy editor, Annette Wenda helped me through the process of the final preparation of the manuscript.

Finally, I thank James L. O'Brien for his unflagging interest in my work, and for the many hours he spent on planes and in libraries while I traced the journey of Gertrude Bell. Writing may be a solitary occupation, but it can never come to fruition without the help and encouragement of others.

GERTRUDE BELL EN ROUTE

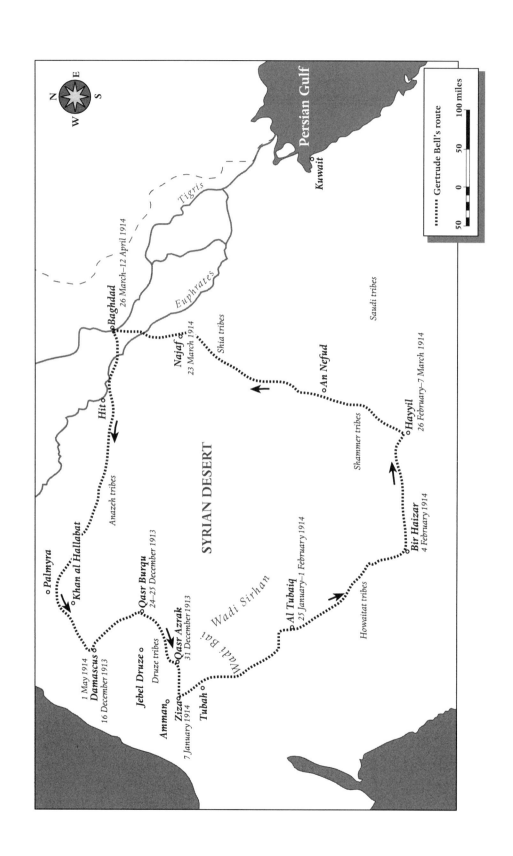

N
W · E
S

Persian Gulf

Kuwait

Tigris

Baghdad
26 March–12 April 1914

Euphrates

Najaf
23 March 1914

Shia tribes

Hit

Saudi tribes

An Nefud

Hayyil
26 February–7 March 1914

Shammer tribes

Anazeh tribes

SYRIAN DESERT

Palmyra

Khan al Hallabat

Bir Haizar
4 February 1914

Qasr Burqu
24–25 December 1913

Damascus
16 December 1913
1 May 1914

Jebel Druze
Druze tribes

Qasr Azrak
31 December 1913

Amman
Zizao
7 January 1914

Tubah

Wadi Bai

Wadi Sirhan

Al Tubaiq
25 January–1 February 1914

Howaitat tribes

········· Gertrude Bell's route

50   0   50   100 miles

Gertrude Bell en Route

On 16 January 1914, an expedition proceeding south from Damascus toward Arabia halted for the night. Gertrude Bell, catching the last rays of the sun, sat down before her tent to begin a special diary intended for Major Charles Hotham Montague Doughty-Wylie, a married man to whom she had a passionate attachment.

In its pages she created a unique and remarkable portrait of a woman explorer during her greatest journey. An Englishwoman who crossed gender and social boundaries to reach fame in the Middle East, she was also an archaeologist and a commentator on the politics of Turkish Arabia. In the 1920s she would become Oriental secretary to the British high commissioner in Baghdad. In that role she played a significant part in the formation of modern Iraq.

Bell loved "wild travel" (G. Bell 1985, v). And so in the autumn of 1913, at age forty-five, she had started the difficult and dangerous journey to Nejd (now Najd), a partly unmapped area of northern Arabia. She thought that somehow she might be able to chart new approaches to the oasis of Hayyil (now Hail), in Jabel Shammar, where she would interview the ruler of the town. If she succeeded she would write a book about it on her return to England. But a stronger and more personal motive lay behind the diaries and letters presented here.

For Bell, the East became the lover she could not have and a refuge from the bourgeois England of her family and friends. She yearned for freedom and found it, traveling the deserts of "the mysterious East" known to all Victorian children from the stories of *Arabian Nights*. She was fortunate in being able to profit from the examples of

3

Gertrude Bell. 1923. Sketch by John Singer Sargent.
Courtesy of the University of Newcastle upon Tyne.

unmarried Victorian women who had used their energy and intelligence to forge independent lives. She spent a large part of hers in a masculine world, yet never lost her feminine interest in clothes and gardening.

Who was this woman, the people of Hayyil must have wondered, when Gertrude Bell finally appeared in their midst in the late winter of 1914? Gertrude Margaret Lowthian Bell was born on 14 July 1868 in surroundings that inevitably contributed to her self-esteem. She could thank her grandfather Isaac Bell for her excellent position in the social hierarchy.

Isaac Bell's youth coincided with the birth of the Industrial Revolution. He studied technology in Germany and came home to expand his father's chemical business into a conglomerate. A boom in railroads in the 1840s created a demand for iron rails; Isaac supplied them and invested the profits in coal and other ventures. England reached its eminence in the world thanks to men such as Isaac Bell and his gifted friends Darwin and Huxley.

Isaac did not confine his interests to business. From 1875 to 1880, he served as a Liberal member of Parliament in Benjamin Disraeli's second ministry. That period saw a shift in British policy abroad from the pursuit of purely economic interests to an interventionist stance. Shares in the Suez Canal were purchased; British regiments occupied Afghanistan. The prime minister blocked Russian ambitions in the Mediterranean by throwing British weight on the side of an incompetent, corrupt Turkish Ottoman empire based in Constantinople. They needed it as a buffer. Gertrude Bell probably learned about international matters earlier than did most children. Her grandfather's political career may have held the key to her adult involvement in Britain's political fortunes.

While the blast furnaces of the family's ironworks sent smoke curling out over the North Sea, young Gertrude played in the nursery of her parents' red-brick mansion in nearby Redcar. The Bells were quintessential Victorian entrepreneurs who knew how to apply intelligence to hard work. They were soon absorbed into the English gentry in spite of being associated with "trade."

Although Bell's childhood was privileged, it was not ideal. Death was the great leveler of Victorian society. The loss of her mother when she was three could hardly have impressed itself on her memory, but its effects undoubtedly remained in the realm of feeling and action. A psychologist today might say her excessive dependence on her father was one sign of childhood trauma and might argue that lifelong bouts of depression and risky behavior were related.

Gertrude Bell was endowed from earliest childhood with a passion for reading, and she soon developed the intense curiosity that is the scholar's habit. Her arresting face, set in a head of reddish hair, signaled what she would become, a serious woman of high intelligence. Her upper lip gave a hint of another side of her temperament: a touch of sensuality, a curve of humor—these, too, would be characteristics of the older Gertrude, along with a powerful and manipulative political personality that surfaced in Iraq in the 1920s.

At age seven an orphaned child cannot help feeling ambivalent about a new parent. In 1877, Florence Olliffe, a Parisian who seemed as stiff as her corset, joined the Bell household as Gertrude's stepmother. She was not pretty, but she was thoughtful—and determined to inculcate in the child the concepts of duty and decorum, particularly since she had heard that Gertrude was undisciplined. It would be unfair, however, to charge Florence Bell with acting the part of the coldhearted stepmother of Victorian fiction. As a playwright and author of children's stories as well as a landmark study of workers at the Bell factories, called *At the Works,* she had a positive influence on Gertrude Bell's intellectual development. In fact, Florence Bell bore the marks of an early feminist, though undoubtedly she would have disdained the term. It would not be an exaggeration to suggest that Gertrude Bell's interest in education for Iraqi women in the 1920s stemmed from the period when, as a young woman, she accompanied her stepmother on rounds of ironworkers' houses to interview the wives. Recognizing the difficulties under which they toiled, Florence Bell organized lectures for them on health, household management, and other topics.

In 1884, Bell's parents sent her to Queen's College in London. From school she wrote lovingly to her father, who was busy with his activities as director of the Bell enterprises. Her letters to Florence Bell were correct, though often petulant, showing resentment of stepmotherly criticisms of her behavior. She made it quite plain that she was not afraid of her father's opinions, in contrast to her dislike of her stepmother's lectures about conduct.

Proximity to leading politicians and statesmen at the London home of Florence Bell's mother, and Bell's stepgrandmother, further stimulated the young student's interest in politics. Many of these public figures would become useful to her in her later career. It was the heyday of the British Empire, and she was exposed to the transcendent dogmas of imperialism whereby Britain had the right, even the duty, to rule and convert native peoples to Western ways. This self-imposed obligation was inspired by the needful economy of an island nation but was naturally described in altruistic terms. Besides economic benefits, empire offered excuses for a curious public to travel to remote outposts they had only dreamed of before the advent of trains, steamships, travel guides, and Thomas Cook and Son.

During this period, changes also were under way in the field of education for women. Since Cambridge opened its doors for women in 1863, women were routinely challenging assumptions that their intelligence was inferior to men's. Bell's teachers at Queen's College saw great promise in her schoolwork and urged her to go to university. But "the serious side of education was not part of the plan our mother made for us," her half sister Molly recalled (Morris 1977, 64). Indeed, most Victorians were known to fear for the health of the too well-educated female and thought she rarely made a good mother (Murray 1982, 213). Nevertheless, Gertrude Bell prevailed, no doubt because her father could seldom refuse her anything.

Oxford was still a cloistered bastion of male predominance in 1886, riddled with contempt for women scholars. Students such as Gertrude Bell, at Lady Margaret Hall, were virtually segregated because of the college's distance from the heart of town. The college visibly mirrored the ambiguity then surrounding the notion of higher education for women. Set apart in classes, forbidden to use the libraries or to receive degrees, they were in a cultural limbo, existing uncomfortably between the myth that using their brains would somehow damage their physiques and their need to put their minds to use. The fact that Oxford women were not permitted to read the "manly" subjects such as classical languages and mathematics did not distress Bell. She had decided to read modern history.

Her letters home were filled with amusing accounts of college life; in one she wrote that a certain lecturer was so disturbed by the presence of young women in his class that he "put us in seats with our backs turned to him" (Goodman 1985, 12). Many of her later writings confirm the influence of Oxford, particularly her theories about political development as a process of continuity from the first institutions to the higher stage of statehood, an idea prevalent among the so-called Whig historians of the Victorian period (Stubbs 1903, 1: 584).

Oxford left her with another legacy: smoking became her permanent habit. She flew around the campus in untidy clothes, a temporary lapse in a lifetime of fashionable dressing. What Florence Bell thought of these manifestations of rebellion can be only imagined, but the Lady Margaret headmistress, Elizabeth Wordsworth, the poet's niece, who envisioned her girls becoming "Adam's helpmates," wondered aloud if a person like Bell was suitable to have in one's bedroom if one were ill (Goodman 1985, 10).

At the end of two unorthodox years she learned that she would be awarded a first in modern history, a triumph for the school. She left in a swirl of balls and parties with friends of both sexes. The contrast between the heady possibilities of independence enjoyed at school and the sedate routines of home must have been sobering. Freedoms granted to the student did not apply equally at Redcar. A trip to London necessitated a chaperone; strolls in London's parks with males were forbidden even if they were friends. She spent the next few years tutoring the younger Bell siblings, relieved only by intervals spent abroad.

One eventful morning in 1892, the post brought a letter to Florence Bell from her sister Mary Lascelles, whose diplomat husband had just been assigned to Teheran. Would Gertrude like to come out for a visit? she asked. Persia, Bell avowed, was the place she had always wanted to see (L. Bell 1927, 1: 24). She immediately sent away for dictionaries in Farsi and Arabic. In April, accompanied by her aunt, her cousin Florence, and two maids, she boarded the Orient Express. The train moved silently eastward out of Paris, through the lighted suburbs and into the night.

Her letters make it clear that she fell at once into the absorbed fascination with novelty that marks the true traveler. She noted not only scenery but also what scenery has to say to a budding historical imagination: she described Constantinople, a city of domes guarding the eastern gates; the Caucasus, ablaze with flowers; camels tossing their heads as they traipsed along caravan trails toward the bazaars; and British residencies where imperial agents kept eyes on the politics of Ottoman Turkey.

After a journey of several weeks by land and sea Bell got her first glimpse of the mud-walled desert town called Teheran. Gardens were unaccountably aflame with roses growing out of the sands. From her bedroom windows she heard nightingales. This world was turned upside down for the twenty-four year old. On daily desert gallops Bell and her cousin were accompanied by a handsome legation secretary named Gerald Cadogan. Before long he and Bell were reading poetry together and roaming around summer palaces where they ate peaches and figs and spoke of the future. Soon they decided to marry.

As before, Gertrude Bell acted on impulse, first accepting the proposal and then telegraphing the news to her parents. The Bells did not approve; they had heard of Cadogan's reputation as a gambler who might be looking for a rich wife. Their daughter was summoned home to England, and not long afterward, as if aware of the opportunity for melodrama, fate disposed of Cadogan. He caught fever and died.

Gertrude was desolate. Her natural ebullience finally rescued her; she discovered that she could write. In 1894, her book *Persian Pictures* appeared. Three years later, her heart still lingering in Persian rose gardens, she published a respected translation of the fourteenth-century poems of the renowned Persian poet Hafiz.

Her representations of Persian life were in many details consistent with the dismissive attitudes of Westerners regarding the inhabitants of imperial outposts. Describing in *Persian Pictures* a plague that swept through Teheran during her 1892 visit she noted that with an epidemic knocking at their doors, the Persians were paralyzed by inaction. They made no effort to quarantine patients or bury the dead, leaving the dying on the streets to spread contagion. This passivity she attributed to Oriental fatalism, which, in her opinion, prevented people from seizing their own destiny.

Further, she characterized the mysterious life in the East as "an existence so different, so misty and unreal, incomprehensible, at any rate unfathomable; a life so monotonous, so unvaried from age to age that it does not present any feature marked enough to create an impression other than that of a vague picturesqueness . . . of repose turned to lethargy" (G. Bell 1928a, 60–61).

Writing was not her only consolation in the aftermath of her Persian experience. She began a series of daring Alpine ascents. In 1902, on the Finsteraarhorn she barely managed to avert disaster during a fierce storm by holding onto several companions by rope while clinging to an icy pinnacle.

Certainly adventure was one way to banish boredom; or was it a sign of some other wish? The issue of suicidal behavior cannot be dismissed in view of Bell's death from an overdose of sleeping pills in Baghdad in 1926. Aside from her daring, sometimes rash, behavior, it is possible, though rare, to discover signs of depression in her writings. As time would show, however, she concealed volcanic emotions beneath the typical English reluctance to expose personal feelings. The truth was that she was leading an emotionally threadbare existence.

Spinsterhood, after all, did not provide much emotional satisfaction. Removed from the temptations and delights of country-house weekends where the flirtations of the smart set lent spice to rounds of bridge, shooting, and bedroom assignments according to current attachments, Bell was left to act as a doting figure to younger siblings and to find the crumbs of social life among married friends, all the while sublimating, in authorship and seeking new adventures abroad, the sexuality that had been awakened in Persia. After the Finsteraarhorn experience, she jauntily remarked that "there was a time when I thought it on the cards [sic] that we should not get down alive" (L. Bell 1927, 1: 145). Bell seems to have sought danger as an aphrodisiac, possibly the expression of thwarted sexuality.

Thus, as the new century dawned on the continued well-being of Britain and her glorious empire, Gertrude Bell reached her thirties seeking a role for herself.

Because the expanding British Empire facilitated touring, women's travel began to present an attractive diversion for the rich. Sometime in 1900, Bell took on a new role, something quite unexpected for a woman of her class—fusing polite travel with an explicit form of information gathering.

At the time, espionage was considered a vulgar profession; an official secret-service bureau was not established in London until 1908, when German imperial ambitions aroused British concerns. Until then, the British Foreign Office routinely used unpaid amateurs (or an occasional adventurer seeking cash) to report on their observations abroad. This system worked reasonably well in tropical countries where British officers were stationed; however, isolated, sparsely populated places such as the Middle Eastern deserts presented serious difficulties. Britain's trading position in the Persian Gulf—where telegraph offices were rare, camel tracks made do for roads, and few travelers spoke Arabic—called for someone of Bell's interests and linguistic abilities.

It is likely that Bell owed her debut as an informal agent to her friendship with a circle of empire boosters close to Foreign Secretary Edward Grey. At any rate, official documents confirm that before 1915, when she formally joined British Intelligence in Cairo at the Arab Bureau, "she had been in the employ [without pay, of course] of the Intelligence Division of the Admiralty" (PRO, L/P&S 10/576).

Whether to call Bell an actual spy matters little. From 1900 until the Great War, she monitored the political pulse of Arabic Turkey; in the tents of powerful Arab sheikhs and the divans of Ottoman officials she spent hours sipping coffee, asking questions, and honing her insights into the state of affairs. According to the social ideas of the time, no one was likely to suspect their honored guest of espionage.

Her new career coincided with a lull in British influence in Constantinople. Sultan Abdul Hamid II's efforts at reforming his crumbling empire were concentrated on retraining his army under German military officers.

Frequently, the king's delegates cooled their heels in the outer waiting rooms of the sultan's palace while German diplomats hobnobbed with the sultan inside. The British Foreign Office regarded German merchants and others setting up shop along the Persian Gulf as competitors and a hostile presence at the back door to India. London was curious to know just how far Germans had penetrated Turkish provinces in Syria, Mesopotamia, and north Arabia. More particularly, were they attempting to poison Arab minds against the British? On her many trips to the East in the first decade of the twentieth century, Bell tried to find answers to these questions for the Foreign Office in London (L. Bell 1927, 1: 252).

It was not her style to stalk her targets in the dead of night. She boldly collected evidence in broad daylight. At the crusader castle at Kerak in March 1900, then used as barracks by German officers for training Turkish soldiers, she reported to her parents that she "walked calmly in, in an affable way, [and] greeted all the soldiers politely." No doubt she made careful notes later (ibid., 73).

At tea with Princeton University archaeologists in Damascus in 1907, she raised no suspicions of her possible involvement in espionage. One of them recalled that she was "dressed in a becoming tailor made suit, a bunch of violets at her waist, some fluffy tulle with a little embroidery in front." Her hosts were impressed by her manner, which they deemed was "found only in women of the highest social rank" (Waldron 1989, 20).

Bell began to find that her budding interest in archaeology provided a useful cover for her presence in southern Mesopotamia (modern Iraq), where German excavators were at work. She developed an expertise in early Islamic architecture and published her findings in books and technical journals.

In 1909, she used German digging methods to study a site in the desert west of the Euphrates near Babylon that she described as the "so enchanting palace of Ukhaidir" (G. Bell 1911, 255). For several years, she worked on her drawings and photographs, attempting to reconstruct the site that she believed contained a mosque of the early-Islamic period.

Certainly, a romantic sensibility about the transitory nature of time and the world fueled her curiosity about the forgotten past. She wrote in 1911:

> Most of us who have had the opportunity to become familiar with some site that has once been the theatre of some vanished civilization have passed through hours of vain imaginings . . . to recapture the aspect of street and market, church or Temple enclosure, of which the evidences lie strewn upon the earth. And even as a thousand unanswerable problems surge up I have found myself longing for an hour out of a remote century, wherein I might look my fill upon the walls that have fallen and stamp the image of a dead world indelibly upon my mind. (Ibid., 143)

The romantically imagined past invited comparison to the lamentable present, particularly the shortcomings of the Turkish administration in its Arab dependencies. There was no central government in the desert, hence no central authority to maintain order. Intertribal warfare was a way of life and a cause of unceasing bloodshed and mayhem. The populations lived in poverty and ignorance. The sultan's position, she wrote, "is that of an alien, governing with a handful of soldiers and an empty purse, a mixed collection of subjects hostile to him and each other" (G. Bell 1985, 139).

Far from improving the situation, the 1908 overthrow of the corrupt bureaucracy in Constantinople by reform-minded intellectuals and Turkish military officers (Young Turks) increased Arab resentment. In her books Bell stressed the need for a British administration similar to the one in Egypt.

It was during her travels in the Middle East that Bell met two dashing Englishmen whose destinies would converge with her own. The first man would pave the way for her rise as a political force in Iraq

T. E. Lawrence. Official photograph,
c. 1914. Courtesy of the Imperial War Museum,
London.

before gaining fame himself as a phenomenon of imperialism in the Middle East and an icon of modern sexual confusion. He was Thomas Edward Lawrence, the illegitimate second son of an impoverished Irish baronet and the governess who cared for his children. The pair fled to Oxford, adopting the name Lawrence, thus providing a precedent for their son, who became, successively, TEL, Lawrence of Arabia, Airman Ross, and Private Shaw, a telling confusion of identities (Mack 1976, 26–29). TEL and Gertrude Bell became friends after their first encounter at an archaeological dig in southern Turkey in 1911, united by their common belief in British imperial destiny in the Middle East.

Bell's fateful involvement with the second man began in Konia in Asia Minor where she stopped to pick up her mail on her way back home from Syria in 1906. It happened to be an unsettling moment for British fortunes in the Ottoman Empire.

Konia, an ancient Seljuk capital, was the hub of the southern Turkish leg of the new Berlin-Baghdad railway. German financial backing had cemented Germany's position in Turkey. The Turks had granted the railway company transfers of public land along the tracks as well as broad rights to archaeological investigations (Earle 1923, 63). By this arrangement the sultan strengthened his grasp of the Arab countryside as well as his hold on army troops stationed far from Constantinople. Germany, among other things, used archaeological excavations as devices to introduce German influence and culture into the area and excavators as a means of keeping Berlin informed (Marchand 1996, 209).

Bell called on the British military vice-consul in Konia. He looked up at her with hooded eyes, which she would learn were a clue to a mystical nature. Charles (Dick) Doughty-Wylie was balding, mustached, and exactly her age. A product of Winchester and Sandhurst, his family members were solid country people from Suffolk, and his uncle was the great Arabian traveler Charles Doughty. Each knew the other by reputation. He was familiar with her books. She had heard of his medal-winning exploits in China and South Africa. In Konia he and his wife entertained a parade of guests at their table, and Bell, among them, failed to notice the grip her hostess had on her husband. Gertrude returned home to write another book.

On the outbreak of the 1912 Balkan war, the Doughty-Wylies were sent to Constantinople by the British Red Cross to organize hospital units for Turkish casualties. Early in 1913, Dick returned alone to his bachelor flat on Half-Moon Street in London to await another assignment. He and Gertrude Bell renewed their acquaintance. If she had been a novelist, Bell might have recognized a familiar plot, suitable for melodrama, in her enchantment with Dick. They were quickly drawn together by a shared sense of loneliness and her belief that he would have been her perfect mate. Once again, as in Persia twenty years earlier, she was madly in love. And, as before, the situation was impossible.

Their letters constitute an excursion into late-Victorian romanticism. His are filled with poetic images of an enclosed garden, his metaphor for their relationship. Invoking, as he consistently did, the pleasures of the mind instead of the body must have seemed a rather breathtaking evasion to a woman long deprived of earthly love. How unfulfilling for her to read in his letters about an imaginary place where the two of them might dwell together in spiritual, if

Major Charles Doughty-Wylie. n.d. Photographer unknown. Courtesy of the University of Newcastle upon Tyne.

not physical, union. It was the latter that Bell both feared and desired, having learned that attachments could be ephemeral. She wanted a commitment; he could not give it. Thus, they reached an impasse that neither was able to resolve. "If you knew the way I have paced backwards and forwards on the floor of hell for the past few months," Bell wrote a friend before leaving for Arabia in November 1913, "you would think me right to try and find any way out" (Winstone 1978b, 132). There would be consolation in the desert. Rumors of increasing Arab displeasure with Turkish rule were an added enticement.

Immersion once again in Arab politics—an expedition to Hayyil—offered the perfect way out. Against all advice, she persisted in her plans. Her friend and fellow archaeologist David Hogarth said that "she had reason to know that [her] project would not be approved either by the Ottoman authorities or by the chief representative of Great Britain in Turkey" (Hogarth 1927, 1). That extra fillip of the forbidden probably made the trip more appealing.

"My dear," Dick wrote that autumn, as she made plans to leave England, "I want to see you but that of course can't be until God pleases—my dear, I wish you the best of luck on your adventure, and may all run easy for you . . . someday perhaps we will do a trek together" (Charles Doughty-Wylie to Gertrude Bell, 6 Oct. 1913). To speak so lightly about danger was part of the sangfroid of prewar Edwardian culture. In truth, she was going headlong into a thicket of tribal war, a place few Westerners had entered and only then when compelled by important errands.

The two major warring tribes in Nejd, the Rashids and the Sauds, were in 1913 proxies of Turkey and Britain, respectively. Even the Turks had long since given up the attempt to assert dominance over Nejd. One result was constant skirmishing for power among the bedouins. One particular family, the Sauds, conquered large portions of the area in the 1830s. Followers of a purifying Muslim sect known as Wahabism, they established their capital at Riyadh.

Restlessly, they pushed eastward toward the Persian Gulf, only to be checked by British power exercised from India. British officials, although initially eschewing involvement in the isolated Arabian interior, limited Saudi reach by establishing a network of treaties up and down the coast with local rulers, thus also holding Turkey at bay. The sultan was reduced to seeking allies among Saudi opponents, settling finally on members of the Shammar federation known as the Rashids. A particularly cruel and violent tribe, ostensible agents of the Saudi state, the Rashids in the 1840s consolidated their position at Hayyil. By the 1880s they succeeded in inciting disaffected tribes, temporarily unseating the Sauds in the environs of Hayyil (Winder 1980, 104).

By the time of Bell's proposed penetration of Nejd, the Sauds, relying on infusions of British gold and weapons, were in possession of most of the Arabian peninsula and were poised to defeat the Rashids. Captain William Shakespear hurried from the British residency in Kuwait to Riyadh to discuss increasing the British subsidy. He hoped that he might be able to prevent the outbreak of a general tribal war. Ironically, Shakespear would be killed fifteen months later in the vanguard of the Saudi cavalry fighting the Rashids. Autumn 1913 was hardly an auspicious time for a woman to pack her bags for Arabia.

Thirty years earlier, Lady Anne Blunt, the only woman to visit Hayyil before Bell, went there with her husband to buy Arabian horses. Charles Doughty, Dick's geologist uncle, departed Damascus in the early 1870s in a pilgrimage caravan, beginning a two-year migration along the border between the Syrian and the Arabian deserts with two visits to Hayyil. Both Lady Blunt and Doughty wrote of their Arabian experiences, and Bell plunged into reading them with the same enthusiasm she showed for scouting ancient Islamic ruins.

Doughty's *Arabia Deserta* is notably eccentric in style. T. E. Lawrence described his idiosyncratic prose as "so tense, so just in its words and phrases that it demands a just reader" (Doughty 1979, 27). For Bell it became a travel bible. In one passage Doughty, having just arrived, was not sure of his welcome. "I sat . . . in the midst of Hayil [*sic*], meanwhile they debated perhaps of my life within yonder earthen walls of the castle" (637).

Lady Blunt assumed that she and her husband would be received with the respect due their station as upper-class Britons. Yet, after a minor misunderstanding with the ruler of Hayyil, she wryly observed in her *Pilgrimage to Nejd* that "[it] was a lesson and a warning, a lesson that we were Europeans still among Asiatics, a warning that Hail [*sic*] was a lions den, though fortunately we were friends with the lion" (1881, 2: 21). Gertrude Bell would never have admitted being afraid of a lion.

HOSTAGE AT HAYYIL

Damascus in November 1913 was awash in the bright colors of autumn. Bell called on old friends and toured the bazaars to buy provisions and purchase camels for the expedition.

Organizing a caravan was an art in itself as well as an expensive proposition. For a journey of the duration she had in mind she was advised to take seventeen camels: "they cost an average of 17£ a piece including their gear. I must reckon to spend 50£ on food to take with us, 50£ for presents such as cloaks, *keffeyehs* for the head, cotton cloth, etc." (L. Bell 1927, 1: 309). Her packing list was only the beginning.

Although her caravan would be small in comparison to traditional merchant or pilgrim convoys, Bell's assembled baggage also included a set of dishes, silverware, linens, the complete Shakespeare and other books, at least two cameras, binoculars, cosmetics, and medicines for various contingencies (Wallach 1996, 106). She would also carry a tent, a portable bathtub, a folding chair and desk, guns, and surveying instruments provided by the Royal Geographical Society. It was part of Edwardian sensibility to endure the discomforts of travel in style.

There were two elements vital to the success of any expedition. First was the caravan leader and his crew. Bell needed to hire perhaps a

Muhammad al-Ma'rawi. February 1914. Photograph by Gertrude Bell. Courtesy of the University of Newcastle upon Tyne.

half-dozen men. Unfortunately, her servant Fattuh, who always came from Aleppo to accompany her in the desert, was ill with fever. Fearful of delay, she decided to depart without him and meet him later at Amman.

Bell's search for an experienced guide ended at dinner in a Damascus restaurant early in December when she met and hired a man named Muhammad al-Ma'rawi. He came with the highest recommendations, and what is more, he knew the young *amir* (ruler) of the Rashids whom she hoped to meet. Bell hired al-Ma'rawi on the spot and thereafter referred to him in her diaries as "M." or "M al M." Muhammad became a vital part of her crew as its leader. He saw to it that the men observed bedouin etiquette of personal honor and courtesy. Resourceful in the face of certain danger, he led his crew through the desert places, the gravelly plains of the Syrian desert called the Hamad, and the largely uncharted Nefud, the nearly impassable mountainous barrier of red sand dunes that separated the Nejd from Syria.

Equally important to the survival of the expedition was that life-sustaining resource: water. The "true" desert of Nejd, in contrast to the more moderate environment of southern Syria, promised virtually no water or vegetation except after winter rains nor hardly any human settlements where food and fodder might be found. One of the legacies in Syria of the eastern Roman Empire of the first century A.D. was the placement of military outposts at important water sources in the desert. Even as moldering ruins they still functioned as gathering places for all who suffered thirst. Caravan routes, literally chains of roads linking one water hole to the next, were an early version of the modern highway. Further south in Nejd, trails dwindled to nothing.

In view of contradictory rumors about the state of tribal warfare, Bell decided to push off from Damascus on the morning of Tuesday, 16 December 1913. She tucked Dick's last letters into her carryall. Even though he had burned all of hers, she would keep his. "Might we have been man and woman as God made us and been happy?" he wondered. "I know what you felt, what you would do and why not—but still and after all you don't know—that way lies a great and splendid thing, but for you all sorts of dangers—" (Charles Doughty-Wylie to Gertrude Bell, 23 Nov. 1913).

Riding down from Damascus to meet her party at its staging ground, she noted "Apricots all in golden leaf, corn springing under the olives, peasants gathering olives" (G. Bell 1913–1914, 16 Dec. 1913). The first days of the winter journey were uneventful. The caravan plodded along on icy volcanic ground, rarely meeting another soul, but a speck of movement or a puff of smoke on the horizon might be cause for concern. "Every Arab in the desert fears the other," one of her men remarked (ibid., 3 Jan. 1914).

Predictably, one morning a shot rang out over her head. A horseman came riding up from behind a dune and circled around her party "like a madman," brandishing a sword and attempting to rob her men of their pistols and cartridges. But for the appearance of two friendly sheikhs, she might have had to turn back. This inauspicious beginning only served as a reminder that for all their aristocratic adherence to a code of honor, bedouin men were raised to consider looting a normal activity. It was generally thanks to the employment of tribal intermediaries (*rafiqs*) that travelers avoided ambush or even murder.

Through the mid-December days she rode onward in rain and fog. At her side Muhammad would dispense various bits of information. "In Taimal, says M. [al-Ma'rawi], there are women who have had from thirty to forty husbands," Bell recorded without even a dash of skepticism (ibid., 22 Dec. 1913).

The party spent Christmas Eve at an abandoned castle (*qasr*) called Burqu, a relatively unknown site with possible Roman remains. It was now a rubble of dark stones scattered along the edge of a water hole. It was a night of particular beauty—starlight cast the remains of a blackened tower into relief, and her camp was enveloped in quiet. The next morning, Bell rose early and without too much regret about missing Christmas at home went climbing among the ruins, measuring and photographing.

The new year began with fresh apprehensions. She turned eastward toward the Ziza station of the Hijaz railway, where she planned to meet Fattuh. She hoped to avoid Turkish soldiers patrolling the area. The attitude of bedouins toward foreigners was generally friendly if they were accompanied by guides, but the same was not true of Turkish officials. In the first place, the sultan, as religious head (caliph) of all Islam, did not make it easy for non-Muslims to traverse the desert provinces. The governors-general of the settled towns, jealous of their powers, had the prerogative of denying permits to any travelers they deemed intruders. Bell had hoped to be able to dodge anyone who might demand to see papers that she did not possess. Unfortunately, on returning to her camp after fetching Fattuh she found three soldiers waiting for her and soon counted a dozen more riding in her direction.

It was a confusing scene. Telegrams flew back to Constantinople regarding the foreign woman; the local Turkish representatives entertained her, uncertain whether to make her turn back or allow her to go on. She was sure, however, that if she had to leave without permission, Turkish soldiers would not follow her very far into the desert.

One afternoon, during this suspenseful period, she attended a wedding, watching with interest as the colorfully dressed guests danced to the music of an accordion, with one man beating time with two sticks. Afterward, she was taken to a nearby house to meet the heavily veiled bride, who had stayed inside during the festivities. According to custom, she noted, the groom would not appear until evening (G. Bell 1913–1914, 14 Jan. 1914).

That same night, Bell signed a document absolving everyone for her safety, and the next morning she rode out of Amman, a free spirit. It pleased her, she wrote, to think that she was now an outlaw. The desert yawned before her, open and "terrifying." Unable, for the time being, to communicate with Doughty-Wylie and having posted her final letters to the rest of the world, she opened a notebook and began a diary for Dick, writing on alternate nights.

Using her daily abbreviated notes to refresh her memory, she described for him the quotidian events of the journey—the sound of a rifle shot that might signal malign intentions of a hostile tribe, a desert shrub in flower, a pond filled with water, a sky alight with stars. She transformed these minutiae into narratives that rank with the century's best travel literature.

A water hole. January 1914. Photograph by Gertrude Bell. Courtesy of the University of Newcastle upon Tyne.

At night after the tents were raised, the camels tethered, and dinner consumed, she joined her men by the coffee fire to hear tales describing past battles and otherwise famous incidents of history and Arabia's great heroes, who exemplified the best of the Arab character.

Bell preferred the company of men wherever she was. She shared their interests and ideas, and women did not usually claim her attention. Not surprisingly, given her contrary nature, she joined the antisuffragette campaign in England. In Arabia, however, she lingered in the bedouin harems, those special areas set aside for females. During the last week of January 1914, when she was a guest at an encampment of the Howaitat tribe, she recorded conversations with some of the Howaitat women.

Sensing a possibly sympathetic ear, the women confided in her the difficulties of their existence. They lived constantly on the move. They ate meager diets of dates and camel milk (and occasionally starved during harsh winters). Their responsibilities included the rugged tasks of setting up and striking the tents, filling the water skins, and preparing food, They gathered camel dung for fires, and often bore the agonies of pain of mothers whose children die of disease and cold (see Appendix 1).

Bell caught some of these women on film for her photographic archive. In spite of the fact that her photographs generally are descriptive rather than composed, as one might expect of documents intended primarily for archaeological purposes, she possessed a sharp eye for composition and the aesthetic potential of the interplay of black and white.

In a snapshot of the Howaitat Sheikh's harem at Tor al-Tubaiq, the dark clothes of the women are balanced against patches of light; a tent pole just off-center stands against the low webbing of the black panels of the tent. On the left, his head invisible but his more elaborate costume contrasted to the sacklike garb of the harem, stands the sheikh, holding his long cloak aside to reveal a beautifully woven belt. This picture captures the cramped existence of the bedouin women. The sheikh appears unconfined by the small dimensions of the tent, while the females crouch together on one side, staring tentatively at the camera.

Bell was now in the third month of her journey, still making copious daily notes about the terrain she crossed and the tribes she met. These details were important for geographers and government officials unacquainted with the territory. Rain had filled cisterns along the way, a sight that should have filled her with pleasure. Instead, a dark depres-

sion began to cloud her spirits. She felt terribly alone and had a sinking feeling that the game was not worth the candle. She was enough of a realist to know that despair at this moment was not only pointless but even dangerous.

If she had received Dick's letters as they trailed her through the desert her dark mood might have lifted. "You give me a new world, you give me the key to your heart," Dick had written at the end of December, "though I have friends, some of them women, even a wife, they are as far removed from the garden where we walk as east from west. . . . I have looked out on the world and felt

Turkiyyeh, Bell's friend at Hayyil. February 1914. Photograph by Gertrude Bell.
Courtesy of the University of Newcastle upon Tyne.

alone and turned to dreams and philosophy and the worship of quiet death." Reflecting on a lonely New Year's Eve with his father in the country (his wife was estranged from his family and stayed away), Dick promised, in imagination, to "sit by your tent and when you sit on your camel and go rocketing away I'll leave my heart in your lap" (Charles Doughty-Wylie to Gertrude Bell, 28 Dec. 1913).

By mid-February, Bell entered a desolate and unmapped part of the Nefud, where she made some important topographical measurements. At noon on the nineteenth she had decided to divert her path slightly to the southeast. She then took her first bearings, working against a bitter wind. She surveyed "an awful landscape, terrifying in its desolation." A wilderness of stone, with blackened crags, ran along one side of her path. "Good God," one of the men exclaimed. "We have come into hell" (G. Bell 1913–1914, 20 Feb. 1914). This nightmarish geography was a fitting prelude to her captivity at Hayyil for eleven days.

On 25 February she was led by a steward named Ibrahim to lodgings in a summer palace in the south wall of the town. The local *amir,* age sixteen and the last weak link in a line of murdered predecessors, was away raiding his neighbors. Ibrahim declined to give assurances about when his guest might leave.

A week passed, and her only companions were the inhabitants of the harem, one of whom became her particular friend. She was named Turkiyyeh because of her Turkish background. Her conversations had a Scheherazade-like quality. She related at length, and on several occasions, the story of her life. She had been kidnapped as a young girl and sold into bondage, and eventually sold again to the ruler of Hayyil. She had at first been unhappy, but then the ruler married her off to a good man. Presumably, her task was to relate to Fatima, the *amir's* grandmother, whatever she had managed to learn about Bell. This mysterious older figure kept herself hidden somewhere in the harem, but Gertrude suspected she, and a eunuch named Sa'id, were the sinister powers behind the throne.

One dark evening Bell was escorted by several torch-carrying slaves through the narrow streets of Hayyil to visit the palace. Ibrahim received her in a large hall with carpets and cushions scattered about. She was too preoccupied to enjoy listening to his stories about the founding of the Rashid dynasty. Finally, with the intervention of two 'Anazeh visitors (present in Hayyil as potential Rashid allies against Ibn Saud), and a good word on her behalf to Fatima by Turkiyyeh, Bell was informed by Sa'id that her caravan could leave. In what might have been a bizarre conflict with Fatima and Sa'id over the fate of their prisoner, Ibrahim soon died of a knife wound. It is a tantalizing but unanswerable question: was Bell's life in the balance?

At Hayyil, she had uncovered some clues to conditions in the Rashid court and observed the characteristics of daily life among town-dwelling Arab women. As the only Western woman ever sequestered in their arbitrary world, she had an opportunity to match the commonplaces of Edwardian drawing rooms to the reality of harem life. The normal practice of polygamy, a custom that Westerners viewed as a confirmation of Eastern decadence, was a prime example. The historian Albert Hourani has pointed out that under Muslim law, men could have several wives, divorce them by "a simple form of words before witnesses," and keep concubines, too (1991, 120). Muhammad al-Ma'rawi had once told Bell that "Arabs divorce in the morning and marry at night" (G. Bell 1913–1914, 22 Dec. 1913).

Westerners, viewing these arrangements from inside their own conceptual framework, ignored the inequities of their own societies. Curious readers might thus wonder how objective they could have been as commentators. Descriptions by returned travelers often read like dark fables, or, as some might insist, like imperialist discourses showing the East in full-blown decay.

In the eighteenth century, Lady Mary Wortley Montague, wife of the British ambassador to Turkey, examined life in the sultan's seraglio. She was amused by what she believed was a unique but not displeasing

way of containing the female sensuality that Muslim men were believed to find objectionable (Halsband 1970, 91). In a less tolerant period, the Victorian traveler Harriet Martineau, an English writer visiting Egypt in 1847, declared after a single visit to a harem that polygamy and the segregation of women were "hell on earth" (Melman 1995, 137).

The required veils had critics as well as adherents. Charles Doughty thought the Arabs "churlish" to cover women's faces,

Seated woman in the harem at Hayyil. February 1914. Photograph by Gertrude Bell. Courtesy of the University of Newcastle upon Tyne.

while many European Orientalist painters found the veil had erotic appeal.

Bell, coming from a world in which women's rights were being debated, saw polygamy's more pernicious implications. No feminist herself, yet she could not accept that the harems of Arabia had the burden of being war booty, frequently exchanged. "Here were these women," she wrote, "wrapped in Indian brocades, hung with jewels, served by slaves. . . . [T]hey pass from hand to hand. . . . [T]he victor takes them, his hands bloody from murdering their husbands and children" (G. Bell 1913–1914, 6 Mar. 1914).

This quote surely is one of the most vivid descriptions left to us from Western female travel in the Middle East; it ranks with Anne Blunt's stunning, if inadvertent, juxtaposing of the description of the Rashid ruler's zoo at Hayyil to that of his harem of tame female creatures (1881, 1: 224–34).

What lesson did Bell derive from her experience? With her focus on the diminishing political prospects for the Rashids future, she did not come away with a zeal for changing the women's lives; in fact, she had registered her dislike of "women's rule" at the court. Only later, in Iraq, did she actively pursue the idea of offering education to Arab women. But, riding toward Baghdad in March 1914, she contemplated her reactions.

She realized that she might fear the lion after all. She recognized it now: "that little restiveness of the mind, like a very fresh horse that keeps on straining at the reins . . . you know the feeling in your hands like an irregular pulse." Still, she admitted, she relished the excitement of it. "But what's very singular about it is that I don't really dislike it." Nor did she attempt to hide the letdown that accompanied each adventure. "[It] always leaves one with a feeling of disillusion. . . . I try to school myself beforehand by reminding myself how I have looked forward . . . to the end, and when it came have found it—just nothing. Dust and ashes in one's hand" (G. Bell 1913–1914, 26 Mar. 1914).

In Baghdad at the end of March, she packed up her diary for Dick and sent it off to him in Addis Ababa, where he was now British representative to a commission marking the southern boundary of Abyssinia (modern Ethiopia). He responded enthusiastically: "My dear, I have read your travel diary with the deepest interest. . . . Of course you will write of this rare journey for it's a great feat—to me it is a fine thing well and finely done, difficulties and dangers surmounted" (Charles Doughty-Wylie to Gertrude Bell, 30 Apr. 1914).

In spite of Dick's compliments, she found the rest of the trip tedious and bore the journey west from Baghdad with ill-concealed impatience. It was too much to expect otherwise, and when finally she rode into Damascus on the first of May, saddle-sore and not at all sure of what she had accomplished, she was utterly exhausted. Even after resting at the house of friends, her dreams were troubled by images of camels shuffling across the sands.

A JOURNEY ENDED

Although Bell was awarded the Royal Geographical Society's gold medal for her trip, the criteria for success in any kind of expedition generally applied only to men; there were no models for women as heroes. Yet, by any standard, Bell had earned the name. She had traveled far on a solitary journey to places partly unknown and had outwardly kept her nerve at dark moments and in tight situations. Her crew respected her, and she had acquired information about Arabia that was to prove valuable to her country in war. Subjectively, she had satisfied her need for action and gained insight into her motives and feelings.

One thing had not changed. Her longing for Dick remained. At home in June 1914, while the English countryside drowsed through the last days of peace, she set the proposed Arabian book aside. Doughty-Wylie was far away in Addis Ababa. On one occasion he wrote: "What wouldn't I give to have you sitting opposite in this all-alone house" (Charles Doughty-Wylie to Gertrude Bell, 17 Oct. 1914).

Hardly a surprise, war came that autumn. "Do you know what it is going to be, this war?" she asked him. "It is going to be a draw. I don't believe either side can win . . . deadlock, vain courage, profitless effort" (Gertrude Bell to Charles Doughty-Wylie, 13 Jan. 1915). Her pessimism was justified. In October 1914, the German army swept through Flanders. A British expeditionary force sent to Ypres to halt their advance was virtually wiped out. Casualties piled up on the docks and at train stations in Boulogne, where Bell and other Red Cross volunteers worked day and night making lists of the wounded and missing for the war office. While Dick's wife was also in France, organizing a military hospital, he was writing to Bell:

> Tonight I should not want to talk. I should make love to you. Would you like it, welcome it, or would a hundred hedges rise and bristle and divide?—but we would tear them down. What is a hedge that it should divide us . . . ? You are in my arms, alight, afire. Tonight I do not want dreams and fancies. But it will never be. . . . The first time should I not be nearly afraid to be your lover?
>
> So much a thing of the mind is the insistent passion of the body. Women sometimes give themselves to men for the man's pleasure. I'd hate a woman to be like that with me. I'd want her to feel to the last sigh the same surge and stir that carried me away. She should miss nothing that I could give her. (Charles Doughty-Wylie to Gertrude Bell, 15 Nov. 1914)

In January 1915, Bell received a telegram saying that Dick would be leaving Addis Ababa and expected to be in Marseilles on the tenth of February. They met and parted. Doughty-Wylie went to war, followed by Gertrude's anguished letters, written against the background of horrifying news from the front, with no end in sight.

She wrote on 7 March 1915:

> I'm alone for the evening . . . and I'm alone with you, and lonely in spite of that. It came over me in waves. . . . I go under for a while and then cling to a floating spar of memory, the echo of a phrase, and coming to

the surface catch sight across the salt and bitter flood, of some cape or headland of Paradise to where I must win, to which I shall win. . . . That headland, I think and think of, what it will be when I reach it.

I am very calm about the shot and shell to which you go. What takes you, takes me out to look for you. If there's search and finding beyond the border I shall find you. If there's nothingness, as with my reason I think, why then there's nothingness. . . . Oh, but life shrinks from it . . . but I'm not afraid. Life would be gone, how could the fire burn? But I'm brave—you know it—as far as human courage goes. Listen, you asked me to cheat life; you told me how to do it. I won't, why, no, that's empty nonsense. I'll do anything you ask and not think twice of it . . . you may do anything you like with what is yours—what's given is given, there is no taking back, no shadow of it. And no reproach. I wish I had given more, except that more of giving is still in my hand for you to take.

On 9 March 1915: "Oh Dick, write to me. When shall I hear? . . . I trust, I believe, you'll take care of me—let me stand upright and say I've never walked by furtive ways. Then they'll forgive me and you—all the people that matter will forgive. . . . [B]ut it's you who should be saying this, should be saying it now, not I. I won't say it anymore."

On 10 March 1915:

[We] thought then of the moment. I think of it still, hourly. But inseparably linked to it is the longing for the fruit of it. What woman fears when that is in the scale? I'm telling you the profoundest secret of life, newly revealed to me, blindingly. Hear me. I tell you solemnly the price was not too great for the short hours of being with you—you said passion would spend itself. You'd sleep. Yes, but between my breasts . . . and my body part sheath to you, part pillow. I've learnt.

On 11 March 1915: "[I]f I had given more, should I have held you closer, drawn you back more surely? I look back and rage at my reluctance."

On 12 March 1915: "I've had a few resplendent hours. I could die on them and be happy. But you, you've not had what you wanted."

On 15 March 1915: "[W]hen my heart quales [*sic*] I remember the morphia tubes and I know there is a way out. . . . [I]f I can't sleep in your arms I'll sleep this way" (Gertrude Bell to Charles Doughty-Wylie, 7–15 Mar. 1915).

Dick replied to this crescendo of emotion in a rather detached manner:

> As to the things you say of some future in far places, they are dreams, dream woman. We must walk along the road—such heavenly madness is for gods and poets—not for us except in lovely dreams. . . . There are some things one cannot argue with, they grow like the night and cover us. . . .
>
> I suppose you won't like the letter of a philosopher—a would-be philosopher. It only means that pleasure is pleasure and fear and doubt and hesitation are thorny ways from which it turns away. It was right in London, and the sober part of me does not regret—the drunk part regrets and remembers until he goes to sleep. Poverty, temperance and chastity. I don't like them. Temperance is tolerable but not more than a matter of good taste—poverty is miserable. Chastity was invented by ascetics—"some have made themselves for the kingdom of God." (Charles Doughty-Wylie to Gertrude Bell, 2 Apr. 1915).

Her morphia letter was answered on 15 April from Gallipoli. He begged her not to do "what you talked of—don't do it, or in some far world my ghost will be the sadder." Ironically, his wife was similarly threatening to resort to morphia in case of his death.

On 20 April he wrote: "Tomorrow I go by collier to run up a beach to land troops, . . . politically, even from a military point of view, I think this takes too many chances. If we fail it is a political disaster." On 26 April, after leading a party of men ashore, Doughty-Wylie was shot in the head and died instantly on the heights above the Gallipoli village of Sedd al-Bahr. He was awarded the Victoria Cross. Unaware that she was writing to the wind, Bell continued her letters until she received the news.

In his book *Gallipoli,* Stephen Snelling suggests that Doughty-Wylie had a death wish rooted in the entanglements of his private life, namely, his "secret liaison" with Gertrude Bell (1999, 67). Naturally, he would have anticipated his own death in battle, but he also seemed to beckon it. Men sacrifice their lives in war for motives of pride, idealism, or trying to reach stated military objectives. In Dick's case, perhaps there was an added element of self-destructiveness.

In the altered perspective of today, it is clear that their relationship was highly unrealistic and even rather impersonal: many written words and too few meetings were in some odd way perhaps a convenience to both. For complex reasons, Doughty-Wylie preferred a not-very-successful marriage, and Bell offered her virginity only when it was too late. The affair resonated with late-Victorian cultural attitudes that en-sured that a potentially perfect match for two brave and questing souls would never materialize. The end of it coincided with the end of a his-torical era and, ironically, the beginning of a defining phase for Ger-trude Bell.

The two women in Dick's life did not die at once, as they had promised to do. Gertrude Bell lived to 1926, Dick's widow until 1960.

AFTERWORD

Not long after Dick's death, Bell received the package containing her letters to him. To close that chapter in her life, she realized, she must find some way to forget.

In November 1915, she was appointed to the Arab Bureau at Cairo, an agency established to collect and disperse Middle Eastern intelli-gence. By now British troops were fighting on two desert fronts, their lines of communication on the Tigris harassed by hostile Rashid tribes-

King Faisal I of Iraq. n.d. Photograph by Lazlo.
Courtesy of the Imperial War Museum, London.

men and threatened at Suez by German-armed Turkish forces composed of Arab conscripts.

In March 1916, as a result of Lawrence's intervention, she joined the staff of Sir Percy Z. Cox, chief political officer in Iraq. In 1916, she became Cox's Oriental secretary—the first woman imperial servant of Great Britain. The East became her permanent home, fusing her deep attraction to the harsh beauty of the land and its people with her interest in politics.

Several distinguishing acts define Bell's influence in Iraq. In 1920, the first Arab council under the presidency of Naqib Gailani was formed, in part according to her judgment, an example of her ability to exercise power through suggestion. In the summer of 1921, she helped execute British policy by persuading Arab tribesmen to vote for Faisal, Lawrence's wartime comrade, as king of Iraq (thereby forestalling promised Arab independence). Third, as the intelligence link between Baghdad and London, it was her voice that spoke to her government about domestic political events in Iraq. And it was her hand, by Cox's order, that set the (contested) boundaries between Saudi Arabia, Iraq, and Kuwait. Finally, the national museum of archaeology that she founded, selecting the best artifacts from various archaeological sites, opened after World War I and gave Iraqis a new context for understanding their past. The museum also houses her personal collection of several thousand books, an invaluable tool for research in Arab literature and history.

History is not always kind to those whose experiments fail. By 1923, Bell had begun to question British purposes in Iraq. Arab nationalism was a growing fact of life. The king was unpopular, and an essentially tribal society was proving immune to adopting foreign institutions. The effort to coax a trumped-up assembly of pro-British sheikhs and town notables to accept a treaty incorporating a League of Nations mandate for British rule in Iraq only narrowly succeeded. It took all of Bell's efforts to persuade the delegates to vote in its favor.

The kingdom of Iraq did not survive for long; it fell in an army coup in 1958, perhaps for lack of a better example of statecraft. It had lasted thirty-seven years before perishing in flames.

The major themes of Gertrude Bell's life—the attraction to unusual men, the risk taking, the passion for politics, and her brilliant literary gifts—come together in her Arabian diaries. They not only chronicle a personal triumph of will over daunting obstacles but also bring alive, to an extraordinary degree, a passage to an unknown world.

If Bell's ghost is hovering somewhere above, it may comfort her to know her book on Arabia is finished at last.

Gertrude Bell's Itinerary, 1913–1914

16 December 1913	Leaves Damascus for eastern desert.
20 December 1913	Reaches Jebel (mountain) Sais, seeking water and pasturage for camels. Turns south.
24 December 1913	Arrives at Burqu ruins after brush with lawless nomads; copies ancient inscriptions.
28 December 1913	Camps at grounds of Jeber Druze tribes.
31 December 1913	Arrives at ruins of Roman fort at Qasr (palace) el Azraq situated near water supplies.
2–7 January 1914	Studies Qasrs el Amra and Kharanah.
7 January 1914	Meets servant Fattuh at Ziza; is detained for ten days by Turk officials, who deny her protection, as does British government.
17 January 1914	Talks her way out of dilemma; studies the Umayyad palace at Tubah.
19–25 January 1914	Traverses valley at Wadi Ba'ir, seeking and recording unknown water sources and tribal units of use to Britain during the war.
25 January 1914	Arrives at stronghold of Howaitat tribes; spends ten days with various families; photographs the harems of the chieftains.
2 February 1914	Leaves with *rafiq* (guarantor of protection on route ahead in the Nefud desert).
9 February 1914	Encounters nomads who threaten robbery.
10 February 1914	Enters sands of the Nefud desert.

19 February 1914	Crosses the southeast angle of the Nefud, the first Westerner to do so, and charts sources of water in the barren black plains.
22 February 1914	Sees first village habitation in weeks.
25 February 1914	Arrives in Hayyil, a walled town currently in possession of the Rashid tribe; is kept under house arrest for eleven days.
7 March 1914	Free to leave Hayyil, turns northwest to Baghdad by way of Hayianiya and Najaf, passing through lands of the Shammar tribes.
17 March 1914	Arrives at Euphrates borderlands and meets several groups of hostile Arab shepherds; spends several days seeking a *rafiq* to conduct her safely forward through camel herdsmen.
23 March 1914	In Najaf at last; within five days passes through Kerbala and arrives at Baghdad.
12 April 1914	Leaves Baghdad, after a side trip to Babylon where she visits German excavators.
23 April 1914	On the road to Damascus after taking the Euphrates road north to Ramadi, then striking to the west, where she is welcomed by the sheikhs of the 'Anazeh tribes.
1 May 1914	Rides into Damascus, exhausted and depressed.
8 May 1914	Leaves by boat for Constantinople to report to the British ambassador.
Around 1 June 1914	At home in Yorkshire.
July–August 1914	War begins, Turkey joins Germany.
November 1915	Bell leaves England for an assignment at Cairo Arab Bureau. She begins a new life in the Middle East.

THE DOUGHTY-WYLIE DIARIES

The Doughty-Wylie Diaries

JANUARY 1914

G. B. to D-W.   *Jan. 16. [16 January 1914]*

Today I returned to the desert and as I rode past the station of
Ziza [Jiza], I stopped and asked whether the missing letters from you
were not, by chance, there. But there was nothing and I, crossing the little thread of rail that binds me here to the outer world, felt like the Fate
with the shears—Clotho, to whom we bow the head. I have cut the
thread. I can hear no more from you or from anyone, and what is more,
do you know that I am an outlaw? [Ambassador] Louis Mallet has informed me that if I go on towards Nejd [Najd] my own government
washes its hands of me, and I have given a categorical acquittal to the
Ottoman Government, saying that I go on at my own risk. This is the
price I pay for having been caught at Ziza. It is not, in reality, heavy; for
in no case could the Turks be held responsible for me, since I travel
without a guard, and British protection is not of great value in these
wastes. If my fellow inhabitants here were to take it into their minds to
rob me, I do not suppose that Willie Tyrrell would send an army to recover my possessions; and if it pleased them to send a rifle bullet my
way, it would be of small satisfaction to me to know that the same
measure would be dealt out in time to them.[1] Still there is something in

1. Private secretary to Sir Edward Grey, head of the British foreign office. Gertrude
Bell stopped there regularly on returning from trips to the East.

the written word which works on the imagination, and I spent my last night at 'Amman sleepless with the thought of it. The desert, there is no denying it, the desert looks terrible from without, and even I, when I find myself in the more or less peaceful routine of a comparative civilization, with a Circassian steam mill puffing over its task near my tents and the quiet village life flowing on beside—even I have a moment when my heart beats a little quicker and my eyes strain themselves to catch some glimpse of the future.[2] But at last, after tossing to and fro with a restless mind for hour after hour of the night, I convinced myself that in the end I didn't mind what happened—and went to sleep. And next day, which was yesterday, I rose out of 'Amman, free and an outlaw, a very harmless outlaw. I did not ride far. I went up to the farm of some Christians, not 3 hours from Ziza, to the north of that place of captivity, and there all my friends of 9 years ago came to see me and I spent the night. They are men these hosts of mine; tall and broad and deep voiced, ready to square all the difficulties which cross their path, the exactions of the government and the exactions of the Arabs. They kill a sheep every night for those who claim their hospitality; they heap up the enormous rice dish, and fill the mangers with corn—I asked them how rural economy bore the strain of such hospitality and they answered with all simplicity: "Where is the inn in this wilderness?" This morning they rode with me to the further side of Ziza, where we sat down by the railway and lunched on the ample remains of last night's feast. They have provided me with camel drivers, for the Agilat whom I brought with me from Damascus [Dimashq, Damas el-Shamas], have returned from Ziza, fearing the risks of the "accursed road" before us; and they have sent with me two *rafiqs,* a Shikari and a Sharari whom they have bound over, by all that any man can call sacred, to see that not a hair of my head suffers injury.[3] And so they left me, with a mighty hand clasp and a thousand deep voiced blessings, rolled their embroi-

2. Circassian, i.e., of Turkish nationality.
3. Minor tribes of the Syrian desert.

dered *abbayas* around their huge bodies and spurred their mares back to Yaduda [el-Yaduda].[4] And I rode on a couple of hours, and found my camp, which had gone before, pitched in the sunshine on the gentle slopes of a wadi. The sun set in splendour, the stars shone out and the late moon rose over us. All the terrors which I conjured up between house walls have fled before me and the desert is clothed once more in abiding security. Thus we turn towards Nejd, *inshallah,* renounced by all the powers that be, and the only thread which is not cut though is that which runs through this little book, which is the diary of my way kept for you.

G. B. to D-W.   Sun. Jan. 18. [18 January 1914]

We have had a delicious 2 days riding across the rolling Shammar country and I am really beginning to enjoy it all. For I must now tell you that I liked the first part of the way so little that I was almost inclined to turn back. The bitter cold, and the absence of Fattuh and one thing and another combined to make a mountain of evils. I did nothing but think and think and my eyes were always turned backwards. But when two days ago I cut myself loose from civilization I felt as if I had cast down all burdens. And I do nothing now but look onwards, till tomorrow, till next day—no further; but it is far enough. And above all I rejoice in the actual moment as it passes. You must now make acquaintance with the members of the expedition. First, there is old Muhammad al-Ma'rawi, Mr Carruthers's companion.[5] In his youth he rode with the *rajajil* of Muhammad ibn al Rashid;[6] in his wiser years he bought and sold camels from Nejd; now he has fallen on lean times and takes whatever odd job may present itself—he has had few odder jobs than me, I expect. He knows all the Arabs of every part. The fathers and grandfathers of all the shaikhs have been among his friends or enemies,

4. A village near Amman.

5. Douglas Carruthers, British geographer and contemporary of Gertrude Bell.

6. Rashid *amir,* "master of Nejd" after battle of al-Mulaidah in January 1891 (Winder 1980, 277).

and his tales of war and adventure are endless, as we ride by day or sit over the fire at night. Next there is his nephew Salim, my own second man. He waits on me and helps Fattuh—a capital boy. He has travelled much—all these Damascenes go camel buying among the tribes—he is an excellent servant, educated and well mannered. Next comes 'Ali, the Agaili post man of 3 years ago. He is an 'ole[?] dog, but I love him. He is as brave as a lion and in the hour of danger as cool as [2 lines heavily deleted] you could wish. He will never leave us. He looks upon himself as a sort of hereditary retainer of mine since we travelled together "in the year of snow." My 3 Agaili camel drivers left me two days ago. First they would come, and then they would not come and then again they would never part from me, and finally when the camels were walking out of the gates of my friends the Christians of Yadudeh; they threw down their camel sticks and declared they would return to Damascus. It was better so; I don't want unwilling men, and they really feared the road. Fortunately we had got another man from Damascus while we were at 'Amman, another nephew of Muhammad's, and he is a treasure; Sa'id, head camel driver. We picked up an Agaili at 'Amman, *meskin,* but he will learn; and my hosts at Yadudeh gave me a third, Mustafa. He is a fellah from a village near Jerusalem, who had been working on the farm at Yadudeh; suddenly he found himself pressed into my service by his energetic employers, and off he went to Heaven knows where. He doesn't seem to mind and he does his work like a man. And then there is a negro who has been with me from the beginning, Fellah. We engaged him as camel herd but he has now been promoted to work in the men's tent and he has the good word of everyone—and deserves it. And finally there is Fattuh, the alpha and omega of all, with his eye on everything although it never appears to be taken off me. At present we have two *rafiqs,* a Sherari [*sic*] of whom I have seen little, and a Skhari [*sic*], Sayyah who is the most delightful of travelling companions. They have a wonderful clear speech, these men of the Sukhur, and he not only tells me exciting tales as we ride, but he gives me, unsolicited, all kinds of interesting information about the tribes.[7] And last night we had a guest, a young shaikhling of the Sukhur, cousin to Hathmel, to whom we are going.[8] He and his slave joined us on the march and lodged with us last night. He was very anxious to come with us to the end of the world, he and the *'abd,* and I am pledged to lodge with him next time I pass this way, to "honour our resting place." A nice boy; he went upon his way this morning. Today we crossed the high ground which parts the waters of the Dead Sea from those of the Sirhan. The undulating, flint covered country was scattered over with the *naga* herds of the Jebbur and the Sukhur—I love to see them.[9] The nagas are just beginning to calve and every herd has a few of the preposterous baby camels, all leg and neck and nothing else. And so we came down to the great Wadi al Ghadaf and to the Ummayad palace of Tubah which I have been photographing all the afternoon. The planning had been done by Musil, but there was, as I expected, much to learn, and I have learnt it this afternoon praise be to God.[10] It was hot today, the first hot day and I dined out of doors in a wonderful afterglow of sunset. We are camped actually within the palace (but half the walls have fallen) and tonight we are the guests of kings. And I am as well content as the receiver of such hospitality should be.

G. B. to D-W.   *Tues. Jan. 20 [20 January 1914]*

The men were not quite so happy as I was at Tubah. They feared a possible *ghazzu* from half way across to the Euphrates, harrying the herds of camels which we had passed on our way. "It is the gate of the 'Anazeh" they said and explained that the desert to the E. of us was "empty" ie there were no Sukhur camps to stop a foe.[11] But none came

7. Bani Sakhr tribe of Syria.
8. Sheikh of the Sukhur (Sakhr) tribe.
9. Nagas are she-camels that breed in winter.
10. Alois Musil, Czech archaeologist, contemporary of Bell. Studied Umayyad caliphate (c. 661–750) of Damascus.
11. 'Anazeh, the largest and wealthiest Syrian tribe.

and we went our way cheerfully, filling our water skins at the big clear pool which lay in the sandy floor of the valley. For yesterday there was no water in the broad valley wherein we camped, and at this time of year there is no fear of raiders there, though in the summer and autumn it is the road of the *ghazzu*. But the desert to the S. is inhabited; Hathmel and his people are all before us. We kept watch, however, for stray robbers, who finding us watchful would turn in as guests, but finding us asleep would lift our camels. They did not come either. This morning as I walked at dawn up the wide desolation of the valley with my *rafiq* Sayyah, he explained to me that a consul like me "they were glad to make welcome" but an *ajnabi,* a foreigner, they would not allow to pass. I told him that the land had never been inhabited and never would be and when we had ended this talk he threw down his fur cloak on the sand and observed that it was the hour of prayer. "Pray" said I "pray, and may God protect you." "Every man" he returned half apologetically "serves his own faith." He prays all the prayers with the utmost assiduity. Our landmark half yesterday and most of today has been a strange group of 3 abrupt sandstone *tells,* rising sharply out of the flint covered plain; the Thlaithuwat—I wonder what caprice of Nature called them into being. We met some of the Sukhur, *rahalin,* moving camp. They gave us a bad account of water and pasturage ahead and added that they were thirsting, they and their sheep. We told them where water lay before them, but they will not drink tonight. In the afternoon we spied two camel riders coming up from behind us and stopped to see who they were. It was Jed'an, Shaikh of the Agaili and one of his men. They had marked us as we passed by the Thlaithuwat, and taking us for raiders, had ridden after us. "We feared you were foes" he called out to me. "No, no" said I "friends, praise be to God." Everyone goes in fear, except only I, who have nothing to lose that matters. And so we came down into the great Wadi Ba'ir, full of tamarisk bushes, and crossing it reached presently the famous well, Bir Ba'ir, which in summer is the only water in all this country; the Sukhur shaikhs camp here with 500 tents. And here stands the last of the castles, Qasr Ba'ir, very very much ruined and never visited before by anyone but Mr Carruthers, who did not even photograph it. There is no architectural feature by which to date it except the plan which I have managed to make out, and that is very old. It is the same plan as Tubah and the placc may be 8th century. It is great fun making the first—and probably the last—record of it. I shall have a morning at it tomorrow. And now I shall go and sit by the campfire for an hour and hear tales.

G. B. to D-W.   *Wed. Jan. 21.* [*21 January 1914*]

I have been beset for the last few hours with a desire to talk to you—see now, I write. We are still at Ba'ir. I spent the whole morning planning the ruins and the whole afternoon drawing out the plan. I think I have got it fairly right but it was a difficult job. At noon I took a latitude and made out our position to be 30° 43´ about; it must be fairly right. Mr Carruthers and I had calculated that Ba'ir should be somewhere a little N. of 30°. And when all was done Muhammad called me and said he wished me to see the grave of al Mara'i who came up with the Beni Hallal when first they came out of Nejd[12] "And conquered Tunis" added Sayyah. The grave was near a dry well; it is some 4 metres square. "This was his length" said 'Ali, selecting one direction at a venture. "They were tall the Beni Hallal." "They were broad too" I observed (Heaven forgive me!) "He was entirely square." "No" replied 'Ali gravely, "it is a chamber." At this I had a *fou rire* [wild laugh] and was so busily choking down my untimely laughter that I scarcely heard the miraculous story of the snake which fell on al Mara'i's head and was killed by a stroke of his good sword. The mark of the snake's body is there upon a stone by the well and the dent made by al Mara'i's sword, if you should doubt my word. We sat down by the edge of the dry well,

12. Possible reference to 'A'id ibn Mar'i, leader of an attack in 1852 against a Turkish force at Hodeida, on the west coast of Nejd (Winder 1980, 182).

Muhammad, Sayyah and I, and Muhammad took up the tale. "My lady" said he "when I first came here, 30 years ago, the big well was filled up. Upon a day of days the 'Ise [sic] fell here upon the Sukhur and the Sukhur killed of them two camel riders and they killed a horseman.[13] The Sukhur took the camels and the two men and threw them into the well and rolled stones on top." "Haram!" said I "it is forbidden." "No wallah" he answered, "the 'Isa thirsted and if they had drunk the water of the well they would have followed the Sukhur and killed them." "It was a good thought" said Sayyah. "Shayyatin al 'Arab," said Muhammad, "they are devils, the Arab." "Shayyatin" said Sayyah. "They are the very devil" said I with conviction—with such conviction that Sayyah looked up at me and laughed and laughed—it was his turn now. How I wish you were here to laugh too. You may take this as typical of our conversations, for Ba'ir is the very trysting place of ghazzus, but not now, the desert to the S. is "closed," Hathmel is there and half the People of the North—so we speak here of the Beni Sakhr. There is a new grave among the castle walls. As I was working this morning Sayyah came up and looked at it. "Sharari" said he reading the wasm, a man of the Sherarat. And then he looked again. "He was killed" he observed. I looked too. The red cotton keffiyyeh and a bit of cotton clothing, thrown down on the stones that covered the grave, were steeped in blood. Occasionally I wonder whether I shall come out of this adventure alive. But the doubt has no shadow of anxiety in it—I am so profoundly indifferent. Last night the talk by the camp fire turned on the years of a man's life. "The limits of man's age are 104 years" postulated Fattuh. "Oh father of Elyas" said Muhammad "call upon the Prophet! there are no limit[s] to a man's age. What says the Injil oh Lady[?]" "The Torat" said I "the Old Testament says that a man's life is 70 years and if he live longer he has little profit." "You have spoken the truth" said Muhammad. I quoted Labid: "And if he live to 70 years and even more, what remains but the stick and the fingers closed over it."[14] And as I

13. Minor division of the 'Anazeh.
14. Abu 'Agil Labid, sixth-century Arab warrior-poet.

quoted, the old words took on fresh colour from the surround[ing] wilderness where first they were welded together, for the stick of Labid's verse is that very camel stick which we all carry every day of our journey, the *asa'i*. Mine comes from Nejd—Muhammad gave it to me and it was given to him by Muhammad ibn al Rashid when he rode with him, raiding, and his own camel stick broke in his hand. I ride with it now—to good or ill, it is all one.

G. B. to D-W.   *Fri. 23. [23 January 1914]*

We have ridden for two days over very desolate country and today it has been quite featureless. I got a bearing back for the first hour but after that there was nothing but my camel's ears. And we were not going straight ahead, for these high uplands are cut by deepish wadis running E and W, down and up which we wound by way of tributary depressions, so that I was forever walking behind and looking through my compass vane to see where we were going. *'Ajist,* as we say, I aged. It's a weary business when it's like this and I don't do it well. You did not teach me enough. However, I have got the general line I think and tomorrow we shall get landmarks. My camels have just come in from pasturing on the dry scrub of the valley bottom where we are camped. They are being fed on their evening meal of *'ajin.* They kneel in 3 groups with a table spread for each, so to speak—3 sacks with the due number of *'ajin* balls for each party. I often join the men in feeding them. I love the great mild beasts. Last night it rained and there were sliverlings of water pools in the first valley we crossed which the camels drank eagerly. They are thirsty. We are carrying water from Ba'ir and using it cautiously for I fear we may find none tomorrow. There are no words to tell you how bare and forbidding is this land. It gleams black with thickly strewn flints, mile after mile of flat black country, and nothing grows, except the scrub in the valley beds. I found a brave little geranium flowering yesterday in the low ground—the only flower I have seen. But that valiant family sends out its colonies to every part—

God give it the reward! No, not the only flower—the marigold is no less courageous. I saw his cheerful yellow face among the stones at Tubah.

G. B. to D-W.   *Sat 24. [24 January 1914]*

We have changed our course a little, for seeing that no rain has come to this country and that the world is all dried up, we decided that Hathmel must have moved east. We feared that if we went down to his camping ground Helbeh and did not find him, we should be uncomfortably far from the well of Hausa—we are rather short of water tonight and there is no other permanent water than Hausa. So we have put Helbeh to the East and turned straight towards Hausa. And Heaven be praised! we have come down from that endless plateau of flints. This morning at 11 o'clock we reached its western limit and climbing up to a *rijm,* we looked through my Zeiss glasses and sighted the cliffs of the Tor al Tubaiq [al-Tubaiq] to the S.—it is on the *Arabia Deserta* map, Jebel Tubaiq. We went down into a wide valley and followed it S.E. In the sand we saw comparatively recent footprints of camels and 'Ali declared that the Arabs must be all round us, "tonight we shall hear their dogs." But not knowing who might be here we turned up a little side valley and camped in a secluded hollow "where they cannot see our fires." When we had got into camp 'Ali, Sayyah and I climbed up a neighbouring tell and scouted for Arabs. When we were little, Maurice and I, we had a favourite game which consisted in wandering all over the house, up and down the staircases, without being seen by the housemaids—I felt exactly as if we were playing that beloved game as we crept up to the shoulder of the tell. But a careful survey through my glasses revealed no housemaids, and we went on boldly to the top where we had a glorious view. Below us lay the sandy bottom of a wide depression, the Ga'ra, bounded to the S and W by fantastically rugged hills and cliffs, the blown sand climbing up their lower slopes. Sand and cliff and rusty outbursts of volcanic rock-cliff and sand and the rusty pallor (is that the way to spell it!?) of the basalt—there was nothing else. I won-

Mountains near Tor al Tubaiq. January 1914. Photograph by Gertrude Bell. Courtesy of the University of Newcastle upon Tyne.

der why one takes pleasure in such a landscape, but the fact remains that one does, and if you were here you would like it as much as I do. Welcome and kinship!

G. B. to D-W.   *Tues. 27. [27 January 1914]*

   We have effected a safe landing in the tents of the Howaitat and this is how it happened.[15] On Sunday we set off in a very still dawn which turned presently into a hot windless day, and rode

15. Auda abu Tayi, sheikh of the Howaitat, was an ally of T. E. Lawrence during the war against Turkey. Bell took some of her most striking photographic portraits at their tents.

down the valley in which we had camped. It was cold and I walked on with 'Ali for the first hour. The footsteps were all round us in the sand. We stopped in a little hollow and looked at them, coming and going. *"Jedid"* said 'Ali, "they are fresh." The valley led us out into a wide flat depression, round which the Ga'rah. Round it stood the broken pinnacles of the Tor al Tubaiq; they stood and watched us; the sunlight crept slowly down their riven sides and there was no sound or sight of human beings. It was curiously sinister. Moreover we did not know where we were. Somewhere to the E. there was a small well called Al Hausah; somewhere further W. there was a *khabra* called Umm al Ruqubbah— we had no water and the camels were thirsty; whatever happened we must reach one of them that night. The well was marked on Mr Carruthers's map; by the light of it I gave the casting vote in favour of a certain block of eastern hills and we turned that way. Where the *khabra* might be neither I nor anyone else knew, and there was a lurking doubt in my mind (which I tried to banish) as to whether we should find water at Hausah. The supply is always small and the Arabs whose footsteps we had seen, might have reduced it to nothing. However, we put our trust in God—there was no alternative. So we marched on for a couple of hours. Then Sayyah called out to 'Ali: "Ya, 'Ali! smoke." Under the black slopes of a tell crowned with pinnacles of rock we saw the wavering smoke curl up and vanish and curl up anew. Whose fire was it? that was the question. The general consensus of opinion was that it was a *ghazzu,* but in any case it was wise to go and see. If they were friends they would give us news of the Arabs and of water; if they were foes they would certainly see and follow us wherever we went. We turned south to the smoke. These are the interesting moments in desert travel. There were two low ridges before us. We topped the first and there below us was the *khabra! "Badhtha tayyib!"* exclaimed one of the camel drivers "Her luck is good." It is a very valuable reputation and I hope I shall be able to keep it up! The camels sniffed the water and set off at a trot. We left the men filling the water skins, and as soon as our camels had drunk, Muhammad, 'Ali, Sayyah and I set out again in quest of the fire. 'Ali was walking. He climbed, bent double, to the top of the second ridge, then stood up and crossed over it. We followed. There was nothing—it all ends in smoke as it began, my story—a few shepherds with flocks of sheep and we knew that we must have reached the winter pasturage of the Howaitat and that their tents could not be far off. The shepherds came up and gave us news. The Sukhur had indeed moved east—we shall not see Hathmel and his people. Moreover their departure had been hastened by a regrettable incident which had resulted in the killing of a Howaitat man [mare?]—the face of my Sukhari, Sayyah, grew rather long over this tale. The big Howaiti people, the Abu Tayyi, were some way S.E., but there was a shaikh called Harb in the hills to the S. and thither we went. The plain from the *khabra* was covered with small plants, so many that in stretches it was quite green—a green which to our unaccustomed eyes seemed dazzlingly [*sic*] brilliant. And the plants were flowering, some of them, in an ineffectual but very cheering way. We failed to find Harb that night—we found nothing but his footsteps. He had moved camp that day. So we pitched our tents in soft red sand among strange rocky tells, with broken pointed heads and black precipitous sides. There were some Howaitat near us who paid us a visit—the "stout nomad native" do you remember they are called in *Arabia Deserta*? They have a redoubtable reputation for courage and devilry. And yesterday we followed Harb and found him camped in the hills. He received us with great cordiality and even welcomed Sayyah, although the night before some guests of the Sukhur had attacked a Howaiti camp—it was the settlement of an old score—killed 3 men, lost one, and taken refuge with Hathmel: so report went. It all happened not far from where we were camped. Harb killed a sheep for me and at night when we were dining then arrived another guest, Muhammad Abu Tayyi, cousin of the great shaikh. A formidable looking person he is, great and stony and flashing eyed—not like the slender feeble Beduin with their restless unquiet glance. He was very polite at first and then the talk took an awkward turn, as to whether I had or had not come with leave from the Government and whether the Beduin liked foreigners in their *diras*. I rose at this and went to bed, leaving Muhammad al-Ma'rawi to smooth matters down, which he did with great success. But the Arabs fell to disputing and shouting—about some private matter of their own—and I lay in bed and listened anxiously, fearing they were quarrelling with my good Sayyah. The fears were dissipated this morning—it was all nothing, as usual, though they made such a mighty noise over it. Today I have spent with Harb, for there is no water but that of the pool below us, 3 hours away, and we had to fill all our water skins before going forward. So I have talked to Harb, and drunk coffee, and talked again and photographed—and taken a latitude I am glad to say—and the day has seemed rather long. I have just been given an ostrich skin and egg as a present. Not a good skin, but still curious.

G. B. to D-W.   *Wed. 28. [28 January 1914]*

I would have you know that the quality most needed when travelling among the Arabs is not (as some have wrongly stated) courage, but patience. My fairy godmothers forgot to endow me with it—you know how little I have it—But perhaps I shall have learnt how to practice it before this journey is done. If I have not, it will not be for want of opportunity. This morning when it came to the question of our new *rafiq*, Harb and his brother and a cousin of 'Audeh Abu Tayyi—the same who brought me the ostrich egg—assembled solemnly in the men's tent and warned me that the road south was full of danger. The Howaitat have left the *dirah* and gone west: the desert is empty—given over to the raiders of the Hetaim, the Fagir, the B. 'Atiyyeh, and I know not whom besides.[16] Anyhow they strongly counselled me not to take that path but go East to the Wadi Sirhan and then S. as I would. And if I agreed to this Harb's brother 'Awwad would see me safe into the Wadi. Moreover

16. Small tribes in Syria.

Howaitat woman. January 1914. Photograph by Gertrude Bell. Courtesy of the University of Newcastle upon Tyne.

my men were afraid of the southern road, even 'Ali who is not easily alarmed. I could not go against this advice—it would have been madness. Specially as it is all one to me which road I take and from here to the W. Sirhan is unmapped ground. Further, I shall see with satisfaction the Hejaz rly [railway] growing more and more distant. Taimah [Tayma] was dangerously near it, it would have been all too easy for Ibn al Rashid's agent then to advise in a manner I should have found difficult to withstand, that the train to Damascus was better than camel riding. So we go east with 'Awwad tomorrow, *wa kasarna yaum* we have broken another day here. In the afternoon I climbed up into the hills and wandered by myself along a high rocky gorge where among the stones I found Spring in the desert—the pallid meagre Spring which is all the desert knows. There were flowers, red and white and purple—we should scarcely notice them in our beflowered England, but here they seemed like separate jewels. Even the thorns were covered with the greenish white seed bags which serve them for blossoming. And when I got to the top I looked out upon fold after fold of golden red sand and smoke grey rock, with the black tents of the Howaitat clinging to the slopes or nestled into the valleys. I longed for you to look with me—it was a sight that filled the eyes and satisfied, for the moment, even the most restless mind. Now the new moon triumphs over the sunset—it is her third night; and presently I shall have the company of the stars to light my dinner table.

A Harb tribesman and his wife. January 1914. Photograph by Gertrude Bell. Courtesy of the University of Newcastle upon Tyne.

G. B. to D-W.   *Thurs 29. [29 January 1914]*

We got off today, with Harb's brother, 'Awwad, as *rafiq*, and riding over the sandy hills we came presently to 'Audeh's big tent. He is away, raiding the Shammar, according to his wont; but I stopped for half an hour, drank coffee and photographed his tent and his womenkind—more particularly his very handsome sister, 'Aliyah. We got news there that the Ruwalla were camping in the W. Sirhan.[17] It was nothing to me where they were camping, but it meant a great deal to 'Awwad, for any man of the Ruwalla whom

Two tribesmen at Sheikh Harb ibn Derwish's camp. January 1914. Photograph by Gertrude Bell.
Courtesy of the University of Newcastle upon Tyne.

17. Ruwalla, a leading Syrian tribe; its sheikh was Nuri al-Sha'lan.

Sheikh Harb ibn Derwish and his wife. January 1914. Photograph by Gertrude Bell.
Courtesy of the University of Newcastle upon Tyne.

we might encounter would cut his throat without a moment's pause. Therefore our *rafiq* fell useless in our hands. We went on our way discussing what to do and finally sent him off to Muhammad's tents, which were near at hand (you remember the formidable Muhammed of two day's [*sic*] ago?) to fetch a substitute. We shortly after came into camp and were joined in an hour's time by Muhammad himself, all smiles, and 'Awwad and others of the shaikhly house. They have brought me a black and white lamb with whom I have come into terms of such intimate friendship that I can scarcely bear the thought of sacrificing it, yet I cannot well carry it with me like Byron's goose. And they have brought me besides a beautiful ostrich skin, black and white too, a full grown male, the price of which I must insinuate delicately into their palms. Muhammad is all for my staying with him tomorrow night, but I have visited shaikhs enough for the present and I long for the road. God seems to have provided a *rafiq* and I hope we shall continue on our way. The shaikhs dine with us tonight.

FEBRUARY 1914

G. B. to D-W.   *Mon. Feb. 2. [2 February 1914]*

It all turned out differently—it always does! Over the coffee fire Muhammad told me of a ruin, in the hills to the W. I had heard of it before but Muhammad himself had seemed so very unwilling that I should see it—this was in the night when he came to Harb's camp—that I did not like to press the point. He said "We do not know that you will not build it up afresh!" They are suspicious and one has to be—patient! Well, here he was pressing me to go to it. I could not say no, and leave a ruin behind me, so rather reluctantly, we turned W. again, rode for a couple of hours and pitched our tents in Muhammad's encampment, near his big "house." Next day I rode off with two guides and one of my own men—5 hours across the hills—and found the ruin which was quite worth seeing. A sort of little *khan* on a *khabra* which had been walled round so as to form a *birkeh* I make no doubt that it was a *menzil* on the road from Ba'ir to Taimah. There was a Cufic inscrip., dated, but alas I cd not make it out with certainty.[18] Anyhow there it is, the only ruin in these parts, good squared stones and mortar brought from far, and I have got it all down in my note books. We worked for 2 hours; it was necessary to hasten. And we got home in about 4 hours, a little after sunset. On the way out I had seen something else on a hill top which I must leave to those wiser than I to explain—a round chamber, beehive domed, of rude stones, surrounded by a completely circular low wall, and yet further outside a row of upright stones enclosing the temenos. What can it be? an ancient high place? some sort of sanctuary I make no doubt, and very ancient. What do we know of ancient nomad faiths? Altogether it was a profitable day. We had sent on camels to water at a distant *khabra,* and to bring us water. It proved to be so very distant that they did not return till 9 PM and then with the news that one of our *dululs* had sat down 6 hours away and absolutely refused to move. They had therefore left her and *ta wakkil Allah!* That's what they do, camels, when they are worn out. You are helpless before them. So we despatched another man next day to fetch her and remained ourselves with Muhammad. The messenger came back at sunset saying he had brought her forward 3 hours and left her with Arabs! There was nothing for it but to go ourselves, but it did not matter, for meantime we had changed all our plans, given up Jof and the [Wadi] Sirhan, fearing that the Ruwalla might stop us, and our road lay past that very *khabra* and past the camel. In point of fact it is much the same road as that which I abandoned when I was with Harb on account of the risks it presented! It is now said to be safe, and good, please God! I don't know, and anyway it is the shortest and so we go and everyone is pleased! The days spent with Muhammad were not wasted. I had never been in a big shaikh's camp before and all was new and interesting. And very beauti-

18. Cufic is early Arabic script.

ful—the sandy valley and M.'s big 5 polled [*sic*] tent where we sat at night, while a man sang of the deeds and days of all the Arabs, and the bowls of camel milk brought in to us when the *nagas* came back with their calves—and not least Muhammad's great figure sitting on the cushions beside me, with the white *keffiyye* falling over his black brows and his eyes flashing in question and answer, I saw his jurisdiction and found it to be just; I heard his tales of the desert and made friends with his women; and I made friends with him. He is a man, and a good fellow; you can lay your head down in his tents, and sleep at night, and have no fear. No, they were not wasted, those days. I learnt much of the desert and of its people. He had a little oryx beatrix calf in his tents— the most enchanting little beast.[19] He promises it to me if I care to have it—I believe I could get it for the Zoo if they wanted it. Muhammad represents his tribe before the Government—he is Shaikh al Dowleh and hands in the camel tax to the *Qaimmaqam* at Ma'an.[20] We have not yet quite reached the independent nomad dominions. The Hajj railay [*sic*] has brought the Govt. into touch with all these tribes. But the Ruwalla are independent—I shall see them, I make no doubt, on my returning way—and so is Nejd. This morning we started once more on our road, with a Sherarat *rafiq,* Musuid. We should be about 20 nights from Hayyil [Hail]. We rode over the hills till we came to their southern brink, where they drop abruptly in great riven crags and tells of red sandstone into a flat plain with endless red tells and driven sand stretching into the furthest distance. Not mountains, these, but low broken gound [*sic*]. At the foot of the J[ebel] Tubaiq we found the *dulul,* apparently recovered, and here we camped—a short day, but the camel pasturage is good here and we have a day with none, ahead of us. I climbed in the afternoon over the sandstone hills. It was cloudy and grey, but far away across the plain the yellow sand heaps glimmered and the red *tells* gave colour and warmth. But what a world! the incredible desolation.

19. Oryx beatrix is an antelope, highly prized by hunters for its curved dark horns.
20. Title of Turkish official.

Abandoned of God and man, that is how it looks—and is. I think no one can travel here and come back the same. It sets its seal upon you, for good or ill.

G. B. to D-W.   Wed. Feb. 4. [4 February 1914]

Whether it is from the pleasure of being at last on the direct road to Nejd, or whether this empty desert delights my men as much as it does me, I do not know, but we are travelling on in the best of spirits and contentment. Also, I think, in complete security; for as luck would have it we met in Monday's camping place a family of Shammar who have spent 5 years in the Howaitat country and now want to return to their own. Hearing that we were on our way thither they proposed to join us and we agreed with alacrity. The benefit conferred is equal on either side, for they would not dare to take this road alone, while we, if we happen to meet a Shammar *ghazzu* have these Shammar to guarantee us. We are in fact a large caravan, for two tents of Sherarat are with us, they and their flocks (6 sheep—or goats, I forget which) and their camels. I do not know how far they mean to go. Yesterday we had rain, heavy showers from time to time during most of the day. We rode straight S. from our camp to *khabra* where we filled our water skins in the rain; and then turned east down a shallow barren valley wherein we ultimately camped. But where we camped it was no longer barren. A thin sprinkling of green plants, mostly of the thistle and clover family had pushed up through the sand, and the "trees" were greening. The camels eat greedily and our Shammari friend rejoiced our hearts by promising us better and better pasturage as we go forward. His words were not empty. The camels have pastured all day today as we journeyed and tonight they eat their fill. I think we shall hunger no more. The November rains, which are the rains that matter to the desert, have been plentiful here. The *khabras* are all full of water—we passed another this morning and filled what skins were empty—and the bushes have sprouted. It's an immense relief; we had only 5 days' *aliq* with us, and if there had been nothing for the camels to eat we were face to face with starvation for them—and what? for us. I had serious thoughts, the last night in the J. Tubaiq, of taking the Jof road after all—we could have got camel food at Jof. And then I decided that in all probability it would mean that we should never get to Nejd, and I took the risk. Luck has been with me. This is real desert as you see it in picture books. It is made of nothing but red sandstone and the resulting red-gold sand. Sometimes the sandstone heaps itself up into a long low ridge and the wind heaps the sand about it into long low hills. Between lie shallow bottoms, *nugrah* they are called, wherein the sandstone lies in floors, with deep sand between, the whole strewn over with mounds of stone, broken and ruined into strange shapes by sun and wind. And here, if you can believe it, the darling spring has not refused to come. The thorny bushes are all grey-green against the red gold of the sand and some have even put forth very faintly coloured flowers. In spite of the desolation and the emptiness, it is beautiful—or is it beautiful partly be-cause of the emptiness? At any rate I love it, and though the camels pace so slowly, eating as they go, I feel no impatience and no desire to get to anywhere. It is cold still. Today, for the first time for many morn-ings, the thermometer was above freezing point when I breakfasted—only just above—and there is a sharp wind all day to temper the sun. The aromatic desert plants give it a delicious scent—"The wind smells of amber" said 'Ali today, when we came into camp in the hard clean sand under a broken pile of rock. Our Sherarat fellow travellers bring us goat's milk of an evening, but I am spoiled by having drunk the milk of the camel from great wooden bowls in the tents of Muhammad abu Tayyi, and goat's milk seems poor and tame after it. Here come my camels—the sun has set—I must go and look at them.

G. B. to D-W.   *Fri. Feb 6. [6 February 1914]*

I feel rather cross this afternoon because we have been induced by our *rafiq* to camp a full two hours earlier than need was by (I believe) wholly false reports that there was no pasturage ahead. The Shammar, who are with us and know this country, came and expostulated when our tents were half pitched, and I suspect they were right. There has been such pressure of public opinion on Masuid that I hope he won't repeat the game and meantime I will comfort myself by writing to you. We marched yesterday across long hills of blown sand, *Tu's* is their Arabic name, naked golden sand dunes. Their softly curving slopes were white with hoar frost until an hour after sunrise; on top they form sharp crests like the aretes on a snow mountain, and drop very precipitately on the W. side, whence comes, I must suppose, the prevailing wind. From the *tu's* we came into a barren world of pebbly floor and sandstone slab and broken sandstone *tells*. Nothing grew on it. We marched till the afternoon and then reached a valley running E and W, with plenty of green shrubs in its sand and water pools lying in the hollows of the sandstone. These we have everywhere, good clean rain water, the result of the rain storms the day we left the Tubaiq. And Heaven be praised for them. So we camped, we and the Shammar and the two miserable tents of the Sherarat, the inhabitants of which are as near starvation as can be and are mainly kept from it by small gifts of flour from us. The children found good entertainment in playing ball with the bitter colocynth gourds which lay scattered over the sand, and so forget hunger for an hour. This morning we were up and off early. One of the Sherarat has a few goats—I told you—and he sets forth before the rest. The Shammari, Ghadi, had taken my rifle and gone ahead a little later, on the chance of an antelope. Then the camels of the Sherarat and Shammar stepped out across the level ground between us and a low ridge and I followed on foot with Musuid, for I wanted to get my bearings from the ridge before I mounted. The sun was not yet up. We had not walked more than 40 yards before I saw the camels of our companions turn and come hastily back towards us. "They have seen foes: they are afraid" said Musuid. Ghadi came trotting up. "What is it?" said I. "*Gom[*"*]* he said—foes. "How many?" said I. "Ten camel riders" he replied and then called to my men *"Ma 'al wad, ma 'al wad!"* To the valley, the valley! The valley was no depression but only a line of low sandy mounds with tamarisk growing on them. Behind these we couched all our camels and the men got out their arms. Ghadi dismounted and walked back across the plain to reconnoitre from the ridge. I sat down on the sand—we all sat down and waited, but one of the Shammar women came to me and said they had a new carpet, might they put it on my loads?—so that it might seem mine, you understand. We took charge of the precious carpet. And my head camel driver Sa'id (bless his kind heart!) sat down by me and told me not to fear, for when the *ghazzu* came he would surely know them, since he knows every Arab in the desert. And that is true. But I was not afraid—only deeply interested. Nothing at all happened, and after a quarter of an hour Fattuh and I and Musuid walked off and joined Ghadi on the ridge whence we scanned the world through my glasses. There was nothing whatever. And it then appeared that the 10 camel riders rested on the ultimate authority of a Sharari boy, he of the colocynth, who had seen, and feared and turned back with the news. My firm belief, and it is now cleared by all the rest, is that he saw the Father of Goats with his flock far down in the plain below when they were pasturing on shrubs and awaiting our arrival. So I took my bearings and we went on our way, but when we rejoined the Father of Goats he was solemnly cautioned and appealed to that he should not wear so deceptive an appearance on another morning—he and his goats. That's the end of my silly story. We marched over sandstone and sand all day, and camped among rain pools and green sweet smelling shrubs—two hours too early as I began by saying. God curse the father of Musuid! But I feel better, having relieved my soul to you. It wasn't much of a burden that was oppressing it after all! Sa'id, I must tell you, is a treasure. May I never travel without him! He works like a Titan and he has a heart of gold. I wish you were here to see this wide desolate landscape and breathe an air which is like a breath from the very fountain of life.

On Saturday we had a prosperous day, passing at times through very gardens of green shrubs and flowering weeds. At night after I had gone to bed, there came to us a guest, who proved to be a Howaiti who had been out hunting oryx. His people were camped an hour or so away and we met them next day moving tents. Their shaikh, a young man called Muhammad, was very anxious that we should all stop and camp where we were, together. He had been spending the winter with the Wadi Sulaiman Arabs, who are a branch of the Fed'an, of the great 'Anazeh stock, and he reported their shaikh to be some 5 hours to the East. Since it was certain that he would hear, or had already heard, of our presence, we decided that we should be well advised to go to him and take a *rafiq* from him; accordingly we turned our course somewhat to the east and reached his tents an hour or so after noon. This man, Sayyah ibn Murted, is a rogue of the first water, cursed of his two parents as we say. He is moreover one eyed—may God deprive him of the other eye also! He received us with all show of friendliness, but over the first coffee cup he was already questioning me as to my knowledge of the country and my purpose in coming. After I had eaten dates with him I went to my tents, where he presently followed me and proceed[ed] to examine all my possessions. As ill luck would have it his eye fell on my Zeiss glass and he fixed his affections upon it instantly. He asked for everything he saw and I refused all. By night fall it was agreed that I should give him a revolver and he would send his nephew with us as *rafiq*. But in the morning he again reverted to the glass and threatened to send us away companionless and fall upon us in the night. This was not said to me, but to Fattuh and Sa'id, with further declarations that no Christian woman had ever travelled here, and none should travel. Whether these threats would have been put into execution or not, I do not know—it is the sort of doubt which one does not bring to the test if one can help it; but Sa'id, who knows the Arabs well and knew this man also, whispered to Fattuh that it were best to give way lest worse should befall, and it ended in our being stripped of both glass and revolver. Our Shammar fellow travellers fared, according to their state, no better, for the Accursed mulcted them of 3 mejidies [Turkish coins] as the price of a safe permit. I shall pay, of course. When at last we were free to depart—I had sat apart, shivering in a bitter cold wind, while these negotiations proceeded—we found ourselves with three *rafiqs*, Sayyah's nephew Zayyid, and two men of the Faqir, Hamid, brother of a shaikh, and Dahir. The Faqir are said to be still more accursed in their ancestry than the Wadi Sulaiman and we feared to go without sureties from them, lest the Shaikh, having seen us in Sayyah's tents, should send after us and rob us. It would seem that we are now perfectly safe— please God!—but there is yet a week between us and Nejd and the vicis-situdes of the wilderness are many. *Khair, inshallah!* Today's journey was very dull, rolling sand hills, stone sprinkled and featureless. The only episode of any interest was that we crossed the track of an ostrich. But we had had enough excitements in the morning and were glad to drowse along in peace. I asked the Faqir shaikh, Muhammad ibn Fendi, if they remembered Khalil who had been their guest in his father's day, and he replied yes, and that he was a good man *wallahi*.[21]

G. B. to D-W.   *Feb. 11. [11 February 1914]*

Yesterday's journey was more amusing. We began to see land-marks; but the country through which we rode was very barren. In the afternoon we came to a big valley, the Wadi Niyyal, with good herbage for the camels and there we camped. And just at sunset the full moon rose in glory and we had the two fold splendour of heaven to comfort us for the niggardliness of the earth. She was indeed niggardly this morning. We rode for 4 hours over a barren pebbly flat entirely devoid of all herbage. They call such regions *jellad*. In front of us were the first great sand hills of the Nefud [al-Nafud]. And turning a little to the west we came down into a wide bleak *khabra* wherein we found water pools under low heaps of sand. The place looked so unpromising that I was

21. Khalil was the name used by Charles Doughty during his travels in Arabia.

Two of Bell's men in the Nefud desert of northern Arabia. February 1914. Photograph by Gertrude Bell. Courtesy of the University of Newcastle upon Tyne.

prepared to find the water exhausted which would have meant a further westerly march to a well some hours away and far from our true road. We watered our camels and filled the water skins in half an hour and turned east into the Nefud. We have come so far south (the *khabra* was but a day's journey from Taimah) in order to avoid the wild sand mountains (*tu'us* they are called in Arabic) of the heart of the Nefud and our way lies now within its southern border. This great region of sand is not desert. It is full of herbage of every kind, at this time of year springing into green, a paradise for the tribes that camp in it and for our own camels. We marched through it for an hour or two and camped in deep pale gold sand with abundance of pasturage all about us, through the beneficence of God. We carry water for 3 days and then drink at the wells of Haizan [Bir Hayzan]. The *Amir*, it seems, is not at Hayyil, but camping to the north with his camel herds. I fear this may be tiresome for me; I would rather have dealt with him than with his *wakil*. Also report says that he informed all men of my coming but whether to forward me or to stop me I do not know. Neither do I know whether the report is true.

G. B. to D-W.   *Feb 13. [13 February 1914]*

We have marched for 2 days in the Nefud, and are still camping within its sands. It is very slow going, up and down in deep soft sand, but I have liked it; the plants are interesting and the sand hills are interesting. The wind driving through it hollows out profound cavities, *ga'r* they are called. You come suddenly to the brink and look down over an almost precipitous wall of sand. And from time to time there rises over the *g'ar* a head of pale driven sand, crested like a snow ridge and devoid of vegetation. These are the *tu'us*. At midday yesterday we came to a very high *ta's* [*sic*] up which I struggled—it is no small labour—and saw from the top the first of the Nejd mountains, Irnan, and to the W. the hills above Taimah and all round me a wilderness of sandbanks and *ti'as* [*sic*]. When I came down I learnt that one of my camels had been seized with a malady and had sat down some 10 minutes away. Muhammad and the negro boy, Fellah, and I went back to see what could be done for her but when we reached her we found her in the death throes. "She is gone" said Muhammad. "Shall we sacrifice her?" "It were best" said I. He drew his knife out, *"Bismillah allaha akbar!"* and cut her throat. All that day the ground was covered with the tracks of the wild cow and my *rafiqs* saw 3, but could not get near them. When we camped we spied camels grazing on the tops of the sand hills. The *rafiqs* went off to see who they were and came back with one of them, 'Audeh ibn

Habrun, a shaikh of the Awajeh. He was ready to come with us, for the other 3 had heard that the Shammar were near at hand and dared not go further. Their fear was born of the raid of 'Audeh abu Tayy. They, being friends of the Shammar had yet given the Shammar no notice of his coming; and for the same reason Masuid, the Sherari, trembled, for he had been in the tents of the Howaitat when 'Audeh set forth and he might have been accused of supplying information as to Shammar camping grounds. Therefore I paid them all off and sent them away—with no regret on my part—and we have now as *rafiq* 'Audeh ibn Habrun who seems to be very agreeable. The Howaitat raid came to very little—we have met stragglers of 'Audeh's band on their way home and heard the tale. They fell by night upon the Swaid, who are Shammar, and drove off their camels. But when dawn came and they saw the brands on the camels, the *wasms,* they found that they belonged to Ibn al Rummal, another Shammar shaikh, who had been camping with the Swaid. Now Ibn al Rummal is a friend of 'Audeh's, and his father-in-law foreby, and he therefore returned all the camels. But a band of the Sukhur, who had raided with 'Audeh, were untrammeled by any ties of friendship, and they kept the camels they had taken. So the net result was that 'Audeh got nothing and his father-in-law was looted by the Sukhur—a typical episode, if you will believe me. We have a wonderfully peaceful camp tonight in a great horseshoe of sand, with steep banks enclosing us. It is cloudy and mild—last night it froze like the devil—and I feel as if I had been born and bred in the Nefud and had known no other world. Is there any other?

G. B. to D-W.   *Feb 15. [15 February 1914]*

We came yesterday to a well, one of the rare wells on the edge of the Nefud, and I rode down to see the watering. Haizan is a profound depression surrounded by steep sand hills and the well itself is very deep—our well rope was 48 paces long. They say it is a work of the awwaliyin[?], the first forefathers, and certainly no Beduin of today would cut down into the rock and build the dry walling of the upper parts—but who can tell how old it is? There are no certain traces of age, only sand and the deep well hole. We found a number of Arabs watering their camels, the 'Anazeh clan of the Awaji who were camped near us. The men worked half naked with the passionate energy which the Arabs will put into their job for an hour or two—no more. I watched and photographed and they left me unmolested, though none had seen a European of any kind before. One or two protested at first against the photography, but the Shammar with me reassured them and I went on in peace. We go two days more through the Nefud because it is said to be the safest road and I am filled with a desire not to be stopped now, so near Hayyil. My bearings are onto Jebel Misma, which is but a few day's journey from Ibn al Rashid. I want to bring this adventure to a prosperous conclusion since we have come so far *salinum*—in the security of God.

G. B. to D-W.   *Feb 16. [16 February 1914]*

I am suffering from a severe fit of depression today—will it be any good if I put it into words, or shall I be more depressed than ever afterwards? It springs, the depression, from a profound doubt as to whether the adventure is after all worth the candle. Not because of the danger—I don't mind that; but I am beginning to wonder what profit I shall get out of it all. A compass traverse over country which was more or less known, a few names added to the map—names of stony mountains and barren plains and of a couple of deep desert wells (for we have been watering at another today)—and probably that is all. I don't know what tete [offer] the Rashid people will make to me when I arrive, and even if they were inspired by the best will in the world, I doubt whether they could do more than give me a free passage to Baghdad, for their power is not so great nowadays as it once was. And the road to Baghdad has been travelled many times before. It is nothing, the journey to Nejd, so far as any real advantage goes, or any real addition to knowledge, but I am beginning to see pretty clearly that it is all that I can do. There are two ways of profitable travel in Arabia. One is the *Arabia Deserta* way, to live with the people and to live like them for months and years. You can learn something thereby, as he did; though you may not be able to tell it again as he could. It's clear I can't take that way; the fact of being a woman bars me from it. And the other is Leachman's way—to ride swiftly through the country with your compass in your hand, for the map's sake and for nothing else.[22] And there is some profit in that too. I might be able to do that over a limited space of time, but I am not sure. Anyway it is not what I am doing now. The net result is that I think I should be more usefully employed in more civilized countries where I know what to look for and how to record it. Here, if there is anything to record the probability is that you can't find it or reach it, because a hostile tribe bars your way, or the road is waterless, or something of that kind, and that which has chanced to lie upon my path for the last 10 days is not worth mentioning—two wells, as I said before, and really I can think of nothing else. So you see the cause of my depression. I fear when I come to the end I shall not look back and say: That was worth doing; but more likely when I look back I shall say: It was a waste of time. It's done now, and there is no remedy, but I think I was a fool to come into these wastes when I have not, and cannot have, a free hand to work at the things I care for. And this reflection is discouraging. It comes too late, like most of our wisest reflections. That's my thought tonight, and I fear it is perilously near the truth. I almost wish that something would happen—something exciting, a raid, or a battle! And yet that's not my job either. What do ineffective archaeologists want with battles? They would only serve to pass the time and leave as little profit as before. There is such a long way between me and letters, or between me and anything and I don't feel at all like the daughter of kings, which I am supposed here to be. It's a bore being a woman when you are in Arabia.

22. Gerald Leachman, an officer famed in the desert for bravery and ill-temper. Murdered in Iraq in 1920. Gertrude Bell disapproved of him.

G. B. to D-W.   *Feb. 17. [17 February 1914]*

We were held up today by rain. It began, most annoyingly, just after we had struck camp—at least I don't know that it was so very annoying, for we put in a couple of hours' march. But the custom of the country was too strong for me. You do not march in the rain. It was, I must admit, torrential. It came sweeping upon us from behind and passing on blotted out the landscape in front, till my *rafiq* said that he should lose his way, there were no landmarks to be seen. "No Arabs move camp today" said he "they fear to be lost in the Nefud." And as he trudged on through the wet sand, his cotton clothes clinging to his drenched body, he rejoiced and gave thanks for the rain. "Please God it goes over all the world" he said and "The camels will pasture here for 3 months time." The clouds lifted a little but when a second flood overtook us I gave way. We pitched the men's tent and lighted a great fire at which we dried ourselves—I was wet too. In a moment's sunshine we pitched the other tents, and then came thunder and hail and rain so heavy that the pools stood twinkling in the thirsty sand. I sat in my tent and read *Hamlet* from beginning to end and, as I read, the world swung back into focus. Princes and powers of Arabia stepped down into their truc place and there rose up above them the human soul conscious and answerable to itself, made with such large discourse, looking before and after—. Before sunset I stood on the top of the sand hills and saw the wings of the rain sweeping round 'Irnan and leaving Misma' light-bathed—Then the hurrying clouds marched over the sand and once more we were wrapped in rain. No fear now of drought ahead of us.

G. B. to D-W.   *Feb. 20. [20 February 1914]*

God is merciful and we have done with the Nefud. The day after the rain—oh but the wet sand smelt good and there was a twittering of small birds to gladden the heart!—we came in the afternoon to some tents of the Shammar and pitching our camp not far off we were visited by the old shaikh, Mhailam, who brought us a goat and some butter.

Volcanic rock in Arabian desert near Jebel Misma. February 1914. Photograph by Gertrude Bell. Courtesy of the University of Newcastle upon Tyne.

Him we induced to come with us as *rafiq*. He is old and lean, gray haired and toothless, and ragged beyond belief; he has not even an *'agal* to bind the kerchief on his head and we have given him a piece of rope. But he is an excellent *rafiq*—I have not had a better. He knows the country and he is anxious to serve us well. And next day we rode over sand to the northern point of Jebel Misma'. Then Mhailam importuned me to camp saying there was no pasturage in the *jellad,* the flat plain below; and Muhammad al-Ma'rawi backed him for he feared that we might fall in with Hetaim raiders if we left the Nefud. But I held firm. Raiders and hunger were as nothing to the possibility of a hard straight road. For you understand that travelling in the Nefud is like travelling in the Labyrinth. You are forever skirting round a deep horseshoe pit of sand, perhaps half a mile wide, and climbing up the opposite slope, and skirting round the next horseshoe. If we made a mile an hour as the crow flies we did well. Even after I had delivered the ultimatum, my two old parties were constantly heading off to the Nefud and I had to keep a watchful eye on them and herd them back every half hour. It was bitter cold; the temperature had fallen to 27° in the night and there was a tempestuous north wind. And so we came to the last sand crest and I looked down between the black rocks of Misma' and saw Nejd. It was a landscape terrifying in its desolation. Misma' drops to the east in precipices of sandstone, weathered to a rusty black; at its feet are gathered endless companies of sandstone pinnacles, black too, shouldering one over the other. They look like the skeleton of a vast city planted on a sandstone and sand-strewn floor. And beyond and beyond more pallid lifeless plain and more great crags of sandstone mountains rising abruptly out of it. Over it all the bitter wind whipped the cloud shadows. *"Subhan Allah!"* said one of my Damascenes, "we have come to Jehannum." Down into it we went and camped on the skirts of the Nefud with a sufficiency of pasturage. And today the sun shone and the world smiled and we marched off gaily and found the floor of Hell to be a very pleasant place after all. For the rain has filled all the sandstone hollows with clear water, and the pasturage is abundant, and the going, over the flat rocky floor, is all the heart could desire. In the afternoon we passed between the rocks of Jebel Habran, marching over a sandy floor with black pinnacled precipices on either hand, and camped on the east, in a bay of rock with *khabras* of rain water below and pasturage all round us in the sand. We have for neighbours about a mile away a small *ferij* of Shammar tents, and lest there should be anyone so evil minded as to dream of stealing a camel from us, Mhailam has just now stepped out into the night and shouted: "Ho! Anyone who watches! come in to supper! I am Mhailam, Mhailam ibn Hamad! Let anyone who is hungry come and eat!" And having thus invited the universe to our bowl, we sleep, I trust, in peace.

G. B. to D-W.   *Feb 24. [24 February 1914]*

We are within sight of Hayyil and I might have ridden in today but I thought it better to announce my auspicious coming! So I sent in two men early this morning, Muhammad and 'Ali, and have myself camped a couple of hours outside. We had a dull day's journey on the 21st, over an endless flat plain, but a most delicious camp in the top of a mountain, Jebel Rakham. I climbed the rocks and found flowers in the crevices—not a great bounty, but in this barren land a feast to the eyes. And next day, what do you think? we were back in the Nefud, for two mortal days, wearily plodding through sand again. It comes down in a long finger here and we had to cross it. On the 22nd we saw the first village—the first inhabited place since Ziza—5 or 6 hours and a plot or two of corn and some big *ithl* trees in a hollow of the Nefud. The men ran out with their guns, taking us for raiders, but finding us to be harmless they ran back and brought us a skin of excellent leben. Yesterday we passed by two more villages and in one there were plum trees flowing—oh the gracious sight! And today we have come through the wild granite crags of Jebel 'Ajja and are camped in the Hayyil plain. From a little rock above my tent I have spied out the land and seen the towers and gardens of Hayyil, and Swaifly lying in the plain beyond, and all is made memorable by *Arabia Deserta*. I feel as if I were on a sort of pilgrimage, visiting sacred sites. And the more I see of this land the more I realize what an achievement that journey was. But isn't it amazing that we should have walked down into Nejd with as much ease as if we had been strolling along Piccadilly!

MARCH 1914

G. B. to D-W.   *March 2. [2 March 1914]*

What did I tell you as to the quality most needed for travel among the Arabs? Patience if you remember; that is what one needs. Now listen to the tale of the week we have spent here. I was received with the utmost courtesy. Their slaves, *'abds,* slave is too servile and yet that is what they are—came riding out to meet me and assured me that Ibrahim, the *Amir's wakil* was much gratified by my visit. We rode round the walls of the town and entered in by the south gate—the walls are of quite recent construction, towered, all round the town—and there, just within the gate I was lodged in a spacious house which Muhammad ibn Rashid had built for his summer dwelling. My tents were pitched in the wide court below. Within our enclosure there is an immense area of what was once gardens and cornfields but it is now left unwatered and uncultivated. The Persian Hajj used to lodge here in the old days.[23] As soon as I was established in the *Roshan,* the great columned reception room, and when the men had all gone off to see to the tents and camels, two women appeared. One was an old widow, Lu.lu.ah, who is caretaker in the house; she lives here with her slave woman and the latter's boy. The other was a merry lady, Turkiyyeh, a Circassian who had belonged to Muhammed al Rashid and had been a great favourite of his. She had been sent down from the *qasr* to receive

23. The Muslim pilgrimage.

me and amuse me and the latter duty she was most successful in performing. In the afternoon came Ibrahim, in state and all smiles. He is an intelligent and well educated man—for Arabia with a quick nervous manner and a restless eye. He stayed till the afternoon prayer. As he went out he told Muhammad al-Ma'rawi that there was some discontent among the *'ulema*[24] at my coming and that etc etc in short, I was not to come further into the town till I was invited. Next day I sent my camels back to the Nefud borders to pasture. There is no pasture here in the granite grit plain of Hayyil and moreover they badly needed rest. I sold 6, for more than they were worth, for they were in wretched condition; but camels are fortunately dear here at this moment, with the *Amir* away and all available animals with him. And that done I sat still and waited on events. But there were no events. Nothing whatever happened, except that two little Rashid princes came to see me, 2 of the 6 male descendants who are all that remain of all the Rashid stock, so relentlessly have they slaughtered one another. Next day I sent to Ibrahim and said I should like to return his call. He invited me to come after dark and sent a mare for me and a couple of slaves. I rode through the dark and empty streets and was received in the big *Roshan* of the *qasr,* a very splendid place with great stone columns supporting an immensely lofty roof, the walls white washed, the floor of white juss, beaten hard and shining as if it were polished. There was a large company. We sat all round the wall on carpets and cushions, I on Ibrahim's right hand, and talked mostly of the history of the Shammar in general and of the Rashids in particular. Ibrahim is well versed in it and I was much interested. As we talked slave boys served us with tea and then coffee and finally they brought lighted censors [*sic*] and swung the sweet smelling *'ud* before each of us three times. This is the signal that the reception is over and I rose and left them. And then followed day after weary day with nothing whatever to do. One day Ibrahim sent me a mare and I

24. The Muslim clergy.

rode round the town and visited one of his gardens—a paradise of blossoming fruit trees in the bare wilderness. And the Circassian, Turkiyyeh, has spent another day with me; and my own slaves (for I have 2 of own to keep my gate for me) sit and tell me tales of raid and foray in the stirring days of 'Abd al Aziz, Muhammad's nephew; and my men come in and tell me the gossip of the town. Finally I have sent for my camels—I should have done so days ago if they had not been so much in need of rest. I can give them no more time to recover for I am penniless. I brought with me a letter of credit on the Rashid's from their agent in Damascus—Ibrahim refuses to honour it in the absence of the *Amir* and if I had not sold some of my camels I should not have had enough money to get away. As it is I have only the barest minimum. The gossip is that the hand which has pulled the strings in all this business is that of the *Amir*'s grandmother, Fatima, of whom Ibrahim stands in deadly fear. In Hayyil murder is like the spilling of milk and not one of the shaikhs but feels his head sitting unsteadily upon his shoulders. I have asked to be allowed to see Fatima and have received no answer. She holds the purse strings in the *Amir*'s absence and she rules. It may be that she is at the bottom of it all. I will not conceal from you that there have been hours of considerable anxiety. War is all round us. The *Amir* is raiding Jof to the north and Ibn Sa'ud is gathering up his powers to the south—presumably to raid the *Amir*. If Ibrahim chose to stop my departure till the *Amir*'s return (which was what I feared) it would have been very uncomfortable. I spent a long night contriving in my head schemes of escape if things went wrong. I have however two powerful friends in Hayyil, shaikhs of 'Anezah [*sic*], with whose help the Rashids hope to recapture that town. I have not seen them—they dare not visit me—but they have protested vigorously against the treatment which has been accorded me. I owe their assistance to the fact that I have their nephew with me, 'Ali the postman who came with me 3 years ago across the Hamad. Yesterday I demanded a private audience of Ibrahim and was received, again at night, in an upper hall of the *qasr*. I told him that I would stay here no longer, that the withholding of the money due to me had caused me great inconvenience and that I must now ask of him a *rafiq* to go with me to the 'Anazeh borders. He was very civil and assured me that the *rafiq* was ready. It does not look as if they intended to put any difficulties in my way. My plan is to choose out the best of my camels and taking with me Fattuh, 'Ali and the negro boy Fellah, to ride to Nejef [al-Najaf]. The Damascenes I send back to Damascus. They will wait a few days more to give the other camels longer rest and then join a caravan which is going to Medina [al-Madinah]—10 days' journey. Thence by train. Since I have no money I can do nothing but push on to Baghdad, but it is at least consoling to think that I could not this year have done more. I could not have gone south from here; the tribes are up and the road is barred. Ibn Sa'ud has—so we hear—taken the Hasa, and driven out the Turkish troops.[25] I think it highly probable that he intends to turn against Hayyil and if by any chance the *Amir* should not be successful in his raid on Hayyil ["Jof" written above], the future of the Shammar would look dark indeed. The Turkish Govt. are sending them arms—a convoy has gone to Medain Salih [Mada'in Salih] to fetch them; but I think that Ibn Saud's star is in the ascendent and if he combines with Ibn Sha'lan (the Ruwalla 'Anazeh) they will have Ibn Rashid between the hammer and the anvil. I feel as if I had lived through a chapter of the *Arabian Nights* during this last week. The Circassian woman and the slaves, the doubt and anxiety, Fatima weaving her plots behind the *qasr* walls, Ibrahim with his smiling lips and restless shifting eyes—and the whole town waiting to hear the fate of the army which has gone up with the *Amir* against Jof. And to the spiritual sense the place smells of blood. Twice since Khalil was here have the Rashids put one another to the sword—the tales round my camp fire are all of murder and the air whispers murder. It gets upon your nerves when you sit day after day between high mud walls and I thank heaven that my nerves are not very responsive. They have kept me awake only one

25. Hasa is a strip of eastern Arabia adjacent to the Arabian Gulf.

night out of seven! And good, please God! please God nothing but good.

Bell's caravan at entrance to Hayyil. February 1914. Photograph by Gertrude Bell. *Courtesy of the University of Newcastle upon Tyne.*

G. B. to D-W. *March 6. [6 March 1914]*

We have at last reached the end of the comedy—for a comedy it has after all proved to be. And what has been the underlying reason of it all I cannot tell, for who can look into their dark minds? On March 3 there appeared in the morning a certain eunuch slave Sa'id, who is a person of great importance and with him another, and informed me that I could not travel, neither could they give me any money, until a messenger had arrived from the *Amir.* I sent messages at once to 'Ali's uncles and the negotiations were taken up again with renewed vigour. Next day

Turkiyyeh, at Hayyil. February 1914. Photograph by Gertrude Bell. Courtesy of the University of Newcastle upon Tyne.

came word from the *Amir*'s mother, Mudi, inviting me to visit
them that evening. I went (riding solemnly through the silent
moonlit streets of this strange place), and passed two hours taken
straight from the *Arabian Nights* with the women of the palace. I
imagine that there are few places left wherein you can see the
unadulterated East in its habit as it has lived for centuries and centuries—of those few Hayyil is one. There they were, those
women—wrapped in Indian brocades, hung with jewels, served
by slaves and there was not one single thing about them which be-
trayed the base existence of Europe or Europeans—except me! I

was the blot. Some of the women of the shaikhly house were very beautiful. They pass from hand to hand—the victor takes them, with her power and the glory, and think of it! his hands are red with the blood of their husband and children. Mudi herself—she is still a young woman and very charming—has been the wife of 3 *Amir*s in turn. Well, some day I will tell you what it is all like, but truly I still feel bewildered by it. I passed the next day in solitary confinement—I have been a prisoner, you understand, in this big house they gave me. Today came an invitation from two boys, cousins of the *Amir*'s to visit them in their garden. I went after the midday prayers and stayed till the *'asr*. Again it was fantastically oriental and medieval. There were 5 very small children, all cousins, dressed in long gold embroidered robes, solemn and silent, staring at me with their painted eyes. And my hosts, who may have been 13 or 14 years old—one had a merry face like a real boy, the other was grave and impassive. But both were most hospitable. We sat in a garden house on carpets—like all the drawings in Persian picture books. Slaves and eunuchs served us with tea and coffee and fruits. Then we walked about the garden, the boys carefully telling me the names of all the trees. And then we sat again and drank more tea and coffee. Sa'id the eunuch was of the party and again I expressed my desire to depart from Hayyil and again was met by the same negative— Not till the *Amir*'s messenger has come. Not I nor anyone knows when the messenger will come, neither did I know whether there were more behind their answer. Sa'id came to us after the *'asr* and I spoke to him with much vigour and ended the interview abruptly by rising and leaving him. I thought indeed that I had been too abrupt, but to tell you the truth I was bothered. An hour later came in my camels and after dark Sa'id again with a bag of gold and full permission to go where I liked and when I liked. And why they have now given way, or why they did not give way before, I cannot guess. But anyhow I am free and my heart is at rest—it is widened.

I have not written any of my tale for these ten days, because of the deadly fatigue of the way. But today, as I will tell you, I have had a short day and I will profit by it. I did not leave Hayyil till March 8. I asked and obtained leave to see the town and the *qasr* by daylight— which I had never been allowed to do—and to photograph. They gave me full permission to photograph—to my surprise and pleasure, and I went out next day, was shown the *modif* and the great kitchen of the *qasr* and took many pictures. Every one was smiling and affable—and I thought all the time of Khalil, coming in there for his coffee and his pittance of *taman*. It is extraordinarily picturesque and I make no doubt that it preserves the aspect of every Arabian palace that has ever been since the Days of Ignorance. Some day, *inshallah*, you shall see my pictures. Then I photographed the *meshab* and the outside of the mosque and as I went through the streets I photographed them too. As I was going home there came a message from my Circassian friend, Turkiyyeh, inviting me to tea at her house. I went, and photographed Hayyil from her roof and took an affectionate farewell of her. She and I are now, I imagine, parted for ever, except in remembrance. As I walked home all the people crowded out to see me, but they seemed to take nothing but a benevolent interest in my doings. And finally the halt, the maim [*sic*] and the blind gathered round my door and I flung out a bag of copper coins among them. And thus it was that my strange visit to Hayyil ended, after 11 days' imprisonment, in a sort of apotheosis! I wanted to ride up to Nejef by the old pilgrim road, the Derb Zubaidah, but at dawn on the morning of my departure there came a slave from the palace, a man with henna dyed beard and blackened eyes, of sinister aspect, and brought me a message to the effect that in my view of my safety, which was of the greatest concern to the *Amir*, I was to take the Western road, since the eastern was *khala*—empty of the tribes and raided by their enemies. I acquiesced—it did not much matter—wondering what was at the back of their mind. For we subsequently learnt that the Shammar lay all along the eastern road which was therefore as safe as any other. I fancy they meant to send me to the *Amir* and thinking he was certain to be on the western road they issued their order. As it turned out I should have met him if I had gone by the Derb Zubaidah, for he moved across ahead of me (so we learnt from the Arabs) and by the time I reached the place where my guide expected him to be, he had passed east. Following an Arab shaikh is much like following a grasshopper and I did not intend to turn out of my way for him, much less back; so in the end I have not seen him! On the second day out from Hayyil we met his messengers who stopped and greeted us and said the *Amir* was expecting me. They told me that he had taken Jof and driven out the Ruwalla without a shot being fired. After 2 days more a couple of his *rajajil* came into our camp at evening on the way to Hayyil and gave us the same news about Jof, with many details as to its capture—mark my tale! We travelled over the Nefud for 4 weary days—but it was starred all over with white and yellow daisies. We followed a road, a *khall,* which I make no doubt is very ancient, worn deep into the sand. And then we came out into great plains, flower covered too—the desert is gay at this season with flowering weeds. We have marched 9 to 10 hours every day, not really long marches, but so wearying to the spirit in this immense monotony that I come into camp every evening giddy with fatigue. Perhaps, too, I am beginning to feel the effects of rather hard camp fare; anyway I shall be glad to reach civilization again, and to rest for a day or two. Two days ago we dismissed our Hayyil *rafiq* and took on another Shammari. This innocent had been with the *Amir* on his recent campaign and he spent the first day in telling us the story of it—wholly unaware of the official version which had been served up to us and to the rest of the world. They stopped short at a fortified village several hours short of Jof—and were turned back by Ibn Sha'lan's garrison. "Did you not enter Jof?" said I. *"La billah"* said he. *"Sahih?"* said I—is it true? *"Egh billah Sahih—w'al shof ma shufn—*and we did not even set eyes on it." *"Wallah?"* said I. *"Egh wallah"* he replied. It's a confusing world, isn't it! But I don't doubt that this last is the true tale.

And now I will tell you my general idea of Arabian politics. Hayyil gave me a sinister impression. I do not like the rule of women and of eunuchs. The unsuccessful expedition against Ibn Sha'lan and the attempt to cover up their tracks with false reports so easily exploded do not serve to modify my views. I think the Rashid are moving towards their close. Not one grown man of their house remains alive—the *Amir* is only 16 or 17, and all the

Member of Bell's entourage, at Hayyil. March 1914. Photograph by Gertrude Bell.
Courtesy of the University of Newcastle upon Tyne.

others are little more than babes, so deadly has been the family strife. I have not seen the man who is Sa'ud's [the Rashid *amir*'s] chief advisor, Zamil, Ibrahim's brother, but from what I have heard I do not fancy that he has great powers of the intelligence. Nor is there anyone who stands out pre-eminent. I should say that the future lies with Ibn Sa'ud. If it is true—as we hear—that he has driven the Turks out of the Hasa, he is a formidable adversary. But the Shammar, with their 80 years of rule behind them, will take some conquering. If Ibn Sa'ud could strike a decisive blow, all the 'Anazeh would flock in to share the spoils and then indeed

Hayyil might be brought low. I cannot find it in my heart to wish the Rashid much good. Their history is one long tale of treachery and murder—you shall hear it some day. I do not know what Ibn Sa'ud is like, but worse he cannot be. So there! my next Arabian journey shall be to him. I have already laid out all my plans for it.

Today we reached the limits of the Shammar and dropped into a big encampment of one of the Shi'a tribes of Nejef, the Ri'u. These transitions are always difficult to effect and we passed a delicate hour in the tent of the Shaikh. It was by no means clear whether he intended to rob us or to welcome us. Finally, after much diplomacy, the scale turned in our favour. We have pitched out tents by his and are to have a *rafiq* tomorrow—and a lamb tonight! They are not Bedu, these people, and they have a bad name. But as soon as we had come to terms with them, and eaten dates and *semen* in the shaikh's tent, they became affable and have spent the rest of the afternoon round our camp fire. Also they dressed up in their best and performed a strange dance, led by their green turbaned *sayyid*, while I photographed them. They sang the while in praise of their patron *sayyid*—it is all very unlike Wahabi Hayyil and I am not very fond of Shi'a—but *khair, inshallah.*

G. B. to D-W.   *March 26. [26 March 1914]*

Baghdad. But what days those were during which we rode up to Nejef. They were the only difficult days of the journey and I am prepared to swear on the book, the book most sacred to you, that the Ri'u deserve all the ill that is commonly said of them. On March 18 we set off gaily with 2 *rafiqs* I must tell you we had all become the greatest friends over the camp fire after dinner. This particular sept was the Beni Hasan with one of whose shaikhs I had once travelled for 2 days before, in 1911.[26] Well, we set off gaily, and rode all day and saw no one and camped *khalawi*, in emptiness. And all was well. So we rode for 2 hours

26. *Sept* is a tribal division.

next morning and then they sighted flocks and tents and were thrown into paroxysms of anxiety. For would it be one of the Ri'u clans who would kill them at sight (our *rafiqs* I mean) or again not? So we all waited in a hollow and they rode off to the tents to find out what men were there. Oh but I know these moments of waiting! we've done it so often. On a careful analysis of my feelings I have come to the conclusion that I'm afraid at these times. That must be fear, that little restiveness of the mind, like a very fresh horse that keeps on straining at the reins and then letting them go abruptly—you know the feeling in your hands, like an irregular pulse. One of my horses at home does it, a very mad one. And then the profound desire to be safely through the next hour! Yes, it's fear. What fun it is to write to you about it, but I expect you don't know the irregular pulse feeling in the mind. But what's very singular is that I don't really dislike it. I dislike it in a way, I suppose, because I wish it were over, and yet I find it exciting. Everybody feels like that I imagine. Well, enough of fear. There was no reason for it that time. The *rafiqs* came back with 2 other horsemen. They were the Beni Salamah, closely allied to the B. Hasan, and they were to come on with us. For there was no doubt as to the sentiments of the B. Hasan; they were afraid and they were not enjoying it. They would not go on another step. We rode on with the B. Salamah men for about 6 hours, and then paff! we saw sheep. You don't think that was alarming? but they did—the men, not the sheep, were alarmed. For the previous hour they had been saying that they would not go on, that they could not possibly camp with us that night. "People we don't know"—the vague phrase which means in the desert *yuth bahuna*—they will slay us. *"Yuth bahuna"* they said when they saw the sheep. Should we camp, or should we go on and look for the tents? The question was settled by our sighting the tents quite close. They would be sure to see us; we must go on. You understand we were a very salient feature, we on camels, in a landscape composed otherwise solely of donkeys. For these Arab don't have camels; only the Bedu have camels. They have sheep and they carry their tents on donkeys. Seeing us they would take us for a small raiding party of Bedu, or a small party of merchants up from Hayyil, and in either case—*yuth bahuna*, if they could! (I love writing this silly story to you.) So then we persuaded one of our horsemen (he was rather reluctant) to ride up to the tents, and we followed slowly. I wasn't afraid that time; I was beginning to be bored. He alighted at the tent and engaged in conversation with the owner; when he saw that we at once proceeded to pitch tents. We were all right. He came back and said they were the Ghazalat. 'Ali and I looked at each other and *Al hamdu lillah!* we said. The Ghazalat are just as impish as the others—accursed of their two parents, all of them—but they are much more powerful, and if we were their guests and got a *rafiq* from them we were safe. And it turned out so. We got an excellent *rafiq,* Dawi was his name. He is *rafiq* to Ibn Rashid's caravans when they come to Nejef for rice, a well known man, grave and silent, with a grizzled beard and a wonderfully fine, clean cut face. We had found a pearl among swine, our usual good luck. But it was indeed good luck. We had come to the end of our water—this was the 5th night from water and we had been very sparing. I had had no bath and scarcely any washing—horrid, isn't it. Therefore we had to fill our water skins next day. We did so at some foul and stagnant pools in a small hollow bottom. And there we found 20 or 30 Arabs engaged in the same task. They would have stripped us to a certainty. They offered Dawi Pound £T30 if he leave us. He could not, of course; but I don't think he wished to leave us. Meantime these sons of the devil were all most merry with us and I photographed them and so on. We went on and saw no more people and camped alone. Next day the 21st, we dropped into the Derb Zubaidah, the high road in the desert up from Hayyil—it was the road I had wanted to take. I thought we really were safe then, but *al khuaf qarib,* as they say—danger is always near. In the afternoon we met a great band of Arab coming up from Nejef—they had been buying provisions. In a moment we were surrounded. Stalwart devils, many of them green turbaned came up on every side, laid hold of our camels by the halters and would have couched them. The Dawi lifted up his voice: in a moment the face of things was changed. "Is that a *Sayyid* I see leading off the *dulul*" said he (it was one of our baggage camels) "amazing *billah!*" The Sayyid slunk off and we passed through. When we were well past them he said to 'Ali "They would have stripped you." "I have news of it" said 'Ali. "Am I not a son of 'Iraq?" That was not quite the end. We turned off the high road for we were going to a place called 'Ain al Sayyid next day; and as we looked back we saw a large caravan behind us on the road we had left, and then we heard shooting in the big valley from which we had turned away, and then we saw men following us, galloping on donkeys. We hurried on. It grew near sunset. At last one of the donkey riders ("Like a horse-man, *wallahi!*" and he did go fast) heaved up on the top of a neighbour-ing ridge. It was no good going on without knowing what they wanted of us; we dismounted Dawi, gave him a rifle, and sent him back to in-quire. It was all right, as usual. It was they who were afraid; they thought us a *ghazzu* and they had sheep in the valley. The shots had been a *feu de joie* [joke] apparently, or so I made out; they may have been more. We camped; the men were not quite happy, but I was sleepy—we had had 11 hours that day—and I slept as soon as my head was on the pillow. If they were going to slay us in the night, why so it would be, *nasib!* But they didn't; no one came. We were about 3 hours from 'Ain al Sayyid and it is 6 from Nejef. 'Ain al Sayyid was once called Qarq-isiyyeh—it was near this village that the riders of Islam defeated the Chosroes. He fled back broken to Ctesiphon, was defeated there again and so ended. At Qarqisiyyeh the history of the world was changed—I wanted to set eyes on the place. Besides there might be old ruins. I knew there was a village there and a castle of some kind. Soon we sight-ed it across that immense flat; we also saw flocks of sheep, but this time we paid no attention until a rifle bullet came whizzing actually between our camels' legs. We heard it with remarkable clearness. It came from one of the shepherds—exploratory, no doubt, rather than aimed in anger, but still disconcerting. Dawi couched his camel at once, lest a second bullet, better aimed, should come, took a rifle and ran out to expostulate and explain. There were two or three of them with the flocks; they looked rather sheepish themselves. 'Ali was very indignant. "Does an enemy come riding over the plain, on camels in broad daylight? no face of God; he creeps up the low ground by night. And if you were afraid the custom is to send a bullet over the heads of the riders, and see whether they are friends or foes—that is the custom." They admitted that they had broken the rules—I was sufficiently content that they had broken nothing else, a camel's leg, for instance. We were only shot at once more before we reached 'Ain al Sayyid, and that was from far off. But there was nothing there, a great spring, old village mounds, and a castle, no doubt on the old site, but itself built not more that two or three hundred years ago, as I should judge—I may say, as I know. I had meant not to go to Nejef but to ride straight up through the desert to Kerbela [Karbala] and touch civilization there, so avoiding the weary high road from Nejef to Kerbela. But my men were rather shaken by the experiences of the last few days, and there was no real reason for more desert, so I gave way. We turned to Nejef—we could see the golden dome glittering—agreeing to camp short of it. I have camped at Nejef before and it's not nice—there is no camping ground and it's alive with robbers. No camping ground near the town because of the graveyards. But there are no trees for the camels to eat for the last 3 hours into Nejef, so we camped at the limit of the trees, at 1 o'clock, in *sabkha*—you know *sabkha*? the salt ground in which palms grow. It was horrid, infested by sandflies, but I sat in anger (because of the sandflies) and wrote up notes and my diary for two hours—jotting down the headings of our adventures—and then it occurred to me to go and ask 'Ali if he thought we were safe camping there—he had chosen the place himself I must mention. And it turned out that he did not think we were safe at all—far from it. We were too near the road, and at night these accursed of their two parents would not know that we had Dawi with us, and in short his mind was very ill at ease. So after some talk—I, thinking it was silly to run the risk of a regrettable incident 3 hours out of Nejef, and for no reason (you see how prudent I am), hustled them out of camp. The dinner, which was cooked, was carried in our good pots, we packed and loaded in half an hour and off we set, with 1¼ hours before sunset. It was a preposterous episode, but Fattuh and 'Ali were deeply relieved at my decision. Just at sunset we came to a small village of wattle huts—*felalih,* cultivation. There were corn fields ahead and the inevitable irrigation canals, probably bridgeless, into which we should slip and founder at night—we turned off and camped near the village perfectly safe at last. Fattuh rose up soon after midnight, and with a guide rode a donkey back to Nejef to secure a carriage for me. I determined not to ride along the high road. We followed at dawn; the canals were difficult with camels but we reached Nejef safe and sound. And then no Fattuh! We searched and searched for him round the town. I went down into the bazaar, found out where he had hired the carriage and that he had gone off in it some time ago, searched again, went into the bazaar again (the people were all mighty civil) and finally learnt that he had gone to Masalla, the first stage on the road. What his idea had been I have never been able to understand; it was all a micmac, but we had wasted 3 hot and weary hours over it. I bought oranges (oh the delicious fruit—I eat 6 running!) we mounted our camels and set off along the Masalla road. And an hour out we met Fattuh, hot and dirty, poor dear, and very anxious, walking back to look for us. He had left the carriage—it was a post carriage and supposed not to stop for God or man—at Masalla; whether it would wait he didn't know. It did wait. We reached Masalla at 1 o'clock—I had camped there 3 years ago and was greeted by many acquaintances. We bundled my personal baggage into the post cart and me after it, and off we jolted. It was 6 hours to Kerbela with 2 changes of horses. The gendarmes came up and chatted with us as we changed horses—each posting station is a *nuqtah* with 3 or 4 gendarmes. I could have fallen on their necks, the good *jonddurma*—I was so much pleased to see them again. "Your Arab are accursed of their two parents" said I and they burst into the relation of their woes and difficulties. The knife, the rifle, the revolver, that was all these 'Arab thought of, and dib! dib! dib!—the popping of the rifle bullets, you understand—where were the days of Nazim Pasha![27] That's the ring of it in 'Iraq—where are the days of Nazim Pasha! The whole thing has fallen to pieces again, the tribes all out of hand, everyone armed—I saw them carrying rifles in the bazaar at Nejef. Turkey moves, but round and round, not forward and we have come to the dark side of the moon again. It's hopeless. They have just sent out a new Vali [governor] here, Jawid, perhaps you know him? a soldier—he is said to have been the only general who remained undefeated in the Balkan war. My own impression is that he has not laid and is not going to lay the fear of God on them. The Nejef post was robbed but a week or two ago and 4000 odd pounds of Govt. money taken—the Nejef post has not been robbed for ever so long before. And our dear little Indian vice consul at Kerbela—oh but I haven't got there yet. We reached Kerbela in the dark, after some trouble with irrigation canals (I thought we were going to spend the night in one of them). I left my baggage at the posting inn and went to Muhammad Hussain Khan—he was an old friend, I stayed with him once before, a nice man. He kept me to dinner (an excellent dinner he gave me) and I stayed talking till past 10—the last lap was of Islam and their law and religion, very interesting. We talked in English—I hadn't heard English since Dec. 15. There were carriage difficulties too, which he arranged for me, God give him the reward! Our talk on religion opened by his saying he was coming to England on leave. "What will you do with your family?" said I. "Oh I shall leave them here" said he "and I shall probably divorce my wife before I leave." "!!!!" said I, or something of that nature. And then he told me his family difficulties—she was not a pleasant wife he said, and he had put up with her for 15

27. Ottoman governor of Iraq, murdered in 1913.

years and could stand it no longer. That led to a long talk and he said many sensible things but I don't think the Abp [Archbishop] of York would see eye to eye with him. So perhaps he will be in search of a bride when he comes to England—I wish I could find him one, a pleasant one. I like the good little man. I got to bed long past 11 and got up at 2, for the post carriages start at 3. I was cross and sleepy and tired and very anxious for my letters—those dreadful anxieties that come out to meet you across the desert—and the wide Babylonian landscape seemed particularly desolate and monotonous *kharban* ruined, nothing left of all its great history and prosperity. We reached Baghdad at 1.30, Fattuh was with me of course, and I snapped at him, Heaven forgive me, being tired and anxious. I asked him to forgive me afterwards and explained how it had been. I went straight to the Residency and got my letters from Col. Erskine. Mrs E. is in bed with a wound in the leg—a fall she had 3 weeks ago. He didn't ask me to stay and I didn't mind, for I wanted to be in peace and read my letters and recover my temper. I read them all the evening till late at night, over and over again—such a pile there were of them and I had not had news for so long. You know the sad Lorimer tragedy? he shot himself by accident in Bushire [Bushehr]. They wouldn't have been here anyway; they had gone to Bushire. But, I am so sorry about it and I miss the dear Lorimers so much. Also Col. Erskine—I lunched with him yesterday and spent a long time with her in her bedroom—of course he knows nothing, having been here some 3 months only, or less. He wasn't even sure who Ibn Rashid was—how Mr Lorimer would have loved to hear my tales and what a great deal we would have unravelled together with the help of what I know! There it is! And the end of an adventure always leaves one with a feeling of disillusion—don't you know it? I try to school myself beforehand by reminding myself how I have looked forward and looked forward at other times to the end, and when it came have found it—just nothing. Dust and ashes in one's hand, dead bones that look as if they would never rise and dance—it's all just nothing and one turns away from it with a sigh and tries to fix one's eyes on to the new thing before one. That's how I felt when I came into Baghdad. And this adventure hasn't been successful either. I have not done what I meant to do. But I have got over that now, since yesterday. It's all one and I don't care. Already I want the next thing, whatever it may be—I've done with that. No, I suppose I haven't really done with it. I don't feel at all inclined now to write about it, but perhaps I am too near to it. Perhaps it will look better when it is a little further off and perhaps I may find things to say about it. I don't know. I think the only things that are worth saying are those that I can't say—my own self in it, how it looked to the eyes of the human being, weak and ignorant and wondering, weary and disappointed, who was in the midst of it. I can't say them because they are too intimate, and also because I haven't the skill. But perhaps after all I may write of it—if I do, will you send me back this little journal, lend it to me? It is yours if you care to have it, but it was written in the midst of it all, with an attempt to[?] the road to one who was only looking on it through my eyes and it may have things of the moment which remind and give the clue to me when I come back to those days afterwards. One doesn't put those things into one's own diary because one is not trying to draw the picture—it is there before one. Perhaps I shall not write—I don't know. Arabia Infelix? I wish I had seen more of it—that name would be too big for what I have to say. But I would like that name.—Well I'm glad I've unburdened my soul to you about the disillusionment that comes with ending. You know it, too, most certainly and you will understand. And I feel as if I had shaken it off now that I have told you it to you. The mail does not go till next week and I may hear local politics which are of interest, and then I'll write them here before this is posted. I've sent word to my native friends that I am here and I am going to see Meissner Pasha—he is here constructing the railway. The first thing I saw as I came into Baghdad was the railway station— it's the only thing that looks like going forward instead of round and round, and I am glad to see it. My camels won't come in till tomorrow. I have some arrangements to make about them and then I think I shall go to Babylon for a few days and stay with my dear Germans. Back to Damascus across the Syrian Desert, travelling very light. I intend to send most of my baggage home by sea. I shall not go by the post road—post road no more, they don't send letters that way now—but by some other places I want to see. It's perfectly safe, the Syrian Desert—one can go where one likes if one has a man (as I have) who knows every creature that lives in it. 'Ali knows them all.

G. B. to D-W.   *March 28. [28 March 1914]*

 I have seen and heard a good deal. Not from the Erskines!—we certainly are an odd nation; they have never once invited me to the house. I have been there twice, on my own initiative and as far as I am concerned, I think honour is satisfied and I need go no more until I am asked. He does not get up till 12 and he is found playing patiences in his room after lunch. He knows no language, not even French and his mind is a complete blank as regards Turkey in general and Turkish Arabia in particular. And this is the man who we send here at the moment when that Baghdad Rly on the one hand and our irrigation schemes on the other are passing from schemes into realities. Good, please God! but I return to where I began—we are an odd nation. Meantime I have made friends with the manager of the Lynch Co, Mr Tod, and his charming little Italian wife. I am going to stay with them when I return from my visit to Babylon. And everyone else, native and foreign, has been exuberantly welcoming. I spent a most interesting 2 hours today with my old friend the Naqib, who is the greatest person in the world of religion here.[28] I should like to tell you also that he receives no woman but your very humble servant. He is too holy to shake hands with me but in the spirit he fell upon my neck and I was vastly amused, as ever, by his talk. Then I went on to the house of another big family here, laymen this

28. Pro-British Arab head of first Iraqi council, 1920, thanks to Bell's advocacy.

time (they have all precipitated themselves to call, my friends) and was again received in a way which warmed my heart. I'm quite right in my impression of 'Iraq—I hear it on every side. The country is entirely out of hand, the reins of government were all dropped during the war (nor held very firmly before) the roads are not safe, trade decadent, the whole thing has gone to ruin. It is dreadful. And they all regret Nazim Pasha now, all these people who hated him while he was here (for he was too strong for them) they long to have King Stork back again. Then I lunched with the Tods, bless them—oh Dick, I must tell you a heavenly tale. There is a very rich merchant of Muhammerah whom they call Hajji Rais al Tujar, Hajji chief of the Merchants. He went to Europe for a journey and when he was about to return he thought and thought what he should bring the Shaikh of Muhammerah as a

Camels watering. n.d. Photograph by Gertrude Bell. Courtesy of the University of Newcastle upon Tyne.

Gertrude Bell and friends in Baghdad. March 1914. Photographer unknown. Courtesy of the University of Newcastle upon Tyne.

present from foreign parts. And this was what he hit on as the best and most suitable that Europe could offer. He purchased 2 life size wax figures of ladies, and had them clothed in evening dress of the latest fashion. "Live women" he explained "would be too dear—and difficult to obtain. But when I saw that these had hands of wood I had them replaced by hands of wax at the cost of 250 francs a hand." So you see they were complete! No not quite complete, for said Mr Wills (who told me the story) "You ought to have had gramophones placed inside them." "*Khush fikr*" said the merchant, in regretful admiration "a sweet thought." Isn't it heavenly?

In the afternoon Meissner Pasha came to fetch me. I invited Mrs Tod to come too and went across the Tigris in his motor boat (disembarking at the Hotel Bagdadbahn!) and saw all that was to be seen. The palms nodded over Tigris bank and on its swollen tide lay a flotilla of ancient boats, their lateen sails furled, their shallow hold filled with wooden sleepers straight from Hamburg. The steam cranes puffed and creaked, the sleepers swung unsteadily over the muddy bank to be carried away by ceaseless streams of ragged Arab, blue clad and ragged, who ran like ants backwards and forwards, singing as they went. Down a wide alley through the palm grove ran the rails and upon them stood locomotives of the latest pattern, some completed, waiting for the fires[?] to move off to railhead, others in varying stages of reconstruction. The muddy waters of Tigris flood, the palms, the ragged singing Arabs—these were the ancient East, and in their midst stood the shining faultless engines, the blue eyed, close cropped Germans, with quick decisive mood[?] and smart military bearing—the soldiery of the West, come out to conquer and conquering, their weapon science. Can you see it at all? I should like you to see it through my eyes. Hospitals, we visited, store houses, the station building, and everywhere reigned the same precision, the same forethought—the ordered Western organization. But the difficulties! they have to import everything. They cannot use the water without straining it because it is salt, for lack of stone they must cast blocks of concrete, for lack of sand (there is not even sand in Arabia, it seems!) they must crush pebbles. "We have neither wood nor water" said Meissner Pasha "stone nor sand nor wood." I dined with the Meissners last night—she was the daughter of 'Abd al Hamid's Armenian jeweller (a rich man as you may think) and was almost is still, a very beautiful woman. It was an immense party. Meissner took me in and on my other side sat Sevian Beg, head of the Regir[?] here. He was in the same fort at Adana [Ataniya] and spoke of you. Do you remember him? After dinner I talked to a Turkish officer, general commanding the second division here, and told him minutely what the

Rashid were doing and how placed. I hope he may take it to heart and not count too much on their help to recover the Hasa from Ibn Sa'ud for they would prove a broken reed. The Turks will never recover the Hasa, in my belief and had best waste no efforts over it. Ibn Sa'ud turned them out without a shot fired, marched the garrisons down to the coast and appropriated all their arms, including some cannon. I think it not improbable that he will hand over half the Hasa to the Shaikh of Kuwait [al-Kuwayt]—a very clever move it would be, for it would then pass automatically under our protection—the Turks may make their devil of it indeed. I have just come in from dining with the German Consul. He is a dull dog. I have known him long. He took me in, for my evil deeds, but on my other side sat Mr Whitley, Jackson's head man. They have finished the Hindiyyeh barrage and the water of the Euphrates now flows gaily down the Hilleh branch. The next under-taking is to be the Habaniyyeh overflow, essential too, because heavy flood would sweep over the barrage and flood the country above it I think. Jackson and Pearson are bidding for the Contract, but Col. Erskine tells me (it is the only thing he has told me) that there is a pri-vate agreement between them and it does not matter which gets it. By the way Meissner—old fox, and Oriental old fox, but mighty civil to me—talked to me of Col. Erskine: "Nous etions tres rassurés" said he "quand nous avons vu le Colonel Erskine. Car c'est evident que si vous auriez en l'intention de suivre une politique agressive dans ce pays vous n'y aurez pas envoyé un consul général qui ne connait ni pays ni langue" [We were very reassured when we saw Col. Erskine. Because it is evident that if you had the intention to pursue a politically aggressive policy in this country you would not have sent a consul-general who does not know the country or the language.] Double edged, isn't it!

And now I think I must end this tale. The mail goes on Tuesday but I go to Babylon on Monday—which is the day after tomorrow—and must deposit my letters at the Residency tomorrow. I do not wish you to wait another week for news of me and my doings, therefore I shall

The yards of the German-built Berlin-Baghdad Railway, Baghdad. March 1914. Photograph by Gertrude Bell. *Courtesy of the University of Newcastle upon Tyne.*

tear out the unwritten pages and let this book go. The rest of the story of Baghdad, if there is any to tell, you shall have in a separate letter before I leave for Damascus. I wonder if you are now at Ad[d]is Ababa? I do not picture the journey nor know how long it takes.

It's after midnight and I must end. I have written to [Ambassador] Louis Mallet and told him I may possibly come to him in Constantinople [Istanbul] on my way home. I shall be a week or less in Damascus first and then up by sea from Beyrout [Beyrouth, Beirut]. I might go and see the diggings at Carchemish and I might go and see those at Sardis, but I don't know. It will be as the fancy takes me and according to the energy that remains in me. But it will England [*sic*] I suppose towards the end of May—a week earlier, a week later it will all be soon enough.

Goodnight and goodbye in this book and for tonight. Mr Tod sends messages.

APRIL 1914

G. B. to D-W.   *Sun. 12. [12 April 1914]*

. . . day of the silk mantles[?]—but I did not go to mass. I packed and had a financial dispute with 'Ali. Mr Wills says that drunkenness and dancing girls have only been common here since the Constitution—they are civilization. The dancing girls are Jewesses, all from Damascus and Aleppo [Halab]. When a Moslem takes to drink, then he is lost. None of the rich men fast. 'Abd al Qadir's brother fasted last Ramazan—he used to come in and tell Mr W. how awful it was and that he wd never do it again. The poor fast, some of them at least; even the poor fast less. The women have more liberty, go about less veiled. They used not to go about at all. The Jews sit in the coffee shops, are well treated, talk and drive with Moslems. Sayyid Daud, who will next be Naqib, was seen driving with an Armenian. He is the Naqib's nephew. At Basrah and here in the desert, people go about openly with dancing girls. They make immense sums of money—the men sit gambling, they come in: when 1 man wins £5 he tosses 2 to a girl. She earns £60 a night. The[y] dance all night in the big kahwah here on the Tigris. No reformed Islam is perceptible. After lunch came 'Abd al Rahman Jamil Zadeh and brought a relative. Then the Tods and I went in 'Abd al Qadir's launch nearly up to Qazimain [Kadhimain] in blazing heat—the river looking lovely, past the Khalif's palace and the *guffa* port on the W. bank. We got out and had tea under flowering Tamarisk and children brought us roses. *Keleks* came down, they and the palms reflected in the river (for our talk go on 4 pages) [see page 110ff]. The sun set and we dropped down, Baghdad shimmering through the heat haze like a fairy city. In the dusk to 'Abd al Qadir's house. Went up through his rose court to his strange drawing room to see a big picture of Nazim Pasha. So home in the night. The cinematograph close by caught fire after dinner and blazed into the night.

G. B. to D-W.   Ap. 13. [13 April 1914]

Feluja [al-Fallujah]. I'm off, but I have not got very far as yet, and I am engaged in wondering whether I shall get any further, today at any rate. There was a battle royal with 'Ali yesterday in Baghdad. Over nothing at all. He disobeyed orders, sulked and called the camels back which I had despatched to Feluja to await my arrival today. I did not know of the last unprecedented piece of villainy till this morning or I would have dismissed him at once. For having issued my commands and told Fattuh to see that they were carried out, I went picknicking [sic] with the Tods up the river and was not to be found when Fattuh came back to report progress. So he did the best he could, got the camels off at last and 'Ali with them (they had heaps of time to reach Feluja by midday) and came at 5 AM with a carriage for me. We got here at 1—no camels, no 'Ali, no anything. It's now 4 and I ought to have been 2 hours out into the desert by this time, pitching tents. 'Ali is extraordinarily tiresome; I have had bother with him before. He is like a naughty child; he never does a stroke of work and is quite irresponsible. But he is very useful as a tongue among the tribes; he knows them and is known by them. And I privately value him for a certain quality of the imagination which he has—it pleases me. Yet I'm afraid I shall have to get rid of him—now, if no good explanation is offered. And anyhow I fear I can't take him with me again. He is too capricious, and disobedient like a naughty child. Behold my writing to you has brought good luck! I see the camels at the other end of the bridge. Let justice be done! I must go and struggle with 'Ali, the kind of job I hate. The camels, for their part, hate crossing the bridge and Euphrates rolls along and doesn't care what happens to any of us. Why should he? we don't matter and he has got to think of his floods and of how to reach the sea. In camp. Well, I continue. 'Ali came in, in the devil's own temper and I dismissed him on the spot. He has had enough money from me (advanced) to cover his wages for the journey, without *bakhshish,* and with that I left him to find his way back to Baghdad. And I shall be suprised [*sic*] if I can't find my own way across the Syrian desert. We picked up a gentleman in the *khan* to take us out to the nearest Dulaim shaikh and off we went.[29] But we did not go to the shaikh. He was a couple of hours away and it was late and my friend suggested that we should camp with him—he is a Dulaimi too. His tents lay on our way, half an hour from Feluja, and here we pitched camp. 'Ali has already turned up once. I have exacted a full apology and he has left. I expect he will come back, but if he does not I don't care. There is a big Dulaim shaikh upon our road tomorrow and I will get a *rafiq* from him.

This is the bit of my other travel diary which I tore out when I sent the latter to you—do you notice? I have begun it at the wrong end, however, because it has a sort of cover this end to protect the written pages. Afterwards you will be able to put the two together, notwithstanding, and keep it, if you want, as one little book. Bother I have left out two pages—I shall go back on them when I finish this page.

My party now is Fattuh, Fellah the negro, and Sayyif the Sherari. Fellah, you remember has come with [us] since Damascus, and Sayyif since Ziza. I have 8 camels, because we did not find a good market in Baghdad and could not sell 2 of those we brought up from Hayil [*sic*]. They have scarcely anything to carry except us, for we are travelling very light. I have left all my baggage in Baghdad to [go] back to London by sea. I have a very small and light native tent, with my bed in a Wolseley valise, and one chair—that's all I have except a bagful of clothes. I could not abandon quite all my possessions because I shall

29. A major Syrian tribe.

want them on the journey to Constantinople. Besides there was no reason for it—the camels are scarcely loaded at all. The men have another very light native tent. We have taken provisions for 3 weeks and a minimum of cooking pots. My one luxury is my canvas bath! It's hot now, you know, and it will serve to water the camels in if necessary. The camels are not drinking now [at all] much; they will not drink till the fresh grass is withered. They are casting their winter coat—it comes off in great handfuls and they look most abandoned. This is not desert; my bed lies on grass and the Euphrates is 10 minutes away. But it is out under the open sky again and at once my heart leaps to it. I like my tiny tent and in theory I like my bed on the ground, but I shall soon weary of that, I know! (Oh Dick! our poor bones! when we lay them at last in our graves, how they will ache.) Here comes the great procession of the stars. Sirius sparkled out long ago—here is the Great Bear with his eternal interrogations, and the sicle [*sic*] of Leo—all my friends. The Twins, and there is Capella's lovely face half veiled in heat haze; Aldebaran, and above me Procyon—a thousand welcomes!

Yesterday the Tods and I picnicked—I told you. We borrowed the launch of 'Abd al Qadir Pasha Qudairi—who holds all Baghdad in the hollow of his hand and has made friends with me because I was friends with Nazim Pasha whom he loved—and steamed in blazing heat up nearly to Qazimain. There we got out and had tea on the bank under flowering tamarisks. Arab children brought us handfuls of roses, the *keleks* floated down the full stream, the sun sank and all the world was transmuted and its glory reflected in the river. We dropped slowly down stream—Baghdad was like a fairy city shimmering through the heat haze; the afterglow of sunset showed nothing but beauty. And in the dark we dropped down to 'Abd al Qadir's house and went in to thank him and say goodbye. It was a wonderful end to Baghdad. But do you know Baghdad has gone to the dogs. Everyone drinks, Sayyids, Shaikhs, everyone is drunk, and gambles half the night through over the *'araq*, and spends the other half with Jewish dancing girls. They make mints

Gertrude Bell's tent. April 1914. Photograph by Gertrude Bell. Courtesy of the University of Newcastle upon Tyne.

of money, these dancing girls, and they are horrible beyond belief, I'm told—the basest creatures. It has all, or most of it, come about in the last four years, since the age of liberty. It is liberty and civilization. Yet I have a feeling that Baghdad has taken to this kind of civilization so quickly and so wholeheartedly because it is a return to what she knew in the gorgeous days of the Khalifate. Not the *'araq,* perhaps, but the dancing girls and the rest. Have you read d'Annunzio's wonderful play, the *Citta Morta*? It is an imaginary picture of the digging up of Mycenae. And as they dig, the ancient evils rise up out of their graves, they are set free again and seize on those who freed them—the old sins, the bitter hatreds and fierce passions—do you remember that I told you these must be immortal if anything lives? And you said No, they faded. Well, they have not faded in Baghdad; they have come out of their graves, and men and women go reeling and dancing, drunken, down to perdition. It's horrible isn't it? Baghdad turned into this ugly rout. I must go to bed—it's past 8 o'clock and camp hours are early. So to my bed on the ground.

G. B. to D-W.   *Ap. 14. [14 April 1914]*

It wasn't nice—I knew it would not be nice. I tossed and turned on the hard ground and was ashamed of finding it so hard! In the middle of the night rose a three quarter moon and shone into my open tent, monstrous, deformed and red on the misty horizon. After that I went to sleep till 4 when I got up and mounted my camel. 'Ali did not return—or he returned only after we left. I have no remorse about him, for the moment he left tongues were unloosed and I heard tales—some of them I knew or guessed and some I did not know. I must tell you the root of the battle in Baghdad was that he wanted me to take with me the son of his uncle who wished to leave hastily in order to avoid his military service. I said No—that was against the law of the Ottoman Govt, and I was their guest. The son of his uncle must do his service. Thereat he was furious, and guess what he did? He mounted the boy on one of my camels and brought him to Feluja, telling him to come and salute me next morning as an indifferent person who wished to go to Damascus in the hope that I would let him come with me. How he imagined that I would not see through the plot I do not know, but when I heard of it I was very angry at this gross insubordination and glad to think that 'Ali and the son of his uncle are now making the best of their way back to Baghdad. The right is with me, as we say; don't you think so? So we rode gaily along Euphrates bank. It was agreeable; I love the Euphrates above all other rivers, for some unknown reason—perhaps because of its splendid name. Anyhow I love it. It is not really hot yet;

the shade temperature in the afternoon is a little over 80° and it will be cooler when we get up into the high Syrian Desert a few days from now. The camels went splendidly; we did an 11 hours' march in 8½ hours. You who are a camel-man know what a satisfaction that is. Tomorrow's march is longer—good, please God! There lives at Ramadi [al-Ramadi] the cheif [sic] shaikh of all the Dulaim and I went straight to him. He lodged me in a palm garden, gave me coffee, and tea with orange flowers in it, and appointed a *rafiq* who is to convey me to Ga'rah where I shall fall in with the 'Anazeh. To them he is to entrust me. His name is 'Adwan; he has a very pleasant, smiling face, is a well known man, and coming from the house of 'Ali Sulaiman commands respect. So I am over the first fence. At Ga'rah—*tawakkil Allah!* I shall get a man there I make no doubt and 'Adwan is bound over to find me his successor. So here I am sitting with shaikhs again and it is all very familiar and pleasant.

G. B. to D-W. *Ap. 15. [15 April 1914]*

They gave me a gorgeous dinner, in the garden at my special request, and the rest of the night was not a success. Any excuse serves for keeping me awake these hot nights, and the chatter of the two watchmen whom the shaikh set over us was enough. At last I rose up in wrath and packed them off, saying I preferred a thousand thieves, who at least would try not to wake me, to watchmen who did not mind whether I slept or not. We were off today before sunrise; it was bitter hot—the temperature was 91° in the shade at 3 PM, I call that hot, don't you? and a weary dull desert and a wearily sleepy person riding through it. Those who sit at home and think what fun it must be to explore waste places, they do not know, do they, the price for it which has to be reckoned in such days as these. Tut, tut! what a fuss I am making about a bad night, a warm day and a dull road! Our destination was Abu Jir [Abu el-Jir], the great pitch springs to which I came 5 years ago when I was looking for Ukhaidir. I kept thinking and thinking in my tired mind of what you said once about the long hot march and the hope of rest and shade at the end of it. Fortunately I did not need to bother much about bearings, for an obliging person at Abu Jir set fire to one of the pitch springs, for fun—they are always doing it—and a monstrous black cloud of smoke rose up in front of us while we were still 6 hours and more away, onto which I could set my compass and troubled no more. So we camped and there came a dust storm which did not make things better and here am I grumbling to you as if I were really undergoing hardships. Please forget, my dear confessor, and try to think of me as a hero regardless of all discomforts. No, that would not be human; take it as it is. Anyhow I feel better when I have grumbled to you.

G. B. to D-W.   *Ap. 16. [16 April 1914]*

It blew like mad yesterday till 8 o'clock, we were heaped in dust but by some miracle the little tents stood firm. When at last it was still—and cooler—I had a bath and went to bed, and thank heaven, to sleep. Today was just as hot but less disagreeable. We rode west for 6 hours and came to a place very famous in the mouths of the Arabs. Wizeh is its name. It is really very singular. There is a little ruined fort, which I have planned and photographed and some 100 paces away an immense rocky hole in the ground. We climbed down a couple of hundred feet—no perhaps not so much—and then entered a rocky underground passage, twisting and turning. We were well provided with candles and we went on boldly through this strange crack in the rocks. Sometimes it opened out into a great hall, sometimes it was so low that we had to creep through it, flat on the sand. And at the end we reached a clear, cold pool, fed by a spring in the rock. We waded into it and filled all our drinking water flasks and one water skin which the men tugged through the passage and lifted over the rocks. We had left lights at various points on the way to guide us back, yet the place was so strange and gate-of-the-pit-like, that I was not sorry when we saw daylight again. "Ha! the light of the world!" said Fattuh. And we came back into the world of men with our treasure of clear water. We had been under the earth for near an hour. In the fort there is a finely built well, now choked up, which they say lies over this subterranean spring, and I should think they are right and that the fort guards the water hole. It is just like the other forts in the east side of the Syrian desert—I must publish them all now when I get back. I can't date them—any age from the 9th century to the 14th perhaps.

G. B. to D-W.   *Ap. 17. [17 April 1914]*

It was quite cool today—comparatively; 85 was the highest temperature I registered and we profited by the weather and made a 10 hours march, without fatigue. A dull part of the desert, this is; long shallow steps leading us up into the high Hamad. I think we have left Mesopotamian heat behind and it looks as if it might rain, in which case we shall be flooded out, being in low ground for the sake of our evening lights, and under such insufficient canvas too. *Khair inshallah!* Today we saw fresh prints of horsemen. 'Adwan (who is a charming man by the way) opined that they were Shammar of the Jezireh [al-Jazirah], Mesopotamia, looking for 'Anazeh, with whom they are at feud. I feel no kind of anxiety as to *ghazzus* while I have 'Adwan with me. A man from the house of the great shaikh of the Dulaim, a relative of his, and employed by the Government in collecting the cattle tax—it would be impossible to find a surer *rafiq*. When I part from him the fun may begin, but perhaps not—the Shamiyyeh [Shamiyah] is tolerably safe. Anyways I don't bother at all; we have been through places so much worse and come out whole and sound. The Government has raised the sheep tax by more than a piastre—I suppose that's the wax[?]. How much of it do they receive, I wonder? 'Adwan says truly that the shaikhs eat more than the Government. The long fatigue of travel is upon me and I talk little while we ride. Whenever I talk 'Adwan greets me with smiles and fair answers. I love these desert people and the sudden heart-whole part they play in your fortunes. And then you leave them and what do they think afterwards? I believe they have a pleasant memory of service rendered and of the quick intimacy of the few days' journey. One of my *rafiqs,* far away on the other side of the Nefud, said once over the camp fire "In all the years when we come to this place we shall say: 'Here we came with her, here she camped.' It will be a thing to talk of, your *ghazzu.* We shall be asked for news of it and we shall speak of it and tell how you came." I expect they will, and it makes me dreadfully anxious that they should tell nothing but good, since they will judge my whole race by me. That recollection very often checks the hasty word when I am tired, and feeling cross, or bored—heavens! how bored, cross and tired some times! Then I try to remember that they will tell how I came.

G. B. to D-W.   *Ap. 18. [18 April 1914]*

Relentless Hamad today, flat, flat and flat, with the tiny 5 foot rises hanging over the mirage for miles away, and then descending as we drew near and sitting down on the Hamad again—no more that 5 ft rises after all. We saw the ruined gateway of the 'Amej [Qasr 'Amij] fort to the right and shortly afterwards dropped into the post road—post road no more, the desert post has ceased to be. Here we met 'Anazeh of the Amarat and asked the news. Where were the shaikhs, what was happening in the Syrian desert? The *ghazzu* of which we saw the footprints yesterday was, as we conjectured, Shammar. They had lifted some 40 camels this morning and ridden away. They would not have touched us, I think, but one is always glad not to meet *ghazzus.* Fahd Beg, the chief shaikh of the Amarat, whom we hoped to meet at Ga'rah (where we are to part from 'Adwan) is probably not there—he was there and has most likely left, as is their habit. There is a nephew of Fahd's camped not far from us; 'Adwan is going off to see him. We may perhaps take an 'Anazeh *rafiq* from here—if we can get one. I have played about so much in the Syrian desert that perhaps I am disposed not to treat it with the respect it deserves, but it's clear we must have an 'Anazeh *rafiq.* You realize what I am busy with? it's the first half of the old road from Damascus to the Euphrates for which I am looking. I have followed the second half, from Muhaiwir [Muhaywir] to the Euphrates; that was in the year of snow. We reach Muhaiwir tomorrow; the road westward is all unknown to me, but I have heard of two small ruins in it which I want. We marched quickly today, and long hours. I succeeded in sleeping on my camel which I have never done before! For a full half hour—I was very proud when I woke up and looked at my watch. There were no bearings to be taken, for we were on the post road which goes quite straight to Muhaiwir. Otherwise I could not have slept. Ibn Sha'lan has been raiding, and Fahd Beg has been raiding—well, I hope they will be content with raiding each other and not bother with us.

G. B. to D-W.   *Ap. 19. [19 April 1914]*

'Adwan came back late last night bringing me word from the shaikh Jad'an that he would give a *rafiq* and in all I wished he was ready to serve me, but would I come and see him in the morning? So I went, rather reluctantly, for I had not slept much and the extra 10 miles ride (he was camped a good 5 miles away) seemed heavy. But what could I do? We trotted out, leaving the men and spare camels to go on their way. As the sun rose we came to Jad'an's immense camp. The tents were all huddled together. The Amarat had taken fright after yesterday's raid. A man came running by our side and told us of it. They had pursued the Shammar *ghazzu,* caught them up, taken 10 of their mares and shot two others—also a *zilimeh,* a man of the raiders had been shot, *dabahnaha,* we slew him. "Did his companions stay to bury him?" I asked, with a sudden picture of the dead man lying in the open Hamad. "No *Wallah*" he answered "they left him to be eaten by the dogs." I could not get him from my thoughts, the dead man lying on the great plains till the dogs came to finish the business. Perhaps now that I have handed him over to you, you will exorcise him. Jad'an was moving camp. We sat in his tent and drank coffee while the women loaded the camels. I thought it would never finish, the slow talk, and I was full of weariness and black thoughts—here was such a long day's march ahead of us and my soul shrank from it. I wondered whether I were afraid and then I wondered whether I should cry out of sheer weariness and what they would think if I dropped tears into the coffee hearth! (Oh Dick, don't let it be known! my reputation as a traveller would never survive these revelations. But I don't mind telling you for I believe you have these black moments, too, when all that one is doing seems such sheer futility and weariness.) And then Jad'an looked at me and said *"La tifkik-eri*—don't be anxious—you shall have all you wish. We are at your service and honoured." He was really very kind and, for an Arab, very expeditious. I got my *rafiq,* 'Asaf is his name and I like him. He is to take us to Buharra, near Palmyra [Tadmur] if I wish, and I think that's the second fence behind us. And with that I parted (reluctantly) with 'Adwan—reluctantly because he has been such a pleasant companion and I love his smiling face—a very beautiful face, also, good to look at. He kissed my hand and went on his way. And we to pick up the camels, and ride and ride and ride hurrying a good deal, but for all our haste it was an 11 hours' day—too long for us and for the camels. As we neared the big Wadi Hauran, two camel riders bore down on us. Fattuh and 'Asaf whipped out their rifles and loaded and the men came in shouting angry questions. But it was all right; they were men of Ibn Mijlad's, an-other 'Anazeh sept, and friends as soon as they found that we were not to be feared. We are camped a stone's throw from the good water of Muhaiwir. Here comes a guest, riding in on a camel—I must go and see who he is—He is very old, and deaf, and lame, the guest, and very dirty. He is another sort of 'Anazeh, the Swailmeh. I'm glad he and all he brings are not going to sleep in my tent. It's cold and rainy this evening.

There was a gazelle faun [*sic*] in Jad'an's tent. They brought it to me and laid it in my lap, where it fell asleep. It lay curled round like a Mycaenean ivory, with one absurd pointed horn stretched out over its ear; it slept through the slow talk. And I looking at the sharp watchful faces of the men round the coffee hearth, and remembering my own probably anxious face, thought that there was none in that company wholly free from apprehension but the little gazelle asleep upon my knee. Its small confident presence was encouraging.

G. B. to D-W.   *Ap. 20. [20 April 1914]*

It rained in torrents last night—winter rain, not spring rain. The men hastily trenched my tent and the swelled canvass [*sic*] held good and let nothing through. Today the thermometer has fallen 20 degrees—a blessed change—and I am much better in consequence. A sharp disillusion awaited us today. When we came down to Muhaiwir the clear pool, which I had thought to be a spring, was dry. It was only a water hole. There was water close by, in the Hauran bed—but such water! fouled by camels. We dug holes in the sandy bank higher up and got water in them, but not much better—all the bank near the pool had been fouled. We filled a skin or two and I have enough of Wizeh water to carry me on, for drinking purposes for a couple of days. It's fortunate to have the feminine fault of drinking little—at least when one is in the Syrian desert. The world was full of camels, the great herds of the 'Anazeh. After we had crossed the Hauran valley and were out again on the huge levels, they drifted across our path in thousands, grazing. It was like some immense slow river, hours wide. I love to see them. From time to time the herdsmen walked or rode by us for half an hour, and heard our news. 'Asaf was careful to tell all and sundry that I was from Hayil [*sic*], which excited much admiration, *wallah!* He is a cheerful bird; he chatters incessantly, or sings. One of our half hour companions commented on the smallness of my caravan. "It is enough" said I. "But I would wish better for you" he insisted. So hear [*sic*] I am in the real desert again, with the real desert people, the Bedu, who never touch settled life. But it is the first time that I have been alone with them, with no one to be voice and tongue for me. Fattuh, for all his eager devotion, is as much a stranger as I am, and I have to be voice and tongue for my-

Fahad Beg's camp near Ga'rah. April 1914. Photograph by Gertrude Bell. Courtesy of the University of Newcastle upon Tyne.

self. I like it; it amuses me to run my own show. And so far all has gone well. 'Asaf, I need not say, has already identified himself heartily with our fortunes. I am half pledged to take him to England and find him a shepherd's job there—I the interpreter till he learns English! In the afternoon the Hamad abruptly ended, and we dropped down a few feet into the Ga'rah jof. (You know what a jof is, don't you? low ground.) On the edge of it we camped after a day's march that was a little shorter than usual, the camels being hungry and rather tired. We have another guest tonight, a man of Ibn Hadhdhal's and going to him, to Fahd Beg. We may see him in the Ga'rah, but I don't hanker after him now that I have got my *rafiq*. Shaikhs always mean delay and he is such a big man that I fear I should have to camp with him. All these 'Anazeh herds mean that we are quite safe for the present, with 'Anazeh tents on every side.

G. B. to D-W.   *Ap. 22. [22 April 1914]*

Yesterday I was busy with a shaikh and with a ruin. They happened to be together and going to the one I fell in with the other. The shaikh was Fahd Beg—but I must tell you who he is. Roughly speaking the 'Anazeh nation are divided into three—the southern 'Anazeh belong to Ibn Sa'ud, the northern are in two parts, the one ruled by Ibn Sha'lan the second by Ibn Hadhdhal. Fahd Beg is the reigning Ibn Hadhdhal. He was camped in the plain under the low rocky cliff which bounds the Ga'rah. I counted 150 tents near him and there were as many more behind grassy ridges stretching half across the wide Ga'rah. An Arab encampment occupies a lot of ground. And just as the camel riders couch their *dululs* before my tents, dismount and come in without questions to dine and sleep, so I couched mine before Fahd Beg's mudif, his coffee tent, went in and sat down at his hearth. He received me with a kindness almost fatherly and I loved being with him. He is a man of 70 I should think; his headquarters are near Kerbela where he owns palm gardens; but every year he turns out for 6 months into the desert with his camels and his clan. And his eldest son, Mit'ab, does the obligatory raiding. He spread out beautiful carpets on which we sat, leaning against a camel saddle. His hawk sat on its perch behind us, and his greyhound lay beside it. We talked and drank coffee; I went to his long haram [*sic*] tent, greeted his latest wife and saw his youngest children. Then I went to my own tent and lunched, mounted my camel and trotted out nearly an hour to the ruin. And it was different from anything I had thought to find in the Shamiyyeh. It was a town—imagine! a town in the heart of the Syrian desert. But a town of a very primitive kind. It lay up on top of the cliff, on a kind of peninsular [*sic*] formed by the winding Wadi Helgum and the only road to it from the upper level was a narrow neck which was fortified by a towered wall. Again all most primitive and terribly ruined; but there it was, a wall and towers guarding the approach to an irregular area which must be a good half mile squared and is completely covered with shapeless ruin heaps. The water was from innumerable wells in the valley below, and the path to these a rough stair down the cliff. Of what its age may be I can form no idea—but isn't it curious? I planned and photographed the gate wall and I would have liked to plot the outline of the peninsular on which the town lies, but by this time the blackest clouds were blowing up and it was clear that I had only just time to get home before they came down in hail and rain. In fact we got in just before they broke—torrents of rain and batteries of hail. When it was over Fahd sent word that he would like to come and see me. He sat in my tent all the rest of the evening. Dinner was served to us there—by far the best dinner I have been given by an Arab shaikh. We eat and the dusk fell and the rain came down again, and still we talked, of the state of the 'Iraq and of the future of Turkey and of our friends in Baghdad, till at last at 8 o'clock he left me and I went to bed. This morning I drank coffee with him and Mit'ab and left amid a shower of blessings. At Fahd's advice I have taken with me a second *rafiq,* a man of the Ruwalla, Ibn Sha'lan's people, who happened to be in Fahd's tents. So I am safe from all the 'Anazeh; but the desert up to Bukharra is *khala,* empty, and though I like the *khala*—I like having the desert to my-self—there is no denying that there is never perfect security in it. We had a trying march, there was a furious cold wind in our teeth—the temperature was 39° this morning—and great rain storms wandered about the world, sweeping us from time to time with their skirts. We struggled on for 8½ hours, crossed the Ga'rah and came out onto a very desolate country with little *tells* and ridges in it, and finally came into camp in too exposed a place, but we could find no better. And I was so dead tired that I went helplessly to sleep for a round hour. Now I'm better. There are two Slubba with us tonight, they and their donkeys and sheep. You know who they are? The strange tribe of hunters and smiths about whose origin all kinds of tales are told. The Ruwaili lost heart in the middle of the morning and wanted to go back—he said he feared the long road and desired to return to his people. Perhaps the wind and rain discouraged him. We represented to him that it was a disgrace for a *rafiq* to abandon his trust and he came on. I expect he regrets it, for it blows like fury tonight and there are scuds of rain. The Beduin shrivel in this cold but I like it and shall presently spread out new green leaves. The wind no one can like. And the dust, which no rain can lay—I sleep on the ground, remember, and I wonder whether my hair will ever be clean again. It's gray with dust. We are 10 days out of Baghdad and there is a long way in front of us—good, please God! But I wish it were over. I feel, as I always do near the end of a journey, as if I should like to sleep for a year. But being me I shall probably sleep for 4 hours or so, and then hurry on my way, wheresoever.

G. B. to D-W.   *Ap 24. [24 April 1914]*

It's still pleasantly cold and I am much better in consequence. Only I have worn out a muscle, camel riding—a muscle down the back of my leg and it goes all the way into my instep—if it's the same one—so that my foot hurts when I walk. A week's rest will set it right, I sup-

The "latest wife" of Fahad Beg, head of a branch of the 'Anazeh. April 1914.
Photograph by Gertrude Bell. Courtesy of the University of Newcastle upon Tyne.

pose; till then it's rather a nuisance. Yesterday—what happened yesterday? we crossed high plains and wide valleys and in one of these I found a ruin and stopped in the middle of the day to plan it. Moreover in the next bit of the plain the old road was remarkably clear. It rained a little all day and again at night, but nothing to matter. Today we went on through the same sort of country, fearfully tiresome to map because it has no features. When we had ridden some two hours we saw objects lying on the ground and 'Assaf observed that they were 3 mares and 2 men who had been slain ten days ago—a *ghazzu* meeting a *ghazzu*. Fattuh rode off to see if he could pick up a spear, but I edged hastily away. If I had seen them I should never have forgotten them and why be haunted by their bloody ghosts? There was no spear; the Slubba had picked up all that was to be found. I told you we had a couple of Slubba with us, they and their sheep? They have left us today, but this morning they started off several hours before us, as was their wont, and presently, after the episode of the dead men, one of our company cried out that he saw *zol,* appearances. I said I thought it must be the Slubba, but 'Assaf declared that he had seen camel riders, in pursuance of which belief he unslung and loaded his rifle. Of course it was only the Slubba and 'Assaf turned to me smiling and said *"Al gom beni Kubais!"*—the enemy are the children of mist. The next valley to which we came was full of ruins, sometimes nothing but indistinguishable heaps of stones, sometimes foundations outlined on the ground. They have no architectural interest but the human interest is great. All this side of the desert must have been inhabited. Every ruin has its well in the valley hard by and some of these wells are still in use—living, as the Arabs say. I have got them down in my map anyway, and this bit of country is quite unmapped. I don't wonder that these valleys had a settled or half settled—more likely the latter—population. They are full of pasture and now, after the rains, of water pools. But we are on barish ground tonight—a very shallow depression just deep enough to hide our tents, in the middle of a huge flat. There are "trees" for the camels to eat—they don't like trees as much as flowering weeds but *yash'abun,* they can satisfy themselves on them. We carry water to Bukharra, for we may find no more; three days I think it should be. And then four days to Dumair [Dumayr]—seven days more camel riding—no eight; for it's a day in to Damascus from Dumair. And we are twelve out from Baghdad.

G. B. to D-W.   *Ap. 25. [25 April 1914]*

The muscle is better, you will be glad to hear. But I think I must have strained my foot—I wonder how? We crossed endless uplands and valleys today, without incident, except that Fattuh once raised an alarm of *zol* and everyone to his rifle. But they were children of mist again. At half past ten I lifted up my eyes to see whether my last bearing was working out right, and on the furthest horizon I saw—mountains! So faint, so far away, such children of the mist, that I would not let myself believe that they were there. But an hour later when we had climbed the next ridge, they were indeed there and unmistakable, beautiful gracious heights, the mountain range of Palmyra. And I have seen no hills since the granite crags of [Jabal] 'Ajja sank below the Nefud. This means that we are further on our way than I thought, and that we shall reach Bukharra tomorrow—Bukharra and the Roman empire, of which it was an outlying settlement. At noon we found an encampment of the Slubba in a valley bottom and alighted at their tents to ask news and buy a little *semen.* One of the men was clad in a robe of gazelle skins. They were very friendly, the good Slubba, pressed us to stay, saying that they had never seen a *khatun*[30] (they were just as much interested in me as I was in them!) and gave us good news of the desert ahead. There is an encampment of Fed'an 'Anazeh somewhere near, against whom I am assured through one of my *rafiqs* and all is quiet. We went on for another couple of hours and came into camp in a solitary valley. My open tent faces the hills.

30. An honorific title: implies a high-born woman who keeps her eyes and ears open for the benefit of her country (Rihani 1930, 3).

We were off before dawn, a clear still morning. And before we had been on our way two hours a great storm marched across our path ahead of us. We, riding in a world darkened by its august presence, watched and heard. The lightening flickered through the cloud masses, the thunder spoke from them and on the outskirts companies of hail, scourged and bent by a wind we could not feel, hurried over the plain and took possession of the mountains. Do you remember Shelley's song to the Spirit of Delight?—

> *I love snow and all the forms*
> *of the radiant frost;*
> *I love wind and rain storms, anything almost*
> *That is Nature's and may be*
> *Untouched by man's misery.*

And after the pageant and the splendour had all passed, malicious little scuds of rain drove before us and tormented us for several hours. What with the weather and what with his anxiety at observing footprints of a large *ghazzu*—so he held it to be—'Assaf missed the way and we went a good deal further north than we need have gone. Finally we hove up against tents and camel herds of the Sba ('Anazeh of Fahd Beg's people) and the herdsmen set us right. We were in fact within sight of Palmyra and I can see the bay of desert wherein it lies from my tent. For we have not reached Bukharra—I don't think we should have reached it even if we had gone straight to it. Palmyra from the desert—it must be nearly 10 miles from us—is a very different Palmyra from the city you come to along the Roman road from Damascus. It is very different in spirit. One looks here upon the Arab Palmyra, facing the desert, ruler of the desert and dependent upon the desert for its life and force. I am wrong to call it Palmyra; that was its bastard Roman name. Tudmor, Tudmor of the Wilderness. And the Sba know it by no other name. In the middle of the morning we met a man walking solitary in the desert. We rode up and accosted him in Arabic—he made no answer. 'Assaf opined that he must be a Persian dervish. We addressed him in Turkish, Fattuh and I, but he continued to regard us in complete silence. Then we tried what words of Persian we could muster—with the same result. With this we left him, after giving him a handful of bread, his acceptance of which was the only act on his part which might be described as intercourse with us. We rode off into the rain clouds to the west and he continued his lonely way into the rain clouds to the east. And what will become of him I cannot tell. He was heading for the heart of an uninhabited desert. Don't you think that an odd story?

G. B. to D-W.   *Ap. 27. [27 April 1914]*

We passed through Bukharra this morning where I photographed a little. Musil was there two years ago, for some days I believe, so I didn't bother about the ruins much. We filled all our water skins at an excellent well and rode on—hours and hours, to a ruined *khan* called al Hallabat. And under it we are camped. But there is no work to be done. It is without interest, mediaeval, I should think; possibly of the date of the mediaeval castle at Palmyra, which if I remember rightly is 17th century. I was thankful not to have to plan it, for I am too tired to do much good at it—yet I suppose if it had been interesting I should have forgotten that I was tired—and my foot is a confounded nuisance. Three days, I think, from here to Dumair—not more than three, I hope. It rained in floods last night and my tent was damp and horrid, but I went to bed and forgot about it. The desert is *khala* again.

G. B. to D-W.   *Ap. 28. [28 April 1914]*

This has been rather an interesting day for I have found Roman milestones all along the way. Most of them are uninscribed; two were inscribed but alas so battered that I could make nothing of them. Such things need hours of time and much patience, and I have neither now. On one I read the letters TRA—Trajanus? the theory is tempting but I fear it won't hold. Palmyra was conquered by the Antonines and why should there be a Roman road before the conquest? Up in the hills I saw a little block house and climbed wearily to it, but there was nothing datable about it. A guard house over the road, the road of the Roman milestones or of the mediaeval *khans*—just like the guard houses in the hills over the Khyber Pass road, you know them. And then I saw another *kahn* about a mile away, looked at it through my glasses and decided that it was like Hallabat and did not go to it. I ought to have gone—but *dunya beni adaam!* it was a mile and more away and the world is so large when you are walking across it on a camel. And yet I believe it's the first ruin to which I have ever turned a cold shoulder. Let's hope it was nothing worth—I think it was nothing worth. It was not on the Roman road; I was on that. There is the devil's own west wind every day—it plagues us terribly, both marching and in camp where it covers us with dust. Nevertheless we have marched over 10 hours today. The map is wildly wrong here. I think I can correct it a little.

G. B. to D-W.   *Ap 29. [29 April 1914]*

Oh we've had such a day! In the (damn this pen) In the middle of the morning we saw a ruin a long way on ahead. Fattuh and I spurred forward to it, leaving the others to follow, and when we had got half way we looked round and there was another confounded ruin several miles to the north. So we turned and trotted to it and the only result of the expedition was to make sure that there was nothing worth bothering about. With that we took a bee line across the hills to the first ruin (which was just as uninteresting) and then we picked up our men and camels and went on our true way. The old road was very clear by reason of a rock cutting. We promised ourselves that we would ride two hours further and then camp, but behold the world was completely barren and there was not a blade of anything for the camels to eat. So we rode on, perforce, on and on, and at last topped a ridge and saw a green valley below which we reached at the end of time. A twelve hours' day and I came in giddy with fatigue and hunger, but tea has made me feel better. There are people camped in the hills above us and I don't care whether they are friends or not, or what they do to us. I expect they are only shepherds from Dumair. Good please God, and all *kahns* to the devil.

G. B. to D-W.   *Ap. 30. [30 April 1914]*

We rode through the hills, we saw the last camel herds which we shall see, we passed through the meagre outlying cultivation where the peasants were plucking the ripe five-inch-high barley out of the ground, and so we came down into Dumair and I took my last bearing on the pediment of its temple. It was still so early as we rode through the village threshing fields, where the barley crop was piled and ready to be trodden out, that we decided to go on for an hour, and lo the earth played us the same trick which it played yesterday—there was nothing whatever growing on it. So we rode on wearily, on and on with the snows of Mt Hermon shining far away before us, and a blazing sun striking us in the face. And at last, after more than 11 hours' riding, we came to the village of 'Adra ['Adhra] and camped there, some five hours from Damascus. It was here that I picked up my camels on the first day's journey out of Damascus, and climbed into the *Shidad* with all Arabia before me. There is a dramatic fitness in our having pitched our last camp on the very same spot whence we set out. But if I had been as tired then as I am now, I should have turned back and not gone forward in Arabia.

MAY 1914

G. B. to D-W.   *May 1. [1 May 1914]*

And today through the vinyards [*sic*] and orchards to Damascus. I cannot tell you what they looked like in the bright morning to eyes weary with deserts—you must think of it, the rushing water and the deep green corn, the grey shade of olive trees and the rustle of sweet smelling chestnut leaves, the pale Damascene roses—a man gave me a handful of them, may God reward him! The first house on the Dumair road as you come into Damascus is the hospital. I reached it soon after 9 and went in to greet the Mackinnons.[31] They have kept me, they refused to let me go any further, and I was all too willing to be made captive. So here I am these kind people—remember them in your prayers!—and in a garden which is one bower of roses, and in a quiet house where no one can bother me and I can lie still and rest. I don't think I ever have felt so tired. I was in bed before 11 AM and slept for an hour or two, but it wasn't much of a success for I rode a camel through my dreams. I expect it will be a day or two before I can rest and sleep. I have a message from [Ambassador] Louis Mallet telling me to come to him whenever I like. My idea is to stay here for a week or so, go down to Beyrout on the 6th, stay with the Cumberbatches or the Blisses till the 8th and catch the French boat up to C'ple [Constantinople] on that day.[32] It reaches C'ple on the 12th or 13th, I may stay there a week or less, and then home by train, ie London about the 23rd. I think that is what I shall do.

By the way, the official envelopes which you sometimes use are, like many official things, so bad that they often, if not generally, arrive half torn open—all the edges frayed. I don't suppose that so far your news has interested the Turkish govt, so it doesn't matter—but they might have had it if they liked! It is as well however to know that envelopes like these are not good covers for letters about political matters which are not public. Therefore I tell you. I meant to have told you before, but I forgot. And before I try to sleep I must tell you a piece of political gossip—have you heard it? My sister Elsa Richmond (her husband is in the Admiralty) writes—you shall have her words for they are interesting: "The story is that Winston Churchill tried to make a coup d'état.

31. Dr. Makinnon, physician at the English hospital in Damascus.
32. Dr. Howard Bliss, president of the Syrian Protestant College, now the American University of Beirut. Cumberbatch, presumably a British official.

He got Seely to agree and though he (Winston) has nothing to do with the army, he was in and out of the War Office the whole time hatching his plot presumably.[33] Warrants for the arrest of Carson and of 200 others were prepared and the troops, without Asquith's knowledge, secretly ordered to move on Ulster.[34] Then all the Ulster leaders were to be arrested and the troops to be (unexpectedly) on the spot to quell in a moment the uprising of the Ulster volunteers that of course would result immediately from the leaders' arrest. Thus suddenly all would have been settled, Ulster cowed, and Winston the man who had done it all. He also ordered a squadron of battle ships to go to Belfast, but stopped them by wireless when the plot was found out. The reason it failed was that Sir Arthur Paget was told to find out from the troops officers under his command if they were ready to go to Ulster—and they resigned almost to a man. Of course then the fat was in the fire, Seely resigned finally and Asquith has made himself War Minister."[35]

From my latest papers it looks as if something of this kind must lie at the bottom of the business—but did you ever hear such a tale! so fatuous a scheme! we might all be living in Nejd—the childish plotting! Can the Govt. survive it? Harold Baker[?] writes to me—his letter is dated before Seely's resignation and he says nothing of the plot—that he feels sure there will be an election in June. With this story for a weapon—true story or no—I do not see how the Opposition can fail to win. But the sorrow of it is that they themselves are such *pauvres sires* [second-rate men]. There is not a man amongst them fit to lead. But I'll write of all this from England.

Tomorrow thank Heaven, I shall not get up at dawn and mount a

33. J. B. Seely, Winston Churchill's classmate at Harrow, war minister in cabinet of H. H. Asquith.

34. Sir Edward Carson, leader of Ulster opposition to Irish Home Rule.

35. H. H. Asquith was maneuvered out of office in August 1916 by Lloyd George, initiating a period in the wilderness for Churchill when four members of the new cabinet refused to serve with him. He became colonial secretary in 1921 and presided at the Cairo Conference, which founded a monarchy in Iraq, carved out of the desert a kingdom called Transjordan, and created an entity in Palestine for Zionist settlement.

camel, I've done with Arabia for the moment. I've crossed the huge Syrian desert for the second time, in safety, in the peace of God. And now it's all behind me and I must try to forget it for a little, till I am less weary and can think of it more soberly and in a better perspective. I'm still too near it—it looms too big, out of all proportion to the world, and too dark, unbelievably menacing. The worst of it is I can't forget it yet. I go on riding camels through my dreams. Perhaps the rose garden and tomorrow's sun will veil it all—and the good Mackinnons will help me to forget it.

APPENDIXES, GLOSSARY
WORKS CITED, & INDEX

Appendix A: Diaries 1913–1914

INTRODUCTION

The foundation of imperialism was not power but information. Bell's daily diary notations were used not only by her but also by imperial administrators, policy makers, and military geographers. Today they will chiefly attract scholars capable of negotiating their way through copious Arabic words and phrases in the pursuit of historical knowledge. Whereas the Doughty-Wylie diaries show Bell imposing a semblance of order on her material, such was not the case with the hastily recorded impressions set down each night, which have rather the aspect of an artist's sketch before the final work begins. A comparison from diaries written on the same date, 19 April 1914, illustrates this point:

> There was a gazelle fawn in Jed'an's tent. It slept on my knee through the long talk, curled up like a Mycaenean [ivory] with a pointed hoof sticking up over its ear. It was the only creature in the company wholly devoid of apprehension.

In the Doughty-Wylie version, she retouches the image in more colorful detail:

> There was a gazelle fawn in Je'dan's tent. They brought it to me and laid it in my lap, where it fell asleep. It lay curled round like a Mycaenean ivory, with one absurd pointed horn stretched out over its ear; it slept through the slow talk. And I looking at the sharp watchful faces of the men around the coffee hearth, and remembering my own probably anxious face, thought that there was none in that company wholly free from apprehension but the little gazelle asleep on my knee.

It was not often that she felt apprehension. Bell's natural courage served her well on her journey; her adherence to the cult of bravery so prevalent among Edwardian males allowed her to range through a universe too alien for many people. Her feeling of connection to nature allowed her to see even in the most barren places some kind of beauty and grandeur, and to derive from them a sense of being at home anywhere.

Sunday 23rd. [23 November 1913]

Rain. Spent the morning reading and writing. Lunched with the Blisses and her fiancé, Mr Dodge, also there. Dr Havard[?] says the Xians behaved shamefully as regards the war—wouldn't serve. The country has suffered from diminution of trade and the people have paid large sums for exemption from service. He thinks the war has diminished the prestige of Xianity as a whole. Most of the emigrants are Xians, but a considerable number of Muslims and even the Bedouin are beginning to go. He also thinks that Muslims all over Turkey have been brought to think seriously of their own incapacity for govt. and to wish for foreign help, but I doubt whether Adana has not largely discounted that. Mr Honey [or Hony] dined. He is directing Jackson's irrigation work in the Lebanon.

Mon. 24. [24 November 1913]

Rain. Mrs C. [Cumberbatch] and I went in the morning to see old Baradi, chemist and collector. He had nothing much. At tea time I went to the College, had tea with the Blisses and a useful talk with Mr Joy about stars.

Tues 25. [25 November 1913]

Came to Damascus [Dimashq] and read *Arabia Deserta* all the way. Still autumn in the Beqa', leaves brown and gold, gold and green on the poplars. So the golden dates were hanging on the palms in Beyrout. Went to the Damascus Palace and immediately to see the Mackinnons, where I found Hochwächter. Dined with Mr and Mrs Brunton (he a nephew of Sir Lauder) who are in the hotel. Also here Mr and Mrs Bray, he a soldier learning Arabic.

Wed 26. [26 November 1913]

Fattuh missed his train at Hamah and will not arrive till tonight. Went to the bank. The Hamiddiyah bazaar not yet quite repaired. Muhammad Bassam came to see me and gave me a most satisfactory account of the desert. There are some good camels to be bought here and everything is at peace. He thinks Nejd [Najd] quite possible and the W[adi] Dawasir, but not 'Asir. Ibn Rashid very powerful and at peace with Ibn Sa'ud. Ibn Sha'lan at Jof [al-Jawf]. He told me with pride of Khalil's gift of a silver bowl. He has been buying lands about Nisibin [Nusaybin] in view of the opening up which is coming with the Baghdad rly [railway]. He has quarrelled with Muhammad al-Na'man who tried to make mischief between him and Nuri ibn Sha'lan. He asked me of the future of Turkey and says the Basrah people want English protection. After lunch went to see Mir Tahir who is also very encouraging about the desert. The W. 'Ali will probably be further east than I want. Fawwas of the

B. Sakhr is the man to go to says Bassam; Hadmel [Hathmel] will probably be east. Tahir says Syria has not felt the war except in diminution of trade. 'Izzet is at Nice. He does not think he will come back for fear of the CUP. He is worth a million liras. The CUP tried to get 100000 out of him in return for making him senator, but he refused. Hochwächter came after tea to see Mr Bray and Mr Devey later. Mr Brunton tells me that what the govt wd like to do in the Lebanon is afforestation, but they can't because so much of the ground is held by the priests and they can't get it. Also the priests own immense herds of goats, fatal to young trees. He says too that no house is built in Syria without sacrifice—a goat usually. The workmen insist, partly because they get the meat, but it is the old custom.

Thurs 27. [27 November 1913]

Better today. Fattuh arrived and we went to see Bassam and his wife. The latter a handsome woman from Nejd. She came via Taif, Meccah and Medinah 8 years ago. Rather difficult to understand her speech—full of invocations to God. Two boys, rather chilifs. The elder is going to Beyrout to Bliss. After lunch unpacked with Fattuh and then went to see the Jesuits—an English man, Burgin, is going to devote himself to the Hauran. He is waiting till his beard grows, which it is not doing at all fast! Then to the Hananers[?] and so walked home through the bazaars and got in at 5. Played Bridge afterwards.

Fri. 28. [28 November 1913]

Went to the bank, walking round the mosque first. Muhammad al Na'man and Abdallah al Khalaf came to see me. M. says Ibn Sha'lan is not at peace with Ibn al Rashid. The present man is Sa'ud ibn al Rashid but he says that 'Abd al 'Aziz ibn al Sa'ud holds all Nejd but just immediately round Hayyil [Hail]. Then to see the Vali's wife Mme 'Arif Bey. An extremely interesting woman, daughter of the Egyptian [space left blank] but they are originally Turks from Kavalla. She says the evils of the Govt weigh hardest on the Turks and there is no talk of reform for Anatolia. Complained bitterly of the Balkan Committee. Desired an English Inspector General for the Armenian provinces, for choice Chermside, but anyhow someone who wd realize that the Kurds have grievances too. The Armenian money lenders get all the land into their hands. 'Arif Bey is an Arab from Mardin; he was Vali at Basrah. His wife loved the journey there and also the people "But of course I can only study the women." Here she says the women are like Moslem women in foreign books—they do absolutely nothing, not even needlework. Most of them can't read. She has an English governess, Miss Green. After lunch walked round the walls with Mrs Brunton and drank coffee at the kahwah near Bab al Salam. Walked round the walls in the afternoon with Mrs Brunton. At tea time came Shukri Beg al 'Asali, and another who had been Mudir at Bab 'Abd al Wahhab and we all talked with Ali Effendi. They talked a good deal of tosh about Arab unity and the feeling of the big shaikhs. Nawwaf ibn Nuri they say is very well educated and a good politician. They also say that Mubarak is summoning Sa'ud ibn al Rashid and Abd al Aziz ibn al Sa'ud to an Arab conference at Hasa or Kwait [Kuwait]. They plead now in Arabic in the courts of law. Shukri is not going to stand again. He says there is no freedom under the C.U.P. Mir Tahir came in and I bamboozled him as to my plans. Dined with the Mackinnons.

Sat 29. [29 November 1913]

Went to Bassam's where I met Muhammad al Marawi and engaged him—a piece of luck. Also 'Ali the Sa'i. Found M. al Na'man in the café near the hotel and sat with him in the sun. He swore he loved me more than his own[?] children, by the Prophet and the Prophet 'Isa and conjured me to take M. al Marawi with me. The wakil of Abd al Rahman joined us and we talked of our journey in the snow—sennet al thalj. Slept after lunch and left a card on Mrs Devey. We have bought 12 camels.

Sun. Nov 30 [30 November 1913]

Went out in rainy weather with the Bruntons to the mosque. Stayed in after lunch. Bassam paid me a long call and after tea talked to Mr Bray.

DECEMBER 1913

Mon. Dec. 1. [1 December 1913]

Shopped in the morning and called on Muhammad Pasha Adam who was not very cordial. He is an old obscurantist and completely pooh poohs the Arab movement. Took observations after lunch. Mr Devey brought me a letter from Dick. Long talk with Dr 'Abd al Rahman, Georges Effendi and 'Abd al Wahhab about the Arab movement. Sayyid Talib, Naqib of Basrah has called a gathering of the Arab Sheikhs. Mubarak of Qweit [Kuwait], the Muntafiqs, the Sha'lans, Ibn Sa'ud, Muhammerah. They are to meet in two months' time at Qweit. The Imam is not of it nor is he so important as al Idasi who is gradually eating up the Yemen. Ibn Rashid has said he wd be represented but he is halfhearted. The Govt has increased his subsidy. They have also given a motor and various presents to the Sherif of Meccah but it is said that a son of his is to go as his representative to Qweit. Facowaz of the Sakh is said to be a good Arab unionist. "The first time the desert has been united since the time of the Prophet" said Abd al Rahman. He says all the leading families here are unionists, or at least all the younger members—the younger Adabys[?], 'Atta Bey Killani etc. Mr M. Philips Price came to see me after dinner, from Aleppo [Halab] and the north.

Tues. Dec 2 [2 December 1913]

Called on Muhammad Bassams wife who told me she never left the house; has been twice to the Great Mosque since she came to Damascus. Bassam says it's all nonsense about the meeting of the sheikhs. They wd never agree. Lunched in the bazaar with the Bruntons, Brays and Mr Price. Went to see Atta Bey Killani and his women—very friendly. Mr Devey came in with Mr Price and his horrid Jew, Reutlinger. Walked with them as far as the mosque and on to the Mackinnons where I had tea with them and Mr Ward. Loytved came to dine. Says England is everything here, partly because of the example of Egypt, partly because we have no military service and partly because we leave trade free. Cumberbatch plays a considerable role, witness his insisting on the opening of the Unionist club in Beyrout. Devey is [illegible] to traffic in arms with the Druzes. He thinks France established here wd be dangerous to our Egyp. Frontier. Talked of Dick.

Wed. Dec. 3. [3 December 1913]

Rainy. Walked out with Mr Price. After lunch called on M. of[?] Kubaisah [Kubaysah]. He is very anxious I should get a permit from the Vali and was very nervous about giving me a letter to Nawwaf. Saw my camels and bought another. The Mackinnons and Dr Ward came to dine.

Thurs Dec 4. [4 December 1913]

Did some work with my theodolite. In the afternoon walked with Mr Brunton to Salahiyyeh and saw the mosques of Muhiyy al Din and 'Abd al Gharni. Beautiful view from the latter. The gardens still covered with brown and gold and green leaf.

Fri. Dec. 5. [5 December 1913]

The Bruntons and I walked out in the afternoon and called on Mr Hope Johnson. He came to dine with the Brays and spent the evening talking to me.

Sat. Dec 6. [6 December 1913]

Called on the Mackinnons—their day. Talked to Dr 'Abd al Rahman who told me how Sami Pasha had imprisoned Nuri ibn Sha'lan with no evidence against him. He had even offered Sami help in putting down the Arab rebellion which S. had refused. He said too the the [*sic*] Wahhabis are everywhere in Arabia—a Protestant movement. There are two Wahhabi sheikhs here in the Maidan, Damascus, who have mosques and large congregations. Not however fanatical though very strict Moslems.

Sun. Dec 7. [7 December 1913]

Dropped my theodolite and went to the Mackinnons in the afternoon where he and Dr Ward put it right. Mr Hope Johnson dined with me and we talked of poetry all the evening.

Mon. Dec 8. [8 December 1913]

Rain. Walked out after lunch up the Marjeh[?] to Sabahiyyeh with the Bruntons. The Mackinnons dined.

Tues Dec 9. [9 December 1913]

Rainy. In the afternoon went with Dr M. [Mackinnon] and Dr Ward to call on 'Abd al Rahman Beg Amir al Hajj. He has not been on the Hajj for 2 years. His grandfather Said Pasha, a Kurd, got an enormous amount of property in this country by fair means and foul. 'Abd al R. had just come back from C'ple [Istanbul, Constantinople] which he reported to be in a very well ordered position. Dined with Muhammad al Ma'rawi in the Maidan. His two brothers there, his son Qasim. Abd al Aziz Humud, agent of Ibn al Rashid, a black door keeper of Ibn al Rashid (eunuch?) in a frock coat and others. We talked of antiquities and 'Abd al Aziz, a strange slight tall figure in [illegible] abayya and immense gold bound agal and gold keffiyeh, spoke of strange worked stones brought into Hayyil, of the Haddaj and its feeling springs, of foundations revealed at Tema [Tayma'] by recent ruins, of the mosques at Kerbela [Karbala] and Nejef [al-Najaf] and the treasures in them. Ibn Rashid and Ibn Sa'ud have lately had a slight disagreement but there is now peace. They asked me of ancient money and when money first began and I wrote for them the Safaitic alphabet. 'Abd al Aziz scarcely moved, spoke in a low soft voice lovely Arabic, kept his eyes mostly cast down; a sly treacherous face with thin black hair on it. My neighbours muttered occasionally Ya Lalif! Ya Manjud[?]. They asked 'Abd al 'Aziz whether any city was fairer than Damascus. He had just come from C'ple which he knows well; was there when the Bulgarians reached Chatalja. He said in respect of air and gardens no place better than Damascus but C'ple bigger. Muhammad al M.'s wife from Tema, a regular beduin woman among all the Shawan. So out into a moonlit night and home by tram.

Wed Dec 10 [10 December 1913]

Walked with the Bruntons to the top of the hill above Salahiyyeh and came down from Kubbet al Nasr. Very nice, a lovely view. Walked up to the Mackinnons after lunch.

Thurs Dec 11 [11 December 1913]

F. [Fattuh] has malaria. Zekiyyeh has come from Aleppo. Called on M. al Bassam and his wife. Dr M. came and saw F. Also took me to Luttickes where Asfar cashed a cheque for me.

Fri. Dec 12 [12 December 1913]

F. still bad. Went up to the hospital in the morning. Dr M. now fears it is typhoid.

Sat. Dec 13 [13 December 1913]

All day busy with F. and with finding a man to replace him.

Sun. Dec 14 [14 December 1913]

Called on 'Abd al Aziz at 8 AM and found there 'Abdallah al Ma'shirek[?] just come from Nejd via Tema and Mu'addam. Abd al A. has the smallest most subtle hands I ever saw on a man. They warned me that the tribes S. of Azraq [Qasr el-Azraq] were much disturbed always. Interviewed cooks and decided to take Salim, Muhammad's nephew. Mr Hope Johnson dined with me.

Monday Dec 15. [15 December 1913]

The camels and baggage got off to Harashtah early. Abu Sa'id, Muhammad's brother, came with a long story of how he had been sent for by 'Abd al Rahman Beg to interview the Vali who told him that M. al M. [Muhammad al Ma'rawi] was not to go with me. He wanted me to take his son with me. I think the rest of the tale is lies. Sat a great deal with Fattuh. Wrote letters and at 3 went with Dr M. to the hospital while F. moved to a hotel in Bab Tuma. Delightful letter from D. [Dick] today. Slept little, with excitement.

Tues. Dec 16 [16 December 1913]

Left the hospital about 7.30 Dr M. in his dressing gown and Mrs M. bidding me goodbye. Jirji drove me and Ibrahim. At Harashtah heard that the camels had gone on. Apricots all in golden leaf, corn springing under the olives, peasants gathering olives. Picked up the camels where the Nebk [al-Nabk] road branches off. M. wanted to camp at 'Adra ['Adhra'] but I refused. So we filled 4 girbehs bought 3 chickens and got off at 11.15. Fortunately fine. Flat dull plain. Got into camp at 2.5 just S. of Dumair [Dumayr]—about 4 miles away I judge. No soldiers there now. Ghiyath in the qishla. 'Ali went off to get a rafiq. Great business getting into camp and finding the things but Ibrahim and Salim most cheerful and willing. I have with me as camel drivers, Ali, Abdallah and Faraj (the latter blackish) and an 'Abd, Fellah, who was sprung upon me,

I having refused to take a 4th man. 'Ali Smugga[?] and Muhammad al-Ma'rawi make up my company. All the 3 camel drivers are 'Agail. The rain fortunately held off till towards 6 by which time we had camped. Quite a good dinner, with meat from Damascus.

Wed. Dec 17 [17 December 1913]

Wind and rain in night and rain at intervals all day. We could not march. 'Ali returned from Dumair not yet having found a rafiq. He went back for wood tibu and cotton cloth for bags, Dumair being our metropolis. The tibu arrived in the middle of the day, but the kham not till the evening with 'Ali. I made the bags after dinner. All day I alternately sat with M. al M. in the men's big tent and read my last weekly Times. Cold and dullish.

Thurs Dec 18 [18 December 1913]

Fine, cold, snow on the hills. We took 2 hrs 20 min. to get off. Left at 8.35 and had an hour's bad struggle through the muddy zera', the camels falling down at intervals. When we were S. of the Roman camp our rafiq joined us, Hamad al Lafi of the Ghiyath. The latter seem to be gom with everyone except the Sayyad and the Jumlan who are fellah tribes of Damascus. But, being with us he does not fear to meet the B. Hassan with whom he is gom. We want one of them as a rafiq. He goes with us for a mej. a day. The big chiefs of the Hasenneh are Sa'ad and Muhammad ibn Milhem who receive ma'ash from the Govt. The B. Hassan are a new group; they were once part of the Ghiyath. We got into the volcanic country at 11.30 and marched over broken ground straight onto a tell called el 'Abd which we reached at 2.30 and found a muddy rain pool where we filled our girbehs. Grass growing between the stones and on the patches of low ground which are free of stones. A man of the Jumlan Sayyad rode out to see who we were; they are camped to the S. of us under the hog's back which was my first bearing, 102° from 'Adra. Got into camp at 4 in a low patch with the Saigal tells immediately in front of us. Beautiful sunset glow. We saw one of the Dumairis at his husbandry. He sowed first and ploughed afterwards. The Jumlani Sayyadi was much surprised to see me, but I offered no explanations. Excellent mushrooms—fitr. We saw a good deal of naitu today but there are no shajar tonight.

Fri. Dec. 19. [19 December 1913]

Woke several times on account of the cold. Ther. fell to 28. Ground all frosted and a thick mist. Broke up camp in under 1½ hours. Mist very tiresome; did not allow me to take long bearings. It lifted a little about 8 and showed us the J. al Sharqi [Jebel al-Sharqi, Anti-Lebanon]; then closed round us till 11. We rode all day through flats strewn with volcanic stones and set with tells; well to the E. of Oppenheim's tells. We passed under T. Milhah Qurunfil, leaving it close to the left, half in mist. Passed a Weli on a hill about 8 and about 12 a couple of walls at right angles, raised ["razed" written above in pencil] to the ground, with a heap of stones behind, like a bustan and a naturah said M al M. I didn't think they were old. All the stones here black when newly broken, weathering white. Lots of Shih. We saw no soul all day and came into camp at 2.15 in line with J. al Makhul. Delicious warm afternoon. We fetched water from a pool not far off, camping here on account of the shih. Lots of paths worn through all this desolate land; but the big tribes have gone to the Hamad. Note Ya Fullan. Allah? Wallah! Teslan[?] Tekrami. Tawakkil Allah.

Sat Dec 20. [20 December 1913]

Horribly cold in night. Ther. fell to 19; 30 when I breakfasted. Sun rose gloriously through mists which at once cleared. We rode over low ground all sailing down to the Khabra Makhul; no water but plenty of grass and shih. At 8 (we had got off at 7—the men's tent was stiff frozen and had to be melted) we sighted J. Sais which we reached at 12. Passed over autumn encampments of the W. Ali and near Sais Muhammad saw two men and was much perturbed. They were probably shepherds of the Sayyad. Passed a Khabra of Sais to the left—dry, but there is a big Khabra Sais to the right about 2 miles away full of water. Also a small khabra under Sais on the NW side in which there was still water. A deep moat round the W and S sides of the volcano ending in a lake on the SE side, full of water. Also N of the ruins some old biyar full of water, very clean and good. We reached the ruins at 12.30 and camped. Plenty of shih and rimth. The ruins consist of a small mosque to the W; a qasr with towers one of which is bigger than the rest and stands two storeys high; and a hammam partly of brick and partly of stone. The mosque is the best building, all of fine cut stones; in the qasr all the foundations are of roughly cut stones, but the inside room of the lower storey and all the upper storey of dressed stones. The masonry of the bath is very rough. Having taken some photographs I climbed to the top of the Jebel which is a perfect round volcano and took bearings and photographs. Lots of big waterpools to the E and South but no Arabs visible anywhere. Saw the J. al Safa and the J. Druze [Jabal al-Duruz]. Came down and had tea. Then from 3 to 5 measured the ruins. Warmer tonight. Note that the small brick vaulted room in the Hammam has no [illegible] but the vault of the big apsed room oversails the wall. The mixture of brick and stone is very curious and inexplicable. Brick only in the big apsed room and the 2 little rooms to the S of it. Looks as if they had been built up with brick after being ruined, but is that likely? and where did they bring the bricks from? In the lower storey of the qasr a fine cut stone vault. It was a gate tower. On the hill opposite the ruins are remains of houses. Fine cut stones. One door standing. I said to Hamad "Who lived in this place?" He replied "We would learn from you. Ya Sitt, who knows? there is no true guide but God."

Sunday Dec 21. [21 December 1913]

Finished my work and set off at 9.15. We presently sighted smoke and flocks. I went up onto a stone heap and looked at them through my glass. No doubt Arabs of the Jebel. Half an hour later a horseman came riding furiously towards us; he shot as he came. Shouted at Hamad who went out to meet him aimed his rifle at him and prepared to ride away. M. al M called to him Ya walad Ibn al Halal, stay! we are Shawam and Agail and Qanasil[?], Tawakkil Allah! God guide you." He circled round us like a madman, shouting that we were gom, Anazeh. He turned out to be a daif, a man of the Sherify not one of the Masa'id. He demanded of 'Ali his rifle wa ludumak. 'Ali threw down his fur. Then came up the Masa'id shepherds riding, running and firing. "Ingil, Ingil!" A man drew M's sword and flourished about with it, hitting at him and me. My camel knelt, he siezing [*sic*] it, and two boys stole some things out of my khurj. But the others, mostly without keffiyyehs and one stark naked except for a handkerchief began stripping my men of their pistols and cartridge belts, shouting and raging the while. My camel got up and I sat watching. Then Fellah wept and called out to them that he knew them and they knew him; he had been in their tents camel buying a year ago. With that my things were returned and presently 2 shaikhs rode up, welcomed us and all turned to smiles and amity. There was really no risk since they were camping Arabs afraid of their enemies—and they have no friends apparently. They asked us anxiously whether we had seen Arabs anywhere. But we have to take a man from them with us and for this end we camped near them at 1 o'clock. The shaikhs sat with us till I tipped them 5 mej. At night they came back singing and brought a man with them 'Awaiseh Abu 'Ali. We sat long over the coffee fire. They say there is an old road from Burqu [Qasr el-Burqu] to Azraq. The frost has gone. Awwad asked me why I travelled here. I said I liked the desert better than cities. "True" said he "I was in Damascus 14 days; it was like a prison and the 14 days seemed 14 months."

Mon. Dec 22 [22 December 1913]

Heavy rain till past 8 and the desert a sticky sop. But a wind rose and dried things and though it was still very threatening I got off at 9.40 and all went well. We rode along the eastern edge of the Harrah all day but had to come into camp at 2.25 under Umm Idu because of the rimth. Our guide Uwaiseh, sits on his camel like a sack and does and says nothing. Abu Naum I have christened him, his name being Abu Ali. The black points of Umm Idu, volcanic, rise above the full khabra opposite my tent, with heavy clouds above them. The stony hills draw together in front of us like the gates of an abandoned Hades. A desolate world, cold and grey. 'Ali has a wife in Baghdad but her doings are not zain on account of her mother who is a kelbeh and has kharrabat her. In Taimal, says M. [Muhammad] there are women who have had from 30 to 40 husbands; this conduct is not approved. Ali thinks one wife and one husband best. M. thinks if a wife has not a child it is better to take another. When a woman is divorced she ought to wait 3 months before remarriage but the Arabs divorce in the morning and marry at night. M. told me the tale of Huber's being murdered by the Harb. His zelameh came into Hayyil wearing Huber's clothes and Muhammad ibn al Rashid sent and caught the Harbi and despached him to Stambul. But nothing happened to him. Huber's two boxes of papers were sent back, but the zelameh stole his money. M. says to the camel drivers "Ya Agail!"

Tues Dec 23 [23 December 1913]

Off at 6, very cold and as soon as the sun rose a thick mist closed round us. I walked till 9.30 the mist in white frost on our clothes. We passed under the Najjar Umm Idu and so out onto a flat plain. From 8.30 to 9.15 not a plant grew—I think this is the W. Muqah marked in the maps. It goes down to the Ruhbah. At 10.30 the fog lifted and we saw the Harrah to the right running NW with the W. Umgad running round its borders. We ourselves were in the valley and remained in it till 12.15 when it went off to the left round the Tell Firdas, whereas we went to the right of Firdas and dropped into the Wadi again at 2.25, just opposite the tomb of Ibn Madi one of the shaikhs of the 'Isa whose camel fell here and killed him about 20 years ago. Under Firdas Awaiseh Abu 'Ali woke up and recounted how his tribe had raided here the 'Anazeh, Ibn killed a man and a horse and taken 40 camels. Since when they have been gom. In the valley, just about where we first touched it, Muhammad al Bassam with 200 camels going to Nejd, had been attacked by the Masa'id and had driven them back, said 'Ali. The ghadir was full of water. After the tombs we marched along the ghadir and came into camp at 3.30. We got heaps of fitr this morning, great big ones growing among shajar and a sort of fennel. Marah of the W. 'Ali in the valley. East of the Harrah all this country is Hamad. As Ali and I walked on this afternoon looking for a camping ground, he stopped and said "Ya sitt, let us wait for the dululs. We have no arms."

Wed Dec 24 [24 December 1913]

Discovered last night that I had left my pistol behind. Ali refused to go back for it so Hamad and 'Abdallah went early this morning. We got off at 7 and rode all up the W. Umbfad till 1 when we reached Burqu. The W. Umgad and the W. Swab both rise at 'Anazah which is some 3 days' due S. of Ga'rah. A sail comes into Umbfad from Khburri. Ga'rah is only a day and a night's ride from Burqu. All the Anazeh tribes camp at 'Anazah, fetching dates from Shethathah [Shithathah] which is 4 or 5 days for loaded camels. No ruins there, but a castle at Al Mat and many tombs and wells. Burqu lies in at [sic] outcrop of volcanic stones; it has a Kufic inscription, apparently of Walid, and a cross over another door. I set to work photographing and drawing it

Qasr Burqu.
Photograph by
Gertrude Bell.
Courtesy of the
University of New-
castle upon Tyne.

as soon as I had had tea. It was warm for the first time, 56°. Many stone tombs with bones in them, bare, perhaps eaten bare. There was a tomb by my camp last night into which the daba' had dug and eaten the body. The square keep stands black against the sky this night of stars. Sirius a green light hung over the tower and Orion spread across heaven above it. I was asked to look through my glasses as we reached Burqu and there was much joy when I reported absence of Arabs.

Dec 25 [25 December 1913]

Worked all day at Burqu. It was so cold in the morning that I could not take a rubbing because the water froze. Breakfasted in a temp of 28°. Read the Kufic inscrip. and found a Greek. So it was a Roman fort after all. Abdallah and Hamad came in safely in the morning, bringing my revolver. Above my camp, W of the birkeh the stones are covered with Safaitic inscrips very difficult to read. Had not time to study them properly before the sun set. The father and grandfather of Uwaiseh are buried here in two of the tombs outside the qasr. The keep must have been 3 storeys high; one sees the sticking out stones for the floors. Part of the NE wall has fallen and been built up. Ibrahim lighted a fire of green shih in the qasr this morning. It smoked abominably and he was rebuked by Ali. "Smoke is seen far in the morning and sound is heard far." For the same reason when we make a fire on the march they are careful to choose dry trees.

Fri. Dec. 26. [26 December 1913]

25° when I breakfasted and a sharp wind all day. We got off at 7 and onto the Harrah at 8.15. Twice I saw a Saf. inscrip; the first only a fragment. We left T el Resai a little to the left and came down into the W. of that name (or Sa'adeh from the low line of hills SW of it). Clear trace of the old road down into the valley. Many deep big wells, some now masdud, most of them empty. But water in the Wadi. Lots of Saf. inscriptions. At Masalla [Khan al-Musalla], heaps of broken earthenware pottery and traces of square rooms, only rude foundations level with the ground. We got in at 2 and I copied Saf. inscrips till 4.30 when it was too dark to go on. No wind and warmer.

Sat Dec 27. [27 December 1913]

Copied inscrips. but badly I fear. We got off at 9 but the miserable Abu 'Ali walked off in another direction and could not be found. He turned up from quite a different quarter in half an hour but meantime Muham. and 'Abdallah had gone east to look for him and we had to wait another half hour for them. Copied 2 more inscrips on the road. We marched first on the W. point of Sa'adeh, then on the W. Ashgaf up the W. Sa'adeh. The position of the hills and valleys is roughly this [sketch]. We camped at 3.20 under the spurs of T. Ta'ainus. Horrible wind all day and bar. very low at night—26.7. But we must have come up a good deal. Very disagreeable march over endless stones with no apparent path through them. The men wanted to stop under Ashgaf W but I wd not and came on an hour further. Ghutba here.

Sun. Dec 28. [28 December 1913]

Raging wind all night and still sharp all today, but behind us luckily. Off at 6.45 and after half an hour's walk reached the ridge which runs NW from T. Ta'ainus and saw 2 days' journey below us. The Harrah stooped down at our feet, to the W. the J. Druze, far away in front a low tell, al Fehdawy, our first for that day. We rode down a valley called W. el Swai'id into immense tracts of Harrah, stonier and stonier till they could grow no worse and grew better. Camping grounds of the Ruwella [sic]. The men in rather a [illegible] lest we should meet Arabs whom we did not know. We saw steps of men and camels and sheep coming in our direction, about a fortnight old. At the lower levels there were tracts of Baida. At 12.50 we crossed a ghadir, but it was dry. A solitary shih plant in leaf among the stones of its banks—strange to see any green thing. The shajar were mainly ghutba and ajrab, the latter with a thistle down or rather daisy like seed. About an hour from Fehdawy a gleam of water in a nearby dry khabra and beyond it a full khabra. But we did not go to the latter because the men sighted pasturing Arabs and were anxious. So we pitched camp in low ground at 3.45. They think we have not been seen. Quite still and a blessed silence. Hamad was sent to the half dry khabra to fetch water. I saw him come back crossing over the red sunset sky. The dulul with her dancing step, and he crouched upon the full skins and holding his camel stick like a sceptre. Mashaban[?] Mashabtain! But the water! pure mud. Abu 'Ali's beard was thick with mud after drinking it. A long sunset glow. Long before it had faded Capella and Aldebaran shone out—Altair stooping his wings to the W (the Nisr they call him). The first stars of Orion swung up. Vega low in the western sky and Fomelhaut. Algerib and Algol in the Milky Way and Deneb shining out of it. Then came the Twins then Sirius rises with his white light and soon after Procyon. And the two Pointers lift themselves up to the N. Star. In the top of the sky the empty square of Pegasus. I can hear the silence tonight. We see the Arab fires twinkling far away—blazing up and dying down.

Mon. Dec. 29 [29 December 1913]

We got off at 6.30 and I walked to the top of al Fehdawi where there are Saf. ins. Saw our road from there and also the smoke of the Arab camps. We crossed a ghadir and passed over a low ridge. Here the men heard the sound of shots—an alarm among the Arabs. M. feared that they would fizz u alaina in the baida at our feet. We left Abu 'Ali on the ridge to meet them and stopped ourselves. Soon a horseman appeared on the ridge and greeted us with the customary shot. Baihr[?] met Abu 'Ali and all was well. They were Adamat, of the Zubaid. We lighted a fire and waited for the horseman. Abu 'A. called out "Sug" but M. Bidna "nasallim 'aly al khteyyal[?]." So we sat down with him and exchanged news "Ahl al Shimal wain?" Wallah ghadi min al Azraq. "Min al Azraq?" "Eh billah." M. "Hayyin hayyin. Tawakkil Allah." "Wa al Sirhan?" "Al Sirhan bil 'Amud wa ghad." "Bil Hamad?" Eigh. "[illegible] ma [illegible] al 'Anazeh?" La billah. Then to us, where we had come from, had we seen Arabs? and where? no one else? and so on. Where had we slept, where was water? So after 40 minutes after we had given him bread figs and tobacco, we went on. He told us that the Serdiyyeh were rahilin that day and presently we saw them coming across our path. A horseman rode out but walking, and came up to us, greeted us and presently took his cartridge out of his rifle and slung it over his shoulder. He was dressed in a blue cloth jacket. Then came several more and finally the shaikh, Ghalib ibn Mit'ab al Gauj[?] and insisted on our spending the night with him. M. also insisted and I gave way reluctantly though it was only 11 o'clock. So we camped and meantime drank coffee with Ghalib. After lunch I walked about, photographed, sat with the women. Ghalib's wife and sister very pretty women. A small son called Sa'ud. Sat with the men and heard of ruins S of Burqa. Doctored a man with a horribly bad foot. Didn't I know a cure from my book? I knew how to read? God sent me. Temp. at highest 56. Mit'ab was a very well known person. New moon. Flocks coming in. Fires in the buyut. A great many questions as to why I came and why travelled in the cold. Ghalib explained at great length how all foreigners wanted to know the history of the land, English, French all. An old mn told me of 2 ruins S of Burqa—one must be I think Graham's Warran of which noone has heard. A road runs from Azraq to Nemara and Burqu. Extremely nasty dinner with Ghalib—sheep and bread in a greasy stew which he mixed up for me with his fingers, saying "Kull hu[?] tayyib—ishtaghalthu be idi." After dinner we talked of maladies, and of a Sherari who learnt all medicine from a Mughrebi and cures every ill. Then compared rifles. I gave Ghalib a cloak and under robe of silk, coffee and sugar. Noise and talk all night.

Tues Dec 30. [30 December 1913]

Off at 6.35, warm and grey with rain hanging about in the W. Nimran the kah-wahji rides with us. I dismissed Abu 'Ali with £11 and 1 mej. with which he was far from content. We rode first over Harrah. Passed a memorial tomb to Mit'ab—he was killed in a ghazzu on the Ahl al Shimal and is buried E. of Azraq. It was all covered with women's hair, bleached by the sun. Nimran said Shufti shughl al harem? Whenever they camp here they come and mourn over it. He died 5 or 6 years ago. The talk was all of ghazzu—M. contributing his [illegible] with tales of raiding with Muham. ibn al Rashid. The Ruwalla are the great foes of the Serdiyyeh. They are the biggest of the tribes and have 5 or 6000 tents. Ghalib has only 150. The Masa'id 7 or 800. We went somewhat E. to avoid war. 'Ali (camel driver) and Salim talked of dreams—'Ali said dreams went by contraries[?]. He dreamt once of a great wedding at which there was nothing to eat. A wise man told him it was a sign that he was to fall very ill, but since there had been nothing to eat he wd recover—if they had feasted he wd have died. And so it fell out—he nearly died. To lose a back tooth means death of a man, a front tooth death of a woman. He knows this is true for he lost a back tooth and heard two months after that his two brothers had died in Nejd, and losing a front tooth his sister died in Nejd. We got to Saikhun at 1, a pointed hill overlooking all the low ground S and W, and crowned by a fort, doubtless Roman. Climbed up with Nimran and saw no water anywhere. I decided that the work wd take 2 hours, that the men had better go on to the Baida springs, while Ibrahim worked with me and 'Ali kept the camels. Worked from 1 till 2.30. The building very rough, mortarless, no in-scrips. Then we rode on over alternate Harrah and Baida, ending in a wide gap full of big ghada bushes and some greening tamarisk and got to Baida at 4.30 finding the men just pitching tents. A tract of sabkha under the ridge of the Harrah, and the wells, very slightly brackish and very cold, in sand and ghada bushes. Nice camp. The new moon with the old moon in its arms. Warm and still. Nimran says that Ghalib is a walad 'adil, no one better. Qabb hu nadif. They never stop raiding. The year of Sami Pasha, Nuri took from them all their camels and possessions leaving nothing but the baits. Ghalib went to Sami and gained his partizanship. He made Nuri return a part[?]. This was when Nuri was imprisoned. The blessing it is to be out of the Harrah.

Dec 31. Wed [31 December 1913]

As the sun rose I was on top of the Harrah taking bearings. Rode off with 'Ali over the Sabhka and reached Azraq. at 8. It lies in an outcrop of Harrah with palms and a mass of reeds and springs at its foot. I left 'Ali with the camels under the palms and went in by the small N. postern through the heavy stone door. In the first room I entered there was a Druze who greeted me with the utmost fervour and gave me coffee saying "This is my lady." I then proceeded to plan and was surrounded by Arabs and a Jofi all shouting that I should do nothing without bakhshish—if I wrote a line they would burn my book. I took them down to 'Ali, but as they had shut the postern and cd not open it we came out of the SW gate. 'Ali talked to them and I thought pacified them, so I went back. But the same scene began again, both the Jofi Nasir and the Arab Nasir declaring that he alone was lord of the castle. An old man uncle to the Nasir took me aside and explained that Nasir's people had been lords here before I was born. Back again to 'Ali who went himself to the castle, I remaining under the trees. At last they all came back declaring that they were entirely at my service. So we went back a second time and they showed me Dussaud's inscrip. and a second, I think new. With that I begun to plan and finished drawing by lunch time. A horrid dirty job, the rooms which stand being inhabited by man and beast. After lunch we did all the measuring and after tea I took bearings. Very hot in the afternoon. Then turned up a man from Kaf with fair hair and blue eyes who offered to take me to Nejd. He is Nuri's man and was formerly with 'Abd al Aziz ibn al Rashid. His name is [space left blank]. The Druze, Faris, is an outlaw. He was with Selim al Atrash nephew of Yahya when the latter was shot. They were 14 of them against a company of Turkish soldiers; they killed 3 and lost 3 themselves. Selim was shot through neck and chest. M. "Did he die hawa, at a breath, or did he linger?" He lingered 13 months. Faris comes from near Imtan but he cannot go back because there are soldiers everywhere in the Jebel. Wild duck and wild boar in the marshes, and fish. So the year ends, with Arabs, Druzes, and the shades of Roman emperors and Mamluks. Heaven send a better one and our hearts' desire for both of us. Faris declares that there is a whole quarter of Druzes in Stambul and that they have a "mosque" under the ground with a secret door. These Druzes came from China. There are 2 Chinas, the outer and the inner. They came from the outer China, passed through Hasan and Husein and so to Homs [Him], Jebel Libnan[?] and J. Druze. His father came to J. Druze when he was a child of 3. Faris was born there. Great talks round the coffee fire. Last night it was all of the sennet al thalj and Ibrahim told a long tale of travel from 'Ain Tab and how they journeyed all night and in the morning heard the muezzin and it was still 'Ain Tab. He is the funny man of the party. Great jokes as today he cd not ride on the bare shedad stripped of khurz[?] and fur because it hurt him. Today the joke was that he thought he saw a snake in the castle. Tonight he told a long Arabian Nights tale, the famous one of the 3 trials ending with the assistance of the ants. The fire flickered up and down and their faces—the dreamy countenance of Nejran, 'Abdallah's laughing face, Ali camel driver with his gray beard, the blue eyed man from Kaf, and Fellah the nigger behind, all grin and white teeth, the Arabs of the castle. Outside the camels and the little moon and the palms and the black walls. Farraj is the other raconteur but I can't understand him.

JANUARY 1914

Thurs. Jan. 1. 1914 [1 January 1914]

Finished my work by 11.30, took a latitude and then the sun went in, leaving me workless. This morning in turning over a big stone, Nimran gave up saying to Salim and Ibrahim "Ya; we are no good for such work, there is no strength in us (holding out his slender wrists) We ride, we can do no other thing. Al Arab ma fi ilhum quwa." Note that Salli alla al Nebi is always an interruption of some one else. In addressing someone they will begin Ya Abu Jasim, yusikum bil khari, or allah yusallimak, while all sitting round the fire. Nuri is evidently in a state of mind about the project of a railway to Kaf. M. has been assuring Nasir, his man, that there is nothing in it. I walked round the marsh after tea. Soft with evening, birds calling and a boy driving back the meagre horses singing. Grass and reeds and sabkha and deep pools with the fort rising black behind its palms. The talk round the camp fire particularly good tonight. Ali told a long tale of a ghazzu of the ahl al Shimal on the Sba' at Ga'rah where they took miri[?] and all the camels and hallal. Also of a ghazzu of the Sherarat on all the 'Anazeh right across to the Euphrates in the autumn when the Anarat camels were away in the desert and the 'Anazeh were as imprisoned in their gardens. The Sherarat sat at Thenail[?] and mopped[?] them all up. Then Nimran told of a raid with Ghalib when they were 4 days without food. Their sight wavered and one man seemed to another like a shadow. The ghazzu in Spring is good, but in the autumn you wd say I prefer the foe and death to this ghazzu. They carry scarcely anything to eat and eat grass in spring and what game they can find. 'Ali: What we have eaten tonight wd serve a man raiding for a month. Then Nimran: a tale of a Sherari on a mare. The Sherari have no horses, they ride on camels. 'Ali: A Sherari can't ride. One riding from here to the castle would fall off. Nimran. So when they saw the foe this mare delighted to see horses made for them and the Sherari could not sop [*sic*] her. The camel riders remained behind, but he dashed on, at the mare's will, she desiring the horses and split up the horsemen so that they turned and fled. When they came back the women aclamed [*sic*] him, but he said "Laud this mare, not me. For it was this mare who rushed on the horsemen." As I went up to the qasr today a small dirty ragged child was climbing up to the gate, singing, with a dry palm branch in his hand. Inside a very old man equally dirty and ragged was walking across the court leaning on a stick—at opposite ends of the same scale. A woman keeps telling me of a treasure which is to found in the qasr.

Fri. Jan 2. [2 January 1914]

Warm morning. Off at 7 with 'Ali and 4 of the Qasr men to look at some stones. They proved to be capitals and engaged columns, the latter on rounded stones of a mihrab or apse. One basket capital. They were used for the graves of the Ruwalla who have a large camping ground below. They come here, but only in great strength, before they go east, when the rains have fallen in the Hamad. The Sukhur dare not attack them. The Qasr Arabs are mostly Sherarat. They pasture the horses of the Druzes and are given flour and coffee by the Druzes. If they see a stray camel in the desert they bring it in, kill it and eat it. They are a miserable lot. The dululs picked us up at the graveyard, having loaded 11 qirbehs of water—all we have. We rode by Wained[?], whence we saw 'Aura. But it was a long way across the flat ground. Near near [*sic*] Nimran told us in his soft feminine voice, the Serdiyyeh attacked the Beni Khadid, killed two women and a child. Ashab al nar are all the Arabs. I changed camels with Ibrahim and rode on with 'Ali getting to 'Amra about 2. It lies delightfully in the valley bed over which are scattered butm. I photographed till 4—badly I fear. The dome is on pendentives. Both these and the cross vault are constructed like the Ukhaidir [Ukhaydir] counterparts, with a bracket of horizontal stones cut to the shape of bricks. No bricks here. All the vaults constructed of thin brick-like stones. Wonderful sunset. This was the first really warm day. Clear glow lasting till 5.45.

Sat. Jan. 3. [3 January 1914]

We got to Kharaneh [Qasr el-Kharana] at 11 after stopping for ½ an hour in the W. al Butm to gather wood. The trees growing in it besides butm are Waizeh and rutm, both looking like broom and gutaf, a small leafed shrub. I rode on with Nimran. He has a wife and 4 small children. Did I see his tent? it was the one with the black foal tethered before it. He has a mare thank God. He has only one camel—he had 3 but the Ruwalla took two in a raid. I said I thought things wd be easier if they didn't steal from one another and enjoyed what they had got. "We follow the ways of our fathers and grandfathers. Hukm Allah. There is no ordinance but that of God."

Presently he thought he saw smoke and looked at it anxiously. It might be a ghazzu he thought. "Every Arab is quick to see smoke. Every Arab in the desert fears the other." Kharaneh is full of splendid surprises. Lots of Kufic. I saw a Kufic inscrip. on the wall of Amrah right of the door. Worked till 4.30. Then came and talked plans with the men. We have found only 2 girbehs of water. None in the W. Mshash [Mushash]. Wrote letters all the evening.

Sun. Jan 4 [4 January 1914]

Worked at the qasr from dawn till sunset and ended rather tired. There is a dead man in one of the lower rooms. They say he must have died in the first cold of winter. His horrible presence is not easily forgotten. Nimran and Ali scoured the country for water but brought in only two skins. Cloudy morning and dew at night. Warmer.

Mon. Jan 5. [5 January 1914]

Worked again all day and finished at nightfall. Not at all tired. Sat with the men at night and 'Ali camel driver told tales of Jinn. Once when he was a boy, in our country (Nejd) he was travelling at night and a Jinneh walked with him for 2 hours. How did he know she was a Jinneh? because her eyes were set lengthways in her face and reached down to her mouth. She was the height of a woman and labiseh hudani. So he kept on repeating Bism[?] illahi al rahmanal rahim. And she echoed with Bis bas rih rah. Whenever he got down into a hollow he hoped she had lost him, but on the other side, there she was. At last she wearied of the Bism ellah and left him. In the middle of the tale Hamad put on a great heap of brushwood onto the fire and it blazed up like a torch. M. rebuked him. Everyone cd see us—look our light shone on the walls of the qasr. I expressed disbelief in Jinn and Ghuls. M. Are not the Jinn mentioned in the Quran? But perhaps they don't exist now. Faraj. Ya M. Sall ala al Nebi! Which are more numerous al nis or al jinn? The jinn are in all the air. As Salim lighted me to bed he concluded that there had been Jinn fil awwal but were no more now. Next day Nimran asked me why all this talk of Ghuls? I said I did not believe in them and he agreed. The Arabs went night and day through the desert and saw none. I. Ya Nimran the ghul is within the heart. "Eh Wallah" he said "al khauf." I said I had only been laughing when I asked 'Ali to tell tales and I thought he had been laughing. Oh [sic] else said N. he imagined them, hallam[?]. All this talk originated with the dead man in the qasr and Ibrahim's betting that for a pound or without a pound he wd go and lay a mark[?] on him. But I intervened saying it was not good for the health to go near a corpse in that state. Yes, only that, said M. Bravo[?] aleyki. The dead can do no harm. I said I wished we cd see the dead khalifs who had feasted here. Here they came yatafantasun said M.

Tues Jan 6 [6 January 1914]

Heavy grey morning, a few drops of rain in the night. About 11 we sighted camels and sheep—much talk as to who they were. I said if the sheikh here was malek al ard I wd not camp with him. But if he were Hadithah? (of the Ahl al Shinal) said Nimran who is anxious to go home to his wife and small children and mare; I wd have let him go. The Arabs turned out to be Jubbur—no horseman rode out so they can have had no horses with them. We did not go near their tents but talked to the ra'yan whom we met. Very horrid water in pools in the ghadir which is an affluent of the Mdaisis. We took some for 'aliq and watered our camels. There were Zahair in the up-per reaches of the Msattara valley, so we went rather S., close to J. Banaya that they might not see us. Ma tara' al kelb w'al kelb yara' said 'Ali. We climbed up and up till at 1.45 we came to the water parting and saw the Belqa hills far away below us. All this is sheep grazing country, soft soil, grass, few shajar and little batab[?]. We came down into the Msattara valley and found good water and camped at 2.45. Saw Muweggar on the hills. Flocks and shepherds on the hillside on the opposite side of the valley. Mshetta [Qasr el-Mushatta] can be seen from above our camp. A gracious country. Nimran was paid off and rode away by moonlight. Went to bed very heavy hearted. My roof pole broke in the night.

Wed Jan 7. [7 January 1914]

A wonderful still and clear aura coming slowly down over soft hill slopes com-forted me a little. We climbed up the hill where we were greeted by a shepherd who said he wd have come to see us last night if he had not feared we had been people not meleh, and invited us to lunch. Wonderful view over the plain with Ziza [Jiza] in the midst and Msetta [Qasr el-Mushatta] to one side. I hastily did up my letters, 'Ali and Salim left for Madeba [Madaba], M. and 'Ali camel d[river] for Madeba. Then we pitched tents and stayed for the rest of day, the others not coming back. Wind.

Thurs. Jan 8. [3 January 1914]

A clear morning, wind later. 'Abdullah went off to see what the others were doing. He returned with 'Ali camel d. and Fattuh! immense joy. F. still looks pale and ill. He brought me the latest letters, one from D. of Dec. 23. After lunch I rode with Ali to Mshetta—or the ghost of it. All standing doors are set back. No sight of the shell niche. Graffiti, I doubt if any are old. As we rode back we saw 3 horsemen com-ing to our tents and when we got there 3 soldiers were seated at our camp fire. They were speedily followed by several more, 10 or 12 in all and a very angry chowwish, Jusef. It seems they have been looking for me everywhere and telegraphing from C'ple. I saw the game was up. After sunset, as a protest from F. of some untimely fol-lowing of me[?], he was sent off to prison in the Qal'ah at Ziza. Also Abdullah, whom

I had sent to Madeba with telegrams was intercepted and taken to the Qal'ah. Men were then posted all round my tent and our arms taken.

Fri. Jan. 9. [9 January 1914]

The temp fell to 22° in the night and our unwelcome guard had a bad time. Spent the day waiting for the Qaimmaqam of Salt. F. and Abdallah came back (the chowwish had offered to bring them back in the middle of the night) and we all spent the morning making a new tent pole for me, the soldiers aiding. Heaps of gazelle in the hills. Sat in F.'s tent and drew out a section of Kharaneh in afternoon. Cold and horribly windy. Jusef Ch. who has been away all day, came back in a good and obliging temper. It is all rather fancy I must say.

Sat. Jan. 10. [10 January 1914]

Disgusting day, cold, wind and sleet. We got out of camp and rode to the station where I waited for the baggage. Jusef Chowwish and 4 soldiers with us. A little way from the station we saw soldiers—it was the Q. who turned back to Zuwaideh [el-Juweiyida] by another road. When we reached Zuwaideh he had gone on to 'Amman with the Yuzbashi. Hurried on and got to the hill down to 'Amman, with little rain. I walked down, got onto Jusef's horse and cantered up to the Serai, where I found the Q, Halim Beg Abu Sha'r, the Yuzbashi, Ishaq Effendi, and the Mudir, Muhammad Beg. All very friendly. I explained my doings, laid my complaint before them about the Yuzbashi and convinced Halim Beg that I was harmless. He telegraphed the same to Damascus. Two young men, Hanna Bsharra, and Ferid, son of Habib Effendi with whom I lodged at Salt. Hanna presently explained to me that Halim, a Xian, did not want to take any responsibility and I had better telegraph to Devey, which I did. My men pitched tents in pouring rain, below the theatre and before the Odeon.

Sun Jan 11. [11 January 1914]

No answer. I drew out Kharaneh all the morning. In the afternoon—after lunch—went to see the Q. whom I found lunching in the house of the richest inhabitant of 'Amman, Muhammad Beg. He has been here 40 years. His house is near the old mosque which they say was built by 'Umar. The Yuzbashi there too. They showed me a Dam. paper with a quotation from the globe about a Russian countess who has left Dam. for the south with 20 camels. This they think is I, as it may be. I called on Ishaq's wife, a pretty little woman from Beyrout. The Q. and I walked round to the Nympheum and up to the citadel. The Moslem building there must I think be Umayyad, or soon after. The Damascenes have asked Halim if he will stand at the next election. He asked my advice. I told him he could do nothing unless he sided with the Committee. He talked politics, inveighed against the Moham. very bitterly but admitted that the Xians were all disunited. He kept the Salt region quiet in the time of the Kerak rising. Says if he had been a Moham. he wd have been a Mutesarrif by this time. They all came to see me in the evening, Muhammad Beg, the Qadi etc.

Mon Jan. 12 [12 January 1914]

No answer. Drew out Kharaneh and in the afternoon went up to the citadel and photographed. The Mudir Muham. a Circassian came to see me. Also a Xian, servant of the Khuri at Madeba who has been robbed of 300 ps worth of raisins by Circassians at Na'um. Undertook to intercede.

Tues Jan 13 [13 January 1914]

Breakfasted with the Mudir and the Yuzbashi. We talked at length of the Govt of which they all complain. They say the Circassians were much mistaken to leave Russia. Ishaq told a long tale of how the English had desired to see the Circassians an independent kingdom, not under Russia; but all the tribes quarrelled together and cd not decide on a single head. Then Russia took them. Then they sent a deputation with presents. They lodged in a hotel and Victoria hearing they were receiving the present then inquired what Circassians they could be and sent for them "took them from the hotel." But she explained that now Russia had taken Circassia, some had become beys and some soldiers, and generals and some officials in Russia, England would no longer intervene. I said what Turkey wanted was not a fleet and an army but gendarmes and trade. Ishaq's wife sent me flowers, marigolds and dark red carnations. In the evening came one to invite me to call on the Protestant mu'allim from Salt. Wonderful night with moon filling half the theatre with light

Wed. Jan 14 [14 January 1914]

Drew out Kharaneh and decided to run away next day when the camel drivers for whom we have sent from Dam. have come. Told the Yuzbashi I intended to go to Umm al Kundum [Um el-Kundum] and very appropriately Shibly Bsharra arrived and I explained to him my plan. He said I would have no difficultly. The soldiers wd not go far into the desert because of their horses; a little money wd buy them off anyway. In the afternoon went to a Circassian wedding. The girls all in their best pink and blue, silver belts and a silver ring on each finger, with high caps, embroidered and covered with tinsel stood in a ring. One played an accordian and the men beat time with two pieces of wood. All the girls plain except one. A man stepped into the ring and took out one of the girls—each one came in her turn. The men made elaborate steps; some were in full Circassian clothes, some in Arab clothes. The girls just minced round, rather gracefully. A very drunken man in top boots.

Thurs Jan 15 [15 January 1914]

Decided to take with us Sa'id ibn Faris, the camel man from Dam. as 4th man. He is M.'s nephew. An Agaili, 'Ali, insisted on coming with us so far, on chance of work. Went at 7 to Ishaq's house and tried to get back my paper. He appeared in underclothes and overcoat and gave me tea in his bedroom! Swore that the paper had been written by Halim who appeared last night from Salt and had gone on with it to Dam. All lies, but I cd not get it anyway. So I rode on with Shibly. We stopped at Juwaideh and had coffee with Selim Abu Jubir and his wife and another. Then on to Yadudeh where I found the two Jawaberi, Abu Salih and Abu Sa'id, men. Great big men, with deep voices. Their father bought the land here, coming from Salt. By origin they are of Nazareth. They have a big house at Salt. They bound over a Sakhary to go with me as rafiq. One very pretty woman in the house, daughter of Abu Salih, and Sa'id, a sickly looking boy. Rock cut tombs and old threshing floors. All the villages here are built with old stones. Drank coffee and rode on to Umm al Kundum where we found Hanna, his mother Umm al Bshara, who is a sister of the Jawaberi, her two daughters, Nur[?] unmarried and another very handsome who is married but has left her husband (a man of Nablus) and come back to live with her little girl. Also Nimrud Hassun whom I was enchanted to see. The uncle, Abu Suleiman Bsharra presently came in. His son Suleiman is the husband of the pretty woman we saw at Yadudeh. The father of these Bsharra boys, Ibrahim is dead. We lunched on chickens and I talked to Nimrud most of the afternoon. They have a great house, madafi, which is full every night—Arabs, soldiers, they have to feed and lodge them all, them and their mounts. Most of their profit goes this way. They kill 3 sheep a week and buy kids for their guests. Hanna talks French and a little English. He has just come back from the university at Freyburg[?] where he has taken an agricultural degree and wants to bring out machines and improve the work here. Nimrud is not doing well. The last 2 years have not given enough corn for his low lying lands and Habib Effendi is dead, while Faris does little or nothing and leaves the work to hired labour. They carried out the big tray, bread steeped in a gravy of dry laban and water, with rice and meat on top, to the guests. Then we dined on lamb and spent some time talking politics. So to bed very sleepy. Their workmen are all Moslems, many Sherarat. They have no trouble about religion. The Bsharras have about 50 workmen. They get in 50 more for the harvest. Their women see no Moslems—they are practically veiled. But not before Xians [Christians]. Wonderful view from the top of this hill over the rolling plain.

Fri. Jan 16 [16 January 1914]

Fearful rows among the men. Fattuh at last got them pacified and they rode off with the camels. Presently M. and Salim returned saying that the Agail had beaten M. with his own sword, and shortly the 3 Agail turned up and said they wd go no further.

We got a Sherari from the farm and took on the Agaili follower, 'Ali. Then I rode down to Yadudeh where I explained my difficulties to the Jawaberi and they said they wd give me two Sherarat if I wanted them. So we all rode off together, with Nimrud, past Tnaid [el-Tuneib] which is now a village with houses. The lands between Juwaideh and Tnaid belong to a Skhari and the lands round Qastal to Fawwaz who has built a house in the camp. They are always ploughing up new land. It is very hard at first and they sow hunta[?]. Turn up the ground ever so little at first. Curious to see the long furrows, often a single line, running out into the desert covered with shajar where no cultivation has been for so long. Nimrud says that Salah al Din transported all the population from here to the Jebel Ajlun where, he says, villages of the same name as these are to be found. The price of land is now £T2 a dallam; when these men's fathers came it was worth a mejideh or less. They complain of prices having gone up—but they themselves reap most of the profit. They send their produce to Jerusalem where prices are higher than in Dam. and get what they don't produce from Jerusalem and Dam. Abu Salih was last year in Egypt and was amazed at what he saw there. He asked me carefully which part of Turkey was richest and I said I thought 'Iraq. "Ya khadrat al sitt. There is a row on here among the Sukhur. Dadagh, brother of the Nahur[?] with whom I dined 9 years ago recently killed his cousin Khazir, brother of Fawwaz—no, Fawwaz killed Khazir and took camels from him. Therefore Dadagh is on the lookout for Fawwaz and F. scarcely dares to stir from his house at Ziza. One night he slept in the house of a Sherari for fear of D. D. has a little band of 9 men—mostly Sherarat boys—with him and goes about plundering as he can. A regular freebooter. They say he is like a madman. He is said to be now E. of the [Wadi] Ghadaf in the Sirhan [Wadi Sirhan]. We asked for letters at Ziza station but got none. Here we saw the camels ahead and just before Ziza F. was waiting for us. M. had stayed at Ziza and said he wd not come on. So F. went back to fetch him and meantime we all lunched on the remains of yesterday's dinner and bread, and oranges and potatoes which Abu Salih had brought. Sun really hot today. F. came back with M. We took a Sakhari called Sayyah and a Sherari boy as rafiqs and bade farewell to Nimrud and the Jawaberi, who poured blessings upon me in their deep voices. An hour and a half further on we found the men encamped by a ghadir; it is near a bridge on the rly, 270.7 kilometres from Dam. Peace at last! and the empty desert. Says Salim Nahna kullna mabsutin; shamaina rihat al hawa[?]. M. very anxious to ride back to Ziza for a debt and Sa'id wants to send money to his family, but I refused to let anyone go. 'Ajezt! hayyat Allah. And the links are cut now. The desert now I am in it again, seems full of security. When I asked the Umm al Bsharra how they cd afford to feed so many guests, she replied Wain al lokanda fi hal barriyyeh? I said to Shibli that I heard Khazir was a rogue. Yes replied[?] but he was a good man, very generous. Yusef Chowwish took away Sayyah's rifle, saying it was a Govt. rifle—and indeed it is numbered. Whereupon Sayyah said he was ma'al sitt and M. observed that there wd be no need to telegraph to the Qaimmaqam. Thereat the rifle was returned!

Sat. Jan 17. [17 January 1914]

Up before 5 and we were ready by 6 though rather delayed by losing 2 hens which were found wrapped up in the men's tent! One of the camels also strayed and had to be looked for. I saw the Scorpion for the first time. Lovely day, but a small and provoking E. wind got up later. We marched all day over rolling country rather short of trees. Talib ibn Zebin joined us with an 'abd. Going to his people. He sleeps with us tonight. Sayyah talks very clear Arabic. We discussed dialects and M. imitated the squeaky voice of the Gahtan. He had heard no ill of them. The Harb near the Hejaz [Hijaz] say ghadweh for bachir. Sayyah observed that the Ahl al Shimal wd not understand and I quoted the Mu'allaqat. Mustafa is a fellah from Abu Ghosh. He came with his family to Ziza 7 years ago and was looking for work at Umm al Kundum where he was impressed into our service. He told his wife he was going as he passed through Zizia [sic]. We saw flehfleh growing today. In the morning encampments of Xians from Madeba with sheep. Later we saw a few herds of camels and flocks of sheep of the Sukhur. We took water from the Rujaimet 'Ali, an affluent of the Hammam and rode up the valley to the water parting. To the S. the land sails to the Sirhan said Sayyah. Shortly after crossing this we camped. Very nice upland, but few trees. Corrected Iskandar's map with M. His names are wild. He was here in 1909, the year of drought—manhush haltak al sehheh. Before we got to the water parting there was an upright stone in the middle of the wadi on which was the wasm of Hamad, cousin of Fawwaz. Sayyah said he fell here on the Ruwalla and Mit'ab ibn Gauj[?] who were there together. The 'Anazeh and the Sukhur are now ashab. 'Ali told the tale of Leachman's being stopped at Kwait. Sayyah was with Shaikh Masa and was much interested in his map. Damascenes are indeed desert people. Sa'id ibn Faris was last autumn S. of Jauf buying camels from the Sherarat and last spring at Tubal trading with the Arabs. Fellah's father was a Shammar. I asked if he was alive. He said Wain rah ba'd ma akhath al 'abdeh! But his uncles are in Nejd. A train passed just as we set out this morning. Sayyah prays all the prayers when we are not actually on the road. Last night he got up and prayed in the tent at 8 o'clock while we were talking. His white robed figure rising and falling and the murmured Allah hu al akbar through our talk of Baghdad and Persia.

Sun Jan 18. [18 January 1914]

Wonderful clear morning and temp 42. Off at 6.15. Talib was very anxious that I should tasherrif wahalna but I promised to come on my return and he rode off after about an hour. We crossed the Bawaliyyat and came down onto the tributaries of the

Atatat and followed the wadi almost down to Tubah. Small marigolds flowering. The ruin stands just a little N. of the junction. Sun hot at noon and temp 62 at 3 PM. Sayyah says that in the summer the Sukhur have from 3 to 400 baits at Bir Ba'ir. The rest go to the W. Sirhan and to Teben, W. of Zizia. He asked me whether we called this desert Syria, and when I said no, Arabia, he said they called it Syria, it was all under Damascus and they came under the govt. in the summer and autumn when they came W and N for water and pasturage—timsikuna. But in winter and spring out in the desert they were free. Fa'iz has about 500 tents, Hathmel 300, Hadithah 200, there is also Khraisah, the Hagaish 200. Early in the morning we passed a good many of the Jebbar, rahalin, with camels, but their chief wealth is in sheep. The camels were wandering all over the Atatir. Flint covered earth, glistening in the sun. The trees chiefly firs which the camels don't like much. Good clear water in the ghadir, a little lower down. Salim ill—temp of 103.5. We got to Tubah at about 1 and I photographed till 3. The work over the doors is quite as fine as Meshatta, but the building is hasty unskilful desert work. No doubt Umayyad. Close with light cloud and wonderful sunset. A few graves outside with the Sukhur dabbus. Curious rounded lumps of sandstone cropping up among the flints. Delicious camp, but the men rather anxious about ghazzus. The desert behind us is fadiyyeh and Tubah is the gate of 'Anazeh raiders. The foes of Sukhur are the Fed'an, the Sba' and all the Jebehiyyeh except the 'Isa and the Serdiyyeh.

Tues Jan 20. [20 January 1914]

Very windy in night and cloudy in morning with a few drops of rain. We marched up the W. Dhurweh (there is dhurwey in it by the way) till 6.50, then came up its edge and left the Thlaithuwat to the E. The point I took for the S. end of the Waqf al Suwan is not really the end, it goes both S and N. We saw al Hadi which is the S point of Khabar al Baid; beyond and parallel lie the J. al Raha, this. But it is called Hadi al Raha. The Thlaithuwat are sandstone; we passed about a mile to the W. At 9.35 crossed the W. al Sai'r flowing to the W. Ba'ir [Wadi Ba'ir] and at 10.20 the W. al Gurdayyeh which must rise near the Hadi or under the Raha. It goes to the W. Ba'ir. At 10.55 we passed between 2 low tells, a rijm to the right, and saw the Metahat Ba'ir. I took the forward bearing here 185 but it was too much. It ought to have been about 166. We came down into the W. Ba'ir at 1. It is deep and big and full of tamarisk and other bushes. It [illegible] under the Thlaithuwat, curls round and goes to the Sirhan where it cuts in [space left blank] to a village called [space]. At 1.10 and 1.45 we crossed a curling tributary of the W. Ba'ir. I doubt whether my bearing of 158 at 12.30 is correct, but it is not far out. I think the qasr may be a little nearer the Matahet which I took 148°. The tributary wadi goes past Ba'ir to the W. As we passed the Thlaithuwat we met some Sukhur rahilin. They had come from the Sai'z and they reported no rain and little fodder. They said they were very thirsty. About 11.45 we saw 2 camel riders following us. They proved to be Jad'an Shaikh of the Hagaish and his man. They had seen us as we rode past the Thlaithuwat and taking us for a ghazzu had come to inquire. I invited him to stay the night but he turned back after showing us the cave. It is hewn out of sandstone and this shape [plan]. The big room about 10 metres long. In one room are small niches, too small for loculi. Full of camels' bones brought in by the dabi'. The Sukhur inquired what pasha I was and a woman called out what was I doing be hal barriyeh? Mudafi they say for thirsty. Sayyah told me this morning that a consul like me was very welcome but an ajnabi they wd not allow to enter. I said they need not fear, the land had never been inhabited. With that he stopped to pray, Kul wahid yehafidh 'ala dinher, he explained. Ba'ir is much much ruined, min kithrat ayyunhu says Mustafa. But the place is very old. The NE corner is entirely blotted out by the Arab watering places round the well. A great marah all round and a rather smelly cemetary [sic] with a big shaikh's tomb. It is the tomb of Asad who is the Jidd of the Sukhur. Whenever they camp here they sacrifice a camel. One of their sheikhs used never to come down from Madeba way without carrying green boughs with which to cover it, but the boughs have been carried off by a ghazzu. Lots of 'ugul, empty cartridges, sticks and a small tin looking glass. At night we talked of Asad and of the age of man. F. The limit of man's age is 104. M. Ya Abu Elyas there is no time limit. What says the Injil ya sitt. I. The Torat says that a man lives to 70 and if he lives longer there is no pleasure in it. M. Teki[illegible] Sadiqti. Igasted[?] labid, and the asai of his verse is the very camel stick we all carry.

Wed Jan 21. [21 January 1914]

Planned the qasr all morning and took a latitude. I make out we are about 30° 43′ which cannot be far wrong. Drew out my plan till 3 o'clock. Then went with M. to look at the tomb of al Mara'i Khalhu Abu Zaid who came up with the Beni Hillal out of Nejd the time they went on and conquered Tunis. A snake fell from the sky on his head here and he cut off his head with a sword. By the bir, now dry, N of the qasr, is the stone with the mark of the snake's body and the cut of his sword. On his tomb is a stone with the tarikh of the snake carved on it. The tomb is about 4 metres square. "This was his length" said Ali "Fawil al beni Hillal." And if this is his breadth said I he must have been ever square. "No" said 'Ali gravely "it is a chamber." As Sayyah, M. and I sat by the dry bir, M. told me that the one in the qasr was masdud when first he knew it. A ghazzu of the 'Isa fell here on the Sukhur, and killed a man and a horse, the Sukhur killed 2 camel riders, threw their bodies into the well and stones on top so that the 'Isa might not drink and follow them. Haram said I. No said Sayyah, fikrhum zain. Shayyatin al Arab observed M. Shayyatin said M. Kethir shayyatin said I with such conviction that S. laughed. The castle well is 10 double outstretched arm lengths deep to the water, and the water is 2 deep. The others are the same depth, but masdud. There is one other still further N of the qasr, besides the snake well. Two in the valley,

S of the qasr, one with some water in it, not much, it is partly masdud, maidenhair growing down the sides. The other is further W, small and dry. There is still another on the high ground S. of our camp, 6 in all. The snake well is the best built. If they dig out any of the dry wells the water comes up, but if they sacrifice a camel the while it is plentiful. They sacrifice camels to al Mara'i—I saw the hole for thė blood. Inside the qasr there is a grave with a Sherari wasm on it. Sayyah looked at it and pointed out that the man had been killed. The red cotton keffiyyeh and a bit of white cotton clothing thrown upon it were steeped in blood. We sent the camels down to the W. Ba'ir to pasture today and they came back at 5. 30 years ago when M. first knew Ba'ir the S wall with the gate was standing and the gate stood much higher than any of the walls stand now. They are now about 3 metres high. M. coming out of Nejd with 85 loads of semneh was attacked here by a mixed raid of Shammar and Anazeh who spilt all the semneh on the ground. He had a Sherarat rafiq with him, but the damage was done before explanations could be made. He afterwards got the whole price from Ibn al Rashid and Ibn Shal'an. But where semneh is spilt the trees will not grow and years afterwards he saw the place makhruq abadan, ai na'am.

Thurs Jan 22. [22 January 1914]

We went by the valley for 10 minutes and then turned up a side sha'ib and got out onto the top at 7.12. The Metahah with its 2 tells in front of us—we passed between it and the 1st western tell—I saw too the Thlaithuwat and the Hadi. Good trees, greening, on the N slope of the Metahah. Over the saddle a featureless country before us. I took bearings back to the saddle. But to the E. I saw the 2 tells of the day before yesterday, and running N. from them the J. Ferid. Further E and S the line of tells called Suainirat—mittel babor. We crossed the W. Ukhaidir. At the further side, on the plain, picked up a slab of flint with Safaitic inscrip. which I carried into camp. We came into camp very early after 6½ hours' march in a very shallow valley with some trees, the Gharrah being too far off with 3 sick camels. Wind, cloud and thunder with a few drops of rain. A very desolate camp. I doubt whether we shall reach Hathmel the day after tomorrow. Skhaif knows this country better than Sayyah. Last night the camels kept getting up, afraid of daba'. Sayyah says they bite the fore foot of the mare, so that she cannot move and then eat her. The Sukhur are practically divided into the Fa'iz and the Zeben. There are besides Khraisah (who is perhaps of the Zeben?) and the Hagaish. I found geraniums flowering in the W. Ukhaidir.

Fri. Jan 23 [23 January 1914]

It rained a little in the night and was very cold in the morning and a cold wind all day. Till 7.25 I took my bearings back to the saddle; after that the country was quite featureless, nothing but the long backs of valleys and no landmarks. At 7.45 we began to go down an affluent of the Gharrah and reached the sha'ib of the latter at 8.15. It was exactly a degree of the aneroid from top to bottom. We then marched up the ghadir till 8.50 when we turned up a side valley till 10.5. We then got out onto an exceedingly flat flint strewn upland, self contained—we passed a dry khabra. The black flints glistened in the sun and there was nothing to be seen. I walked and rode and tried to keep my bearings. At 1.20 we came suddenly onto the brink of the W. Hasa, so called because of the cliffs further down, about 4 hours from the Sirhan. Where we cut it 2 tributaries flow together and form the Hasa. We camped just at the junction. Good trees, plenty of shih, but the rain seems scarcely to have reached here. We found small pools in the W. Gharrah which the camels drank eagerly. The Hasa is not nearly so deep here, not more than 100 ft or so. Sayyah did not pray today. Salim asked him in the morning whether he had prayed. He said no, his clothes were dirty. But Salim turned to me and said "Haik al Arab! if it is cold they don't pray." At night we talked of riches and of how every man thought only of gain and if it were not for money they wd all stay at home. I told the story of Croesus with great success. Sayyah talked of sorcery. There was a man of the Sukhur who had 3 wives and one wrote a hijab; put in it a lock of hair and a piece of charcoal, tied it with a brown cord and placed it in an old tomb near Ziza. The man sickened and they took him to a doctor in Jerusalem "Perhaps he was a Jew" said S. "I think perhaps he was a Jew" (the Jews are reported good sorcerers). The doctor took out a book and read and said that there was a hijab etc describing it. Then he read and read and read, and finally he lifted a corner of the lubbad and there was the hijab ["nijab" written above in pencil] beneath it. "Lan ma hkatt hu taht al lubbad min qabl" said Sa'id—the spirit of scepticism is rife! But Sayyah "Wain Zizia wa wain al Quds!" I "did this man recover." S. "No he died, Allah yerhamhu." He said too that for casting devils out of madmen the Abu Sihr wd bring a boy and put before him a cup of oil, covered over. And the boy wd talk to the jinn in the man and the jinn wd answer but only the boy heard. Then the magician puts a book on the man's head and reads and the man recovers.

Sat. 24. [24 January 1914]

It was 28° this morning, I was very cold. We went up a side valley and I got a bearing back at 6.16. Then endlessly winding up till at 8.51 we came upon the brink of the head valleys of the W. Hedrij [Wadi Hadraj]. The Gharamil to the left and straight ahead a small tell with a rijm which Sayyah said was our road—it was 105°. But presently I found when we had wound a long time up a side valley that we were going much more to the S. We got up onto a rijm and I think our way from the wadi must have been about 170. Here we saw low ground before us, the W. Sahb, and beyond it dimly the cliffs of the Tor al Tubaiq. Our way on was 168 into the W. Sahb and then 152 and 153 down the valley, which runs into the Ga'rah. At 1.55 we passed the Sabia' Biyar in the middle of the valley. They are filled up with sand (they say da') and are said to be salt. Stones round them and stones forming watercourse and basin for watering camels. On the banks of the valley tombs with upright stones set on them. Outcrops of volcanic rock along the valley banks. We saw footprints of camels going and coming, in the sand and camel droppings but the latter not fresh. I had taken my bearing on a high tell but at 210 we turned off into a little side depression and camped at 2.15 where no one could see our fires. Ali, Sayyah and I went scouting Arabs up onto the tell. We saw a [illegible] which S. said came from the Arabs, they must be close. Ali swore that we shd hear their dogs at night. I said to S. "Are they not the footsteps of your own people?" He replied Wallah ma nidri. We went cautiously onto the shoulder of the tell and looked through my glasses all over the Gar'ah. There was no one. So we climbed to the top and took bearings. Back to the rijm of 11 o'clock was 338. In front was the great mass of broken rugged hills and table topped tells of the Tor. To the W. the 2 big tells at the end of the high ground with a very small tell below them, which mark Umm al Rqubbeh. The Arabs drink from here when they are camped at Helbeh. We were not where al Hausah was—Sayyah does not know the country from this side. Ghineh was to the E, a little SE, we could not see it. It is a sandy bottom between several small valleys [illegible] together; very good pasturage. They drink from Umm al Rqubbeh which is a khabra. We decided not to go to Helbeh, for seeing that there had been no rain and all the world was dried up, we think that Hathmel must have moved E, to the W. Sirhan or to the Hamad beyond. We feared that when we got there we might find it very far to the water of Hausah tomorrow. The Jafar [el-Jafr] is also a jurah like the Ga'rah. It lies between Bir Ba'ir and Ma'an, not a dulul day's journey from Ma'an. The Waqf is N of it. There are no buildings there or at Waisit but wells in both places. We are rather short of water tonight. We came in with only 2½ qurah[?]. I saw the footprints of the Oryx Beatrix in the sand of the W. Helbij. The sandy plants of the Nefud grow in the sand here. Rusty outcrops of volcanic stone on the tell near our camp.

Friday. Sun Jan. 25. [25 January 1914]

Very clear frosty dawn. We have had no dew since Kharaneh. I climbed to the top of the bank before my tent and watched the sinister silence of the sunrise. We were off early. I walked for an hour with 'Ali down the W. Sahb—camel prints everywhere. We stopped in a sandy hollow for the others and we lighted a fire. The footsteps everywhere, coming and going. Jedid said Ali. Then we débouchéd into the wide Ga'rah. The fantastic broken hills stood round, the sun crept them and all was silent and empty. Neither M. nor Sayyah knew the way. It was 7.50 when we left the W. Sahb. We rode straight on till 9, they discussing[?] where was al Hausah where Umm al Rqubbeh. I threw in a casting vote for an [illegible] for Hausah. At 9 we turned to 94°. At 10.5 we saw smoke under a black tell with riven rocks on its head like the ruins of a castle. The men discussed whether the smoke meant Arabs or a ghazzu and favoured the idea of a ghazzu—gomani or ashab ma nadri wallah. S said to me: What will you do if they are foes? salute them? I. I have no foes. S. And I? I. No, you are with us. The rafiq has no foes. S. Sadiqti wallah. Small plants were growing on the plain and the camels eat. The silence and emptiness and the smoke were extraordinarily menacing. At 11 we came to the khabra of Umm al Rqubbeh and found water. The camels drank thirstily and the men filled all the skins. The water very red from the red sand. Ali had gone on to look over a low rise at the smoke. I saw him creeping up the slope; he climbed it and disappeared. Sayyah and M. followed and I followed them. Over the rise no tents, but the smoke under the tell. Then we saw sheep and shepherds and knew that all was well. There was a reedy khabra over the brow and we sat down in the hot sun and waited for the shepherd. I lunched. He came, a very small black haired man, with very clean cut features. A Howaiti. He told us there had been a row between Hathmel and the Howaitat, the Sukhur had killed a man [mare?] and Hathmel had moved E. 'Audi Abu Tayyi he also reported to be E; Harb not far off in the hills. So we went off thither at 12.15, marching between broken hills. The low ground covered with green plants and even some little flowers, white, purple and yellow. The green looked startlingly brilliant. The hills are rusty red with a dropping of coal black stones down their steep sides, the sand red on the outskirts and yellow further in. We passed between 2 steep pointed tells and M and Sayyah scouting round, learnt from a woman that Harb had rahal to the hills of al Hausah; we found nothing but the traces of his camels. There was nothing for the camels to eat but dry ghada trees, but it was too far to go back to the herbage so we camped. Two men, of the Howaitat came in to see us. Very keen faced and restless eyed. They drank coffee with us and kept asking what we carried. Ali Alieh al jemal[?] w'al selain[?]. They. Wa thabah? I. Shu nashil be hal[?] bar-riyyeh? They had come from Ma'n where they had been looking at the pasturage. The stout nomad nature of the Howaitat says Doughty, and they have a great reputation. Thijal! says Ali. 'Audi raided across to Shethathah and held up the Amarat. But he feared the soldiers and came back without loot. No moon tonight, it is the first night of the moon. But countless moths. The Sukhur think it 'aib to sell their semneh—it is for the guest. A man who sells his semneh will find no one to marry his daughter. The Sherarat wander about singly, a man and his wife and children and his camel will cross the whole desert. M. had an interview once with Lord C[romer]. He was going from Egypt to Nejd and he brought 9 rifles which had been stolen from the soldiers. They were siezed and he was taken up and brought before the Lord. He described him as having long moustaches so that a man's heart trembled when he saw them. He explained that he bought and sold camels and did not traffic in rifles. Let the men who sold them to him be punished. So they were brought and one said he was Namsawi and ma' salameh. And the other said he was Fransawi and got off free. But the turj-man told M. that the Lord had seen he was a true man and he might go. The rifles however were confiscated. Next time M. came from Damascus to Cairo he bought the Lord a present of almonds and fastuq in sugar, shughl al-Sham.

Mon. Jan. 26. [*26 January 1914*]

We set off this morning to Harb al Daransheh (ibn Derwish). On the way we met a man who told us there had been a regrettable incident last night. A man, by origin of the 'Atiyyeh but camping with the Sukhur, had an old grudge against some of the Howaitat. He raided them, a little to the S. of us, and carried off some sheep. He was killed in the business and his brother killed 3 of the Howaitat. Hathmel's uncle happened to be daif in his tents at the time and his people packed up and hurried off to join the Sukhur. This news made Sayyah very anxious. I assured him that I wd not desert him whatever happened. We found Harb camped among low hills with a few tents about him—the ard is not qowwiyyeh so they have to split up. He explained that they had come to the end of almost all their provisions and gave the men a lunch of bread and oil which I did not share. He sent out to some neighbouring tents for the evening's sheep, he having none. They complain much of the dowleh. I asked whether the railway was a profit or a disadvantage to them. He said both. I. It brings the dowleh nearer. He. If the govt. had a kanun it wd not matter. But we bring in 200 camels to be counted for the tax, they reckon them 250. There is no settlement of a suit but with bakhshish—the piastre is hakim. They are all very much afraid of the Shammar, who they say will rob me and kill my men. In the summer when the khabra of Umm al Rqubbeh is dry they dig for water and find it, but mostly they have to go to the wells at Ma'an and between Ma'an and Tebuq [Tabuk] and then the govt. catches them. At night while we were dining one arrived. Man al daif? said Harb. It was Muhammad ad Dhailan Abu Tayyi cousin of 'Audeh. He had heard news of my being here from the shepherds at the khabra. He is a man and no doubt of it, with a fine bold bearing. Harb engaged in some description of a dispute. Muham. Ya Harb, ya Ibn Derwish, yusikum bil khair. Tisma'. "It was so and so Tisma'." When he arrived Harb who knew M. greeted him with many enquiries after his family and then Kaif dowletkum? kaif hal al Muslimin? At night the talk took a dangerous turn as to whether I had or had not come without permission and whether the Arabs were gom to me or not. I left M. and Ali to solve these questions with Muhammad. They talked long and loud—of their own affairs as it turned out—but I lay sleepless fearing that it was of me or of Sayyah.

Tues Jan 27 [*27 January 1914*]

Very cold wind. I took a latitude in the morning to the great interest of Harb and his son Qasim. Harb keeps repeating when I show him instruments "Mesaqin bal Arab!" After lunch I photographed them and sat in Harb's tent with Sa'id. Great success with Iskandar's pictures. There is a gossip that the Ott. Govt. has sent a present of arms to Ibn Rashid—at first we heard 70 camel loads, then 75, 1000, 1500. It is to help him against Ibn Sabbah Sa'ad. 'Audeh Abu Tayyi has gone off raiding the Shammar. A cousin of his brought me ostrich eggs and skin.

Wed. Jan 28. [28 January 1914]

Today I thought to start and go S. to Ibn Jazi. But Harb, his brother 'Awwad and 'Audeh assembled in the men's tent and said that Ibn Jazi had gone W—we hear he is at the Tor—the desert towards Taimah is empty and raided by the Hetaim, Harb, 'Awagi, Faqir and others. By the life of this dawn said Harb. They strongly advised me to take the Sirhan road. Moreover my men were frightened, even Ali, so I could do nothing but agree. 'Awwad is to go with us, but his hajin is azar and has to be fetched today. So we leave tomorrow, sending for water tonight. There is a gossip that Ibn al R., if I arrived at Taimah wd sallim me to the dowleh and the rly, but they cannot know this. I climbed up into the hills this afternoon by a stony gorge, full of the meagre Spring of the desert. Flowers, white and red and purple, even the thorns covered with white green [illegible] They were poor enough but they looked like separate jewels. I have some on my table tonight. Moreover from the top I looked over fold after fold of golden red sand and smoke grey ridge, with the black tents of the Howaitat scattered up and down. Harb's favourite phrase is la al Qallil wa la al kattur. The moon is in her 3rd night; we saw her yesterday very slender and Salim stood with open outstretched palms and gave thanks. Salim and F. think nothing of the Arabs. S. Alhamdulillal who did not create us Arabs. F. Alh. who created the Turks! I. Alh. that there is no rly in the W. Sirhan. S. Who would make a rly into this Jehannum? M. today took a prophecy in the sand Min aimta surt rammal? said F. You make the mark of thumb and little finger 4 times [five dots] Then strokes made by 2 fingers between each [three dots followed by ten small downward strokes] Then a long stroke at haphazard in the middle and a long stroke 3 on either side, then 2 then 3. At the last there will be some of the finger marks over at either end—6 is unlucky, anything short of 6 is all right, but best if the number is uneven.

Thurs Jan 29. [29 January 1914]

We got off yesterday with Awwad and rode through rolling country full of camels and an occasional single Sharari tent. We stopped to drink coffee in the big tent of 'Audeh who is as usual away raiding the Shammar. Photographed his sister 'Aliyah and his wives. Shammariyyat. He has 2 Shammar wives cousins. A Shammar shaikh quarrelled with Ibn Rashid, came and camped near 'Audeh and raided Nejd with him. Hence these marriages which otherwise are unusual. He has a Howaitiyyeh wife also and one other a Ruwalla woman. (Harb has recently married a young wife.) I photographed her with Qasim, son of the old wife. He called her 'ammeti. Here we heard that the Ruwalla were in the W. Sirhan and it presently turned out that Awwad could not go there for they would kill him at sight. He had already told us he could not go to Jof. We sent him off to Muhammad's tents to bring a Sherari and came into camp early. Good trees, greening. Awwad returned with Muhammad, Audeh, Haddaj (whom I had photographed in Shaikh Audeh's big tent). They brought me a lamb and an ostrich skin and stayed to dine and sleep. We sent for the Sherari who duly appeared but I had heard of a ruin at the Khabra of Kilweh and decided reluctantly that I must see it. Muhammad says "Oh Listeners." His duty with the Govt (he is Shaikh al Dowleh) is to collect the miri which is ½ a mej sagh. He receives a fourth for his pains. There is another Sh. al D. for the Ibn Jazi, M. is only for the Abu Tayyi. Their people in Egypt are the [space left blank]. They went at the conquest. They have lands near Tauta. When a Howaiti falls out with the govt here he goes to Egypt. But the Ott. Govt try to prevent them. The year of the war M. wanted to go to Egypt but was not allowed.

Fri. Jan 30 [30 January 1914]

We rode to M's tents and camped. Very pretty to see the valley with tents and camels in the clean sand. Lots of Sherarat with camels. They have no dira. They are foes of the Howaitat, Sukhur and B. Atiyyeh country. In the summer they stay about the wells on the edge of the Nefud, and Mujharrieh[?] and Fajr and "live like wild animals" said Muhammad. The Howaitat guard the Hajj line from Kerak to Tebuq, the Sukhur north and the Harb S. Sami imprisoned Muham. for 4 months but he has nothing but admiration for him. He has 4 Howaitiyyat wives. One, Hileh, came and sat with me. She has had 4 children, all have died. Muham. has only 2 children. She did not want to marry. Ma istahait al rigil—but her father beat her. She showed me a white scar on her breast. Ahubb al bint she said. But all the girls must marry— the children die young of travel and t'ab and the women suffer terribly after childbirth from the constant moving and work. "We do not rest an hour" she said. She had the most pitiful face. Muham. has a young Beatrix Oryx in his tents. Fine picture of the men sitting round the coffee fire by the big dallas. Ya dunya! murmured one old man. The Sherarat came in too and were given coffee, but last of all, and an old aunt of Muhammad's. In the pictures such as there is none but he! Ya tabb! The Jidd of all the Howaitat is one of the Ashraf of Mecca. He was sent as a child into the mts of Aqaba ['Aqaba], married there and is the father of all. In the afternoon Muham. and I sat in F.'s tent and drank tea. He talked of his work for the miri and all it entailed, and of his work with the tribe as judge and lawmaker—they come to him to settle disputes. He takes the miri from the Sherarat who camp with him. Some of these are very rich—60 nagas, but they all live in the same miserable way, dying of hunger. They drink the camels' milk as long as there is any. They never sell their camels. The money for the miri they earn by working in the cultivated places—Jizia [sic], Kerak. Muham. has battal ghazzus since he was imprisoned at Dam. Shuft al mant wa battalt. His little daughter, very handsome and black eyed came and was given sweetmeats by F. I sat in M's tent at night. Interesting talk about the worship of ancestors. The tomb of their Jidd is at Ma'an and they do the usual sacrificing. Hajjaj the man from Jof accused them of honouring their ancestor and praying to him more than to God. Muham and the coffee maker Su'ud indignantly protested la hayyatak wa hayyat Allah, they knew there was none but God and M. his Prophet. They admitted that when the Sukhur came into the W. Ba'ir they could not free themselves from it save by sacrifice but it was not the dead man who prevented their departure, but God. Ya Hajjaj yusikum bil khair. Hajjaj sang Qasidubs[?] to the rebaba. M. al M. then told the tale of the accession of M. al Rashid and the murder of his relatives. Two were killed and thrown into a well. Ashab al nar said I. Ai billah said Shaikh M. After the Friday prayers it is the custom for all the people to come to the Amir's reception. They sit in 4 rows before him. And Hamud used always to sit on the other side of M. al R.'s cushion. Hajjaj who knows Hayyid said Ana nashud or Unshud billah. M. turned to me and said that for 4 years after his accession Muhammad used to go at night through the streets with 2 slaves and a ladder. A slave wd climb up to the window of the house, if it was lighted and listen to what was being said. "And if he heard M. al Dhailani or M al-Ma'arawi or the Sitt speaking against him, next morning he wd either imprison him or cut his throat." Wonderful sight in M's tent with the fire and the ring of stones round it. At the outer side 2 big stones supporting an upright slab like a tombstone. The big dallals and the people sitting round. Little boys of 6 or 7 sitting solemnly like grown men. One had come to my tents the night before and ridden back with us on a mare. You see tiny mites riding on the rump of a camel hobbling the mare like grown men. Beside me M's large figure with the white linnen [sic] keffiyeh over his dark brows and the narghileh between his heavy lips. A slave brought his fur cloak with the long sleeves and threw it over his shoulders. Outside a mare tethered to the long rope. The nagas came in and they brought us great bowls of milk. The camel mothers and their calves lying in the sand beyond. As I walked back to my tent in the frosty night the little moon hung like a boat in the W. and Sirius showed his white flame gloriously. I saw an immense falling star as I sat in the tent. It fell across half heaven. There is some dew in the Tubaiq. I see the frost on the sand of a morning and my tent flies are wet.

Sat. Jan 31 [31 January 1914]

Off before sunrise with 'Ali, Awwad and a man of M's called Audeh to Kilweh. We rode across endless small ridges and valleys. Near our tents in a valley the rain of the early winter had ploughed a deep ghadir in the sand where there had been none the year before. Awwad told of the great raid of last year, across to the Euphrates. They took 1200 camel riders, were away 3 months but not a man died. They crossed the desert to al Mat, were 3 days in the W. Hauran [Wadi Hawran] and came to Kubaisah. They held up Fahd ibn Hadhdhal at Ghazazeh but did not take many camels as they were all away. 200 said Awwad. Therefore Audeh determined to extend operations. He divided his people into 3, sent ⅔ [two-thirds] home and with 100 riders went N. to near Haleb [Aleppo] raiding the northern Anazeh, Fedah and Sba'. He mainly captured camels of the fellahin near Homs and Hama [Hamah] and they complained to the Govt so that he had to return the camels afterwards. The Anazeh wd not complain to the Govt—it was the fortunes of war, so Muhammad told me at night in the big tent. The whole expedition was for nothing; they got nothing out of it. But it was [illegible] said 'Ali. We crossed a biggish valley which goes to the Sirhan and another which goes to Umm Rqubbeh. Here a Howaiti met us and told us of a qasr on the hill, al Za'udiyyeh, whither we went. We had a glorious view from it and I think it must have been a sort of high place. A round building of dry masonry, uncut stones; it must have been a sort of bee hive vault. A circular wall round it; it did not stand quite in the middle and round that a row of upright stones following the contour of the hill. This is the red sandstone country and so continued till we got down to Kilweh. The khabra has been made into a big birkeh, there are traces of a strong dam on the lower side. The first building is a cistern with a hole to admit the water from the khabra. The other 3 are lodgings. No decoration; carefully plastered inside and over the roof of stone slabs a covering of mortar and small stones. The same lines the cistern. A Cufic inscrip. scratched in the plaster of the door. No decoration save a sort of pyramid pattern of plaster and pebbles over one of the doors. No arches. A few Arabic letters written on a bit of sandstone in the cistern. The rest of the buildings are of volcanic stones and the plaster must have been brought from far. Under a little tell we saw scattered fragments of it and the place where it had been burnt. Other small ruins scattered over the plain but no mortar and the stones not squared. So rode back with a strong cold wind behind us and got in soon after sunset. Lovely in the early morning to see the nagas and their calves near the tents. Our dululs had gone to a khabra to fetch water. They did not return till past 9 and then reported that one had sat down 6 hours away, and refused to move. They had left her. So we had to send for her and no marching tomorrow! I sat in M.'s tent and Hajjaj sang to the rebaba of Audeh's raids invoking 'Aliyah. (There is dew here. The sand is frosted.) No one had any water till the camels came in—neither Arabs nor we. An old woman came and told Muham. that her man[?] was ill and wd he send someone.

FEBRUARY 1914

Sun. Feb. 1. [1 February 1914]

A man went after the dulul in the night and returned at sunset having brought her 3 hours on the way but no further. We spent some time conversing (an Agaili) a Shammari from Nejd who promised to come with us, but after extracting a real from me next day as we were departing, appeared no more. His name is Hussain, from the Sinjari. I sat with Muham's harim late in the afternoon. They were sewing his white cotton robes. His sister, a very pretty graceful creature, unmarried, Hamdeh. There are 4 other sisters, married. I talked to one of the wives. She has had one child which died. The baqr calf came in and sucked our fingers—it was hungry. Muham. hung round, played with it and eat dates from Jof with us. Excellent dates. The women do not ride the dulul on a shedad. They put libads on the hidaj and curl on top. They wd not sit with the men as I did—nishtahi. But Hamdeh showed no shyness with Sa'id and Fattuh. I did not see Hileh again. 'Ali the Agaili is continually nagging at Mustafa. He declared he wd leave us (Mustafa had complained to Muham.) and I seized on the occasion and dismissed him—a bad fellow. I wanted to send Sayyif back, but he cried and said he had been in the house of the Jawaberi since he was a child and did not know his way among these people and I have kept him on. Our rafiq is Musuid a Sherari. He has hired a camel for 10 mej. I went at dusk to Muham., handed him the 10 mej. He called 10 men to witness that he had them "Al jalisur, minkum 'ashara? Audeh wa Awwad wa Hajjaj etc" and then said that they were to testify that if Musuid returned without a letter bearing the seal of M. and of me, he was to hand over 20 re-als. We have given[?] by Jof, M. fearing that as Nawwaf is not there, the 'abd might re-tain us till he had sent word. Moreover we have Ruwalla camels bought from the Miri with the Wasm upon them. So now we turn SE as originally intended. Musuid swears we shall put 'Audeh's ghazzu to the left and the others to the right. Muham. says that the Howaiti dira used to be as safe as possible. You cd put a bag of gold on your head and walk through it in peace. But last autumn a caravan of merchants from Ghazzeh with a Howaiti rafiq was attacked by a Howaiti, cousin to the rafiq, who killed his cousin and the merchants and took the booty. This has ruined the dira since there is blood between the men of the tribe. Sa'id says that 'Audeh is mild and kind in his own tent, speaks to everyone, is just to everyone, but madly furious when angered. Last year a Sherari killed a Sherari who was with M.'s people. M. caught the man, cut off his hands and feet and left him in the desert to die, which he did. He has brought back immense numbers of camels from his raids. He puts his wasm on them and confides them to different people that if a ghazzu comes they may not all be found round his tents. When he sells he confides the money to merchants at Ma'an or Kerak. Yesterday when I was away the herdsmen on the hills quarrelled and one stood on the top of the ridge and waved his kerchief on his asa'i. In a moment all the outlying tents had driven in their camels and were running, men and women into the centre near M's tent. The great oath is al hayyat al 'ud wa rab al ma'bud wa khatim Sulaiman ibn Daud. Hayyat ul Sabah. Hamdeh came to my tent and smoked a cigarette. Sa'id came and told her that M. had come and wd see her smoking. I. Is it mamun'? She. No but we have little tutun—the tutun is for the guests.

Mon. Feb. 2. [2 February 1914]

Off at last with many leavetakings. M. has given us corn, but only ½ a load. I gave him a Zeiss glass. He interceded for 'Ali but I explained and he agreed. Everyone asking for tutun. Grey cloudy day and very cold later with no sun. The Arabs are moving—work for the women who complain bitterly of the constant moving. We crossed over to a valley to the W and marched up it—it drains[?] to the Hausah—till we came to the edge of the hills. They drop down abruptly in a great broken mass of sandstone. Great scramble down. In the sandy valley I found the curious awaiherri growing, rootless and leafless like a big asparagus. All the plants green, ghutba with its [illegible] like green and others. From below we can see very clearly the conformation of the hills, red sandstone below and grey volcanic rock above. The outlying tells table topped. The sandstone all riven and broken, without water to smooth it. Great purposeless ruined gashes running up into the hills. We found our dulul here and camped on account of the trees. Read [illegible] Feverel and walked over the broken tells. The sandstone at the top granulated; the hill tops strewn with what looks like petrified camel droppings. We are on the brink here of the Ga'rat al Tubaiq. Beyond a red welter of small tells standing in sand—a barren world which leaves its seal on the soul. Cloudy and windy. The camel had wandered up the valley without a shidad. She had a sore on her back and the crows made it bigger. The men branded her below the wound, behind the ears, on the nose and on the tail with a burnt stick. It is so cloudy I said to the men Yeji matar? They answered God is he who sends good. But there is probably rain S. of us.

Tues. Feb 3 [3 February 1914]

We parted with Awwad today to whom I gave a chokh and a keffiyyeh—he thought it too little I fear. We rode out over the Ga'rat al Tubaiq to the Khabra al Ghdai which lies in the W. al Ghdai. The latter begins at the Khabra al Mufa' and goes to the Khabra al Masawid, about an hour from where we camped. We rode down this valley after we had filled our waterskins and I walked out 25 min. from camp and got the whole of the J. Wai'leh. I saw the Thenit al Rilan which seems to be the eastern continuation of the Tubaiq. The W side of the Tubaiq is called the T. al 'Afa, the N.E the T. al Aswad. In the heart of the Tor lies the W. al 'Asreh wherein no one wd cut trees for firewood or a branch for an asa'i. But camels and sheep may graze there. There is a big khabra, al Husenneh left of the road from Mufa' to Mughairah [Mughayra']. It is full when there has been rain in winter and is full now, but the danger round it is not qowwi. There is a tell in the heart of the Tor called Tell Jad'an and when the winds blow from it, it smells of amber. All these legends are known best by the Sherarat whose dira this originally was. M. ibn al Rashid protected them and suffered no one to encroach on their dirah, but since his death the Howaitat and [illegible] al Shimal have come to it. These two had an immense battle some 4 years ago near Tell Mugyah and about 300 men were killed. Since then they have made friends. Musuid tells sort of Æsop stories of animals, the asad the nimr and abu'l Hussain and how they quarrelled over the body of the arnab. We began to see 'uslib and green trees today. After the khabra we were joined by Ghadi who is of the Ibn Rummad and after 5 years sojourning with the Howaitat is going back with his camels, his mother, brother and sister, to his own people. We are to serve as mutual rafiqs. Most fortunate. He wd not have dared to come by this road without us. Rain today and all day cloud and cold wind. I said to 'Ali this morning that people in my country wd fear this emptiness. Yes, he said, this maku. Talked to F. of Islam and Xianity and said that Jesus was a better nebi than M. He said They are like people who are lost. We have many feasts and we know exactly when each one is. They have but one and they never know when it is—they have to watch the moon to find out. I quoted Blessed are the merciful a propos of Fellah who had nearly quarrelled with F last night because he swore Wallahi that he had picked up the sack he sleeps on in the desert whereas F. bought it in Dam. F. said Why did he swear by God—did God know? Yes he knew. F. had Fellah seen him? The other night we talked of the Moham. swearing and both Sa'id and Salim said it was not good or necessary.

Wed Feb 4. [4 February 1914]

Clear cold morning and we rode off at 6.45 to the Khabra Musawid which we reached at 7.15 8.10. At 6.55 I climbed onto a rijm which marks the Khabra and took some bearings onto J. Wai'leh, Thenit al Rilan, behind Wai'leh and Umm Inhaileh far behind both. We saw too Mlaih and the Swaiwinat al Hawi. At the khabra we were joined by Ghadi and his family and 2 baits of Sherarat who are with us. We had crossed at 7.30 the sultaneh from 'Arfajeh to Mughanah. We watered our animals and filled the empty skins. Our bearing now was onto the Abrak al Swaiwineh. We crossed the low lying Nuqrat al Hamra, flat slabs of red sandstone, ruined tells of the same and golden red sand between, and reached the Abrak at 11.25. The Nuqrat stretches from the khabra to the Abrak. Here I got bearings onto Shibliyyeh Wai'leh, Tell Saifur and J. al Sdar. We rode over the Swaiwineh, sandy hills, till 1.52 and then dropped down into the Nugrat al Rshaidan. Before doing so I got a bearing on the table topped Mlaih. We camped in the Nugrah in deep sand, quite hard and holding our tent pegs, under a small sandstone tell at 2.10. I got a bearing from the tell onto the sandy hillocks called Tu's Nuqrat al Rshaidan. All the trees have greened. The camels eat the whole way and we went slowly. The Nuqrah is delightful with its grey green trees and red gold sand. Cloudy in the afternoon and evening. Everyone in the best of spirits. The trees have greened because of the early rains, the Matar al Thurriyyeh ["Thrui" written above] which fall in November. They say: [half a line of Arabic script] Ghadi spends most of his time drinking coffee in our tent but they don't camp near us. Musuid told me he wanted to go with me to the bilad where my father was the lord of hills of nihas and fahm, that he might come back to the sheikhs and say he had visited my father who had clothed him in lots of gold. Beautiful grey green of the shrubs against the red gold sand. Some have put out colourless flowers and some smell deliciously aromtic. "The wind smells of amber" said 'Ali when we came into camp. Our Sherarat fellow travellers bring us goats' milk.

Thurs. Feb. 5. [5 February 1914]

The sand hills were all frosted this morning. They rise to sharp ridges like snow aretes and fall steeply on the W. side. We crossed the Tu's of the Nuqrah, long lines of dunes, apparently continued in the Tu's al Swaiwineh. At 8.15 we had the broken tells of the Swaiwinat al Howi in front of us. We marched over a stretch of da', absolutely barren and got into the tells at 9.30 marching pretty direct onto the Qulaib al Swaiwinah which I photographed. Here we found rain water pools in the hollow places of the sandstone slabs. At 11.32 we came out of this low ground and saw Mlaih to the SE. It consists of a table topped hill which is my bearing here 135 and is also the hill onto which I took all former bearings of Mlaih. Further E. a large table topped hill, the middle of which is my bearing here 126; and finally a tell (119°) called Barud al Mlaih. The well is somewhere under the middle hill but there is also water in the Barud. At 1.25 we came into camp in the W. Fajr [Wadi Fajr] where there are plenty of rain water pools due to the rain of 3 days ago—thank goodness—and plenty of trees, green. The Fajr goes past a big khabra (I think further W) al Howi, from which the Sherarat drink all the summer if there have been good rains; it ends in the W. Sirhan. The Sherarat with us are miserably poor. A starving woman and boy came begging for some flour today. The Arab children found Hanqal gourds in the valley and played with them. Ghadi and one of the Sherarat went off to scout for bakr but found none. On the da' we saw round hollow patches, the threshing floors of the Sherarat wherein they beat out the semh seeds. They are about the size of a round soldier's tent.

Fri. Feb 6. [6 February 1914]

We were off before dawn. The Father of Goats had gone on ahead and Ghadi and a Sherari with 2 of our rifles to look for bakr. The Shammar and Sherarat camels had started and I followed them on foot with Masuid to take bearings from the ridge ahead. After about 50 yards they turned back and Musuid said "Khayyifin. They have seen gom" They had turned from near the brink of the ridge having met Ghadi, the Sherari and a boy and he of the colocynth balls yesterday. I said to Ghadi What is it? He answered Gom. I said How many? 10 camel riders he said—they afterwards swelled to 20 and dropped again to 15. Ma'al wad, ma' al wad! he shouted to my men. We couched the camels behind the sand banks and tamarisk of the valley and got out all our arms. I sat down Sa'id sat by me and said La takhafi. There will be acquaintance between us. I know all the Arabs. The Shammariyyeh with the baby came to me and said they had a new gatifeh and might they put it on my loads? Fellah transferred

Domed roof of unfinished Umayyad desert castle (c. A.D. 743) in Tubah, Jordan. Photograph by Gertrude Bell. Courtesy of the University of Newcastle upon Tyne.

it and I saw her afterwards bring her tent cloths and lay them among our camels. Her baby who had cried to see me yesterday, smiled today. Tasababua[?]. The men stood round the warm ashes of the camp fires, Masuid in his white robes shading his eyes from the low sun. Ghadi had gone on to the ridge to scout. Through my glasses I saw him creeping up. Nothing happened. Fattuh, Masuid and I walked over to the ridge, crept up, joined Ghadi and scanned the world. We saw nothing, not even the Father of Goats. Ghadi waved with his keffiyyeh to the others to come on and I took bearings, onto the W end of the W. Mlaih tell (1) and the J. Anfad or Fuwad (equally good both names) ahead. Our road lay down the slope between the Swaiwineh hills, just to the E. of Anfad. All the way down it was da' and nothing grew. Then we came to sandstone and sand, rain pools and trees. This is the end of the Swaiwineh. And here we met the Father of Goats who was probably the cause of our false alarm. The evidence rested on a Sherari boy, the colocynth boy, and on the Sherari hunter who was cautioned not to go on next day and see ghazzus. F. There were 3 men, one drank arak, the other wine and the third hashish. And when they rose to go out of the house they looked at the door. And the Father of arak said It is a[s] great as the door of a khan, we can never open it. The Father of wine said It is open and the flood of a river is flowing through, we cannot pass. But the Father of hashish said Then we must climb the wall. And he climbed the wall and dropped into the street. And wallahi the door was nothing but a house door. On the first sandstone mound I got bearings onto Mlaih 1 and the Tu's al Jaifeh which run out from under it to near where we are camped. Also onto the Jraniyyat to the W. a line of tells. The Anfad are also a line of tells. At one, we reached a region called the Mara' al Malaidah where there were plenty of pools and trees. Here the early rains are said to fall always. Masuid said there were no trees further on. Ali and Ghadi were on ahead; they rode back very angry and said there were plenty of trees, and the Shammar all protested. I was very cross, but the deed was done. Sweet smelly air, keen and clear.

Sat. Feb 7. [7 February 1914]

We got off at 6.18. The ground became better and better till under the Anfad it was a regular garden. The large purple flowered weed Khazameh, and a quantity of the small flowered (white to purple) Terbeh. Of trees Jeraifeh with small dull purple flowers and pea-like pods; the Arfej, yellow flowered and with an aromatic smell; the 'Irfa, a leafless broom like plant, and the small flat leafed dhammah with a pale small mauve flower almost like sorrel. At 6.45 I got bearings of the N face of the Anfad and the E. face of the Jraniyyat. We turned round the eastern end of the Anfad and saw a nugrah with the Qlaib al Musawid in the middle of it. At its SE end the 2 flat topped hills Mugharawain and behind them the J. al Tfaihah which were about 2 miles to the E of us at 9.23 and curved back away from us. The Anfad stretch a long way to the S in broken tells. I took bearings on the S. tell at 9.23 and at 12.10 and of the whole E. face at 1.20. At 11.10 and at 1.20 I got bearings on Umkur al Haujah; at 11.10 on the W. end of Mlaih 1 and at 1.20 on Barud al Mlaih. The other bearings on Anfad are all the NE tell, 148° at 6.45. Before we rounded the Anfad Ghadi met a camel rider who told us that Audeh with the returning ghazzu was just ahead and further on there were Arabs of the W. Sulaiman camping. (These are the Awajeh, a part of the Fed'an who are also seated about Homs and Hama.) Masuid reported that he had seen two hajun riders with a kasb camel—but of the rest of the raid we saw nothing. They wd not come back together but wd split and separate with their kasb. Nor have we seen the Awajeh. After the rich 'aishb we rode over a barren stretch—the trees not green—and then coming again to trees and aishb camped at 2 o'clock. Sa'id when he buys camels pays half in money and half in hudum. He will take with him all he can collect, 400 to £800, not all his own I gather. A very cold SE wind all day. Last night I said I must take a rafiq of the Beni Ma'az which created great mirth, the Father of Goats, Salim, rolling with laughter. The Sherarat children and the sluggah dog haunt our camp for food.

Sun. Feb. 8. [8 February 1914]

Last night a Howaiti came into our camp, having traced us by our footsteps, he being out hunting. The Sherarat thought him an enemy and took his sword and gun from him, but Musuid knew him and brought him to us. He rode with us next day through the Garameh to the people of Muhammad ibn 'Id, a Howaiti who has spent the winter with Sayyah ibn Murted—or Mu'rted? We found Muhammad moving camp. He wanted to pitch tents and spend the night with us while he fetched an 'ajleh for me, but I refused and we altered our course so as to camp with Sayyah tonight. Muhammad came with us. Our direction had been 147° onto the SW tell of the J. Tfaih; we now turned to 100 onto a pass called al Mausafeh which we crossed at 10.30 and dropped down into a long valley-like depression. Got bearings onto al Helwat which are the tells I took for Umm Gur yesterday. We reached S's camp at 12.35. At 6.40 we had crossed the W. al Agail which comes from the Agailat (water, I gather khabras, it is only rain water) lying E of the road from Mughairah to Taimah [Tayma'], and ends at the Qulaib of yesterday. Sayyah ibn Zaid is one of the 2 shaikhs of the Ibn Mu'rtad, the other being Guwairan ibn Fahad. We drank coffee and eat dates in his tents. He questioned me closely as to my knowledge of the country and was angry when I admitted to knowledge of the name of the Helwat. He blamed Musuid for telling me and said he was inclined to slay him. Whereat Musuid kissed his hand and I said it was only that I might know where he, Sayyah, was. He then came to my tent saw my glass and asked for it. Then he went to the men's tent and looked at everything. Finally he came back with M. al M., asked first for the glass and then for a pistol, which latter I fear we shall have to give him. M. al M. says the Wadi Sulaiman are the W. Shaitan which I well believe, but that he will send a rafiq with me. Inshallah! We met 4 camel riders of 'Audeh's raid this morning. 'Audeh and some of Hathmel's people raided the Beni Rammal with whom 'Audeh is friends, so when he saw the awsam on their camels he returned his part but the Sukhur, who wd not have ventured so far south without him, kept theirs. 'Audeh then raided the Swaib, who are Shammar, but got nothing. So they say.

Mon. Feb. 9 [9 February 1914]

We had a difficult 3 hours this morning. First Sayyah told M. al M. that we ought to take a man of the Faqir, since one of their Shaikhs, Muhammad ibn Fendi, was in his tents. Then, having received the revolver, he came to F. and said he wd not let me go without the glass and £10—was not a Xian? We waited about in a bitter cold wind and I went over to his tents and finally refused the 'ajleh though

Muhammad ibn 'Id kept 5 mej. for his pains and the trouble of those who had brought her. Then I went back to the camels and presently they all came out of the tent towards us. F. came and told me there was no help for it, I must give the glass. I gave it and took back the revolver. Then I mounted and rode on a little. More talk with F. and Sa'id. Sayyah declared he wd send no rafiq and wd rob me in the night; that no Nasraniyyeh had travelled here and none should travel; that it was a disgrace that a Nasraniyyeh should take back a revolver from a shaikh. Sa'id said to F. "Ya F. ukhlusna ba'dain besir mush tayyib." So F. gave the revolver also. We have as rafiq, Zayyid ibn Mhailan cousin of Sayyah. Hamid ibn Fendi al Jebel, brother of the Faqir Shaikh Muhammad, and another of the Faqir, Dahir. I asked Muhammad if they remembered Khalil and he answered yes and that he was a good man. He rode away shouting to M al M "I confide to you my brother, wrap him warm at night." Once when Sayyah spoke to me "Ya sitta, ya sitta" I sat on my camel and looked down at him saying nothing. "Why do you not say ha!" he said. I said "I will say no word to you." We rode over very featureless country all day, rolling sand, stone besprinkled. Once we crossed the track of an ostrich, the 3 great pads. My bearings bad, nothing to take them by and I did not like to question too closely as to our direction. In the middle of the day Hamid called out to me a blessing "our journey shd be prosperous, please God, and water present and pasture also (mara') and might I travel ever in safety." It was perhaps a sort of olive branch. Sayyah is known to be mal'un al walidain, but M. al M. says the Faqir are still more accursed in their parentage. M. ibn Fendi, like Sayyah has a long thin face, and a long black beard, square at the end like an Assyrian. Sayyah mulcted Ghadi of 3 mej. or else he wd not be answerable for the safety of their camels. M. al M. stood surety for him, since he has nothing. The Sherarat we have left to continue the process of starvation with Sayyah. We camped in a district called al Wasmiyyeh on account of its 'aishb. There is not much, but the trees are pretty good. White aromatic daisies round my tent jehowiyyan, a sort of caromel[?]? Musuid sometimes prays and I saw some men praying outside Sayyah's tent last night. I bound up the burnt feet of the Shammari Sluggah puppy. The Shammar were deeply distressed at Sayyah's behaviour to me and promise me a different reception among their people. F. says Sayyah proposed to Sa'id that they shd kill the Nas. and the Arabs wd give my men half the goods.

Tues Feb. 10 [10 February 1914]

We got off at 6.15 and rode over the same pebbly sandhills as those over which we passed yesterday. At 8.5 I got a bearing onto a hill which I noted as Bhaibat al Baid but if that name was correct I never saw it again. At 8.35 we saw Helwan al Khunfa [al-Khanfah] and at 9.46 I got a series of bearings onto Helwan [Halwan], Senam, Mshaid and Dhaiban (but I am not quite certain of the correctness of the 2 last, they were so insignificant from this distance) and to the right onto the Tu'us which are the SW end of the Nefud and a day's dulul journey from Taimah. Our road lay just to the left of them. At 10.55 the low rocky tells Thlaithuwat lay to the left and I got a bearing onto what was perhaps Mshaid. We then crossed a dry khabra, Umm al Tarfa. I took a bearing onto the Thlaithuwat at 11.45 and again at 12.30 when I also saw Helwan and Senam. We had been riding since the khabra over pebbly ground, black pebbles, slowing rising and very flat. At 12.50 I got the Thlaithuwat again and the Asafiyyeh [al-'Assafiyah] a tell or tells standing on the S. side of the Wadi Niyyal [Wadi Nayyal]. Below them are more than 100 jelib but there is water in them only when the Wadi sails. I got too Helwan, Senam and Dhaiban, this time I think correct. We came into camp at 1.30 in the W. Niyyal, about 3 hours above the Asafiyyeh. It flows from the Ghamariyyeh to a khabra called el 'Arus. Musuid showed me how the Shararat crouch in cracks of the sandstone heaps when it rains and once he said, pointing to one of them, we take shelter here from the sun in the gaith. The Faqir have no enemies at this moment but the Hetaim but my Faqir, Hamid, and also Zayyid, are in fear of the Shammar, because they knew of 'Audeh's coming raid and did not warn their friends the Shammar. Musuid also is afraid. Dahir is of the Sirhan a branch of the Faqir. Cold wind all day, but hot sun when we camped. Good 'aishb. There has been great dispute over our road. 'Ali and Ghadi wanted to drink at Asafiyeh and go thence, a short day's journey to Shmukka which is a themail in the Nefud. Thence to Haizan [Bir Hayzan] is the same as from the khabra to Haizan. Whether through fear of the Shammar (the Swaid were at Shmukka when 'Audeh raided them but have now moved east) or because, as they say, the Tu'us are very large by that route, the others elected to take the khabra road. I do not think there can be much difference in time. The Amir is not at Hayyil but N. near Haiyaniyyeh [al-Hayyaniyah]. I think this is unfortunate for me. They say he has notified all men of my coming but whether to stop me or to forward me I do not know. Neither do I know whether this report is true. Sunset and moonrise almost together and moonset and dawn.

Wed. Feb. 11. [11 February 1914]

We got off at 6, but it was cloudy and we did not have the full glory of the moon. We climbed up the opposite bank of the wadi and rode from 6.20 till near 10 over a jellad (they call it in 'Iraq haswah) a pebbly floor, hard and entirely without herbage. Till about 10 our bearing was still east of the Tu'us or close onto the Tu'us, then we turned more W over rolling sand hills, rather pebbly and near 11.30 reached the wide khabra of Fasfas, a hard pebbly bottom with water pools under low sand-hills. We stopped at a good pool at 11.30, watered our camels and filled our waterskins in half an hour. A most desolate place but I rejoiced to see the water for if it had been exhausted we should have had to have gone on SW to Beid, all too near Taimah and waste of time. Zayyid was most anxious to camp ¾ of an hour from the water where there were trees, but I insisted on going on. We were abreast of the first sand hills of the Nefud at 1.30, the big Ta's onto which I had taken bearings being just to the left. Immediately we found abundance of herbage, 'adil an upright plant with slender branches already green, the dry subat grass, this is the Faqir name, M. al M. calls it kharshaf, shkhi a big thistle just greening, and a low growing plant called hammat also just greening. Also ghada trees and a green tree called alandal which camels do not eat. Irta just greening in long slender green threads 'alga found only in Nefud. We came into camp at 2.45, a good day. Hamid says the Faqir guard the Hajj line from Dar al Hamra to Medain [Mada'in Salih] and receive a yearly surra of money clothes and zohab and a ma'ash when the Hajj passes. They used to carry down to the Hajj bundles of subat grass which Abd al Rahman wd buy for the Hajj camels. Now this trade is over since the Hajj passes in the train pt[?]! We are camped in deep pale yellow sand. The Nefud is delightful. Guarding the line are Sukhur, Howaitat, B. Atiyyeh, Faqir, 'Aida, Billi and Jeheyna, Harb. The Faqir, B. Atiyeh, W. Sulaiman and all the Annezeh all spring from 'Annaz ibn Wail. The other old tribes they know are the Temun and the Qahtan. The 3 rafaqa showed me their rifles which are all marked with the crown and V.R. I said if I were a great shaikh I wd forbid the entrance of all firearms into Arabia. Zayyad declared it wd be much better wallah, they wd return to the lance and the stone if only none had rifles. They have now no good mares left. Only Ibn Rashid and ibn Sha'lan have cannon—madafi'. There is one cannon at Jof, a good one. All my rafiqs pray, but they do not take off the abbaya to do so.

Thurs Feb. 12 [12 February 1914]

We were off soon after 6 and took a pretty direct course onto the ta's called·al Sabi'. Thence I got bearings onto Dhaibat, the ta's above Shmukka, and Irnan. Also onto Ghnaim, hills which are only an hour from Taimah, the plain of Mhaimeriyyeh near Taimah, the whole of our road back to the first sand hills of the Nefud and our way forward to Haizan. The tu'us are heads of sand with no herbage on them. They stand up pale yellow out of the Nefud and have a sort of moat round 3 sides, the 4th being generally a deep depression. The sand banks run mostly in an east-west direction, more or less. The valleys between them have a way of dropping suddenly into a very steep hollow called a Ga'r which on these edges of the Nefud has sometimes jellad at the bottom. The tu'us have a very sharp E and W ridge, the steepest slope being as far as I have observed, generally to the N. While I was climbing up Sabi' the camels came up and F. reported that one had sat down and wd not move. M. al M, Fellah and I went back to her with some 'aliq and found her lying on her side, twitching and evidently dying. M. said "Rahat hadhi, Nahallalha?" I said Ahsan and he cut her throat, thrusting his knife into the big jugular vein and giving it a sharp turn to one side, with the words Bismillah, Allaha akbar. It was a disease called al tair. Fortunately she was one of the weak camels. Lots of baqr tracks. The rafiqs saw 3 baqr but failed to get near them. Also fresh tracks of Arabs and as we camped we sighted ba'irin far off. The rafiqs went off to see who they were—pray heaven they bring back no bad tidings! The sand often very soft and exceedingly heavy going for the camels up and down hills. We cannot keep to the bottoms because of the deep gu'r. Sun hot in the middle of day, but the air cold directly after sunset. M. once rode with letters from the Vali to M. Sa'id Pasha who was returning with the Hajj in 3 days from Damascus to Ma'an. He left Dam. at dawn and the following dawn was at Fdainmar Umm el Jemal, the next at Annezeh near Keframeh[?] and by 8 AM next day at Ma'an. Between the W. al Hesa [Hasa] and Ma'an he met M. ibn Jazi and 8 horsemen. He was gomani with the Ibn Jazi on account of a dispute over some camels. It was before the days of rifles and though he had a good Egyptian rifle they had only one between them. M. ibn Jazi called on him to stop and asked him who he was. He had couched his camel and was standing beside her with his rifle in his hand. He cried out I am M., M. al Ma'rawi. Ibn Jazi levelled his lance at him. M. cried I am M. al M. and you are M. ibn Jazi. If you cast your lance I shoot. He had determined to shoot as he saw the lance cast so that they might both die together. Ibn Jazi cried Udbuh al kelb 3 men threw their lances at him from behind; they touched him but only grazed him. Then Ibn Jazi siezed [sic] the rifle from the Howaiti and shot. The shot passed under M.'s arm through his clothes. Whereupon he shot aiming between M. ibn Jazi's legs and the bullet passed between them. Thereat Ibn Jazi mounted his mare and rode away, calling off his men. It wasted more than an hour. Sa'id said "God delivered you from the Howaitat M. got a fresh camel at Fdain from the Khraishan and at Annezeh (he met Khraisah [sic]) God sent him Ibn Jebel on his way to join Sa'id P. at Ma'an and he gave him a fresh dulul. Both times the dulul he was riding broke down in the night.

Fri. Feb 13 [13 February 1914]

It froze hard in the night and was cloudy all day. The 3 rafiqs had come back bringing with them 'Awwad ibn Habrun of the Awajeh, for they said they dared not go on, fearing the Shammar because they had not given tidings of Audeh Abu Tayy's raid. Musuid also feared because he was in the Howaitat tents and wd be accused of having given information as to the Shammar camping grounds. So we took 'Awwad, at a mej. a day; the others came on with us to our camp where I paid them and they went away. Musuid 1½ mej. a day (I might have got him for 1) Zayyid 1 mej. a day and 8 for clothes, Hamid ditto, and Dahir 8 mej. all told. They had been with us 5 days—very dear terms. We rode over very high ground; the bar at 8 was 26.5 and it fell to 26.45. At 9.15 we saw Helwan and at 9.30 I got bearings onto Irnan, Haza'ib, Zebuch, Helwan and Bird. Also onto the ta's above Haizan; it is called Zebran. Just before we came into camp we passed a ga'r which was an almost perfect horseshoe, but lower on one side than on the other; and we are camped in a place which is in 2 stages of ga'r, one above the other on the intervening platform. They are a wide irregular horseshoe. Ibn Rashid is reported to have sent a large convoy to fetch the goods (arms?) which have come from the Ott. Govt. to Madain [Mada'in Salih]. They are said to be watering today at Haizan, hence the fear of the rafiqs. 'Abdullah ibn al Jullul conveys them. The rafiqs came back this morning in new clothes which they had bought from a merchant whom they found in the Awajeh camp. M. al M. knows him; he comes originally from Meshed [al-Najaf] and his name is Sadiq abu al 'Ajineh. There was a good deal of nusi' today, besides subat, alga, hammat, 'vita and alanda. 'Ali says [illegible] Allah. F. to Abu Q. Taht 'amrak. Abu Q Layla! istaghfir allah! al 'amr hillah. Ma fi 'asur ghair lillah.

Sat Feb 14. [14 February 1914]

Off at 5.50, before sunrise. Very wonderful to see the light come over the Nefud touching the top of the tu'us about Zabran and creeping down their flanks, the nazi, into the shadowed ga'r. We passed to the east of the Zabran group. I climbed up the south eastern ta's, with great labour, and took these bearings: Bird 208, Haizan 197, Helwan 188–200, Labueh, two points (I took the centre) 175, Dalma 173–4, Haza'il 162–5. These make a practically continuous ring of high ground on the edge of the Nefud; beyond them is jallad. Then 'Irnan 126–140 and Misma far away 90. The chief Ta's, Fabran lay to the W of where I stood. Back to Subi' was 348. We came into camp at 9.10 about ½ a mile or less from Zabran to which the bearing was 306, while back to my Ta's it was 180. I went on with the camels to Haizan which we reached at 10.25. The well lies in a very deep cup—the Bar fell 2 points from the lip to the floor. There is only one well now in use, Haizan; our well rope was 48 paces long. A little to the S. is another well, Haizal which is masdudeh, maiteh. In the days of M. ibn al Rashid the Ruwalla took possession of these wells and barred the way to the Shammar. M. ibn R. drove them out and blocked one well, Haizah, the least good one. It has not been used since. Both wells are lined with roughly squared stones and the lower part cut out of the solid rock. The bottom of the cup was jellad, partly white encrusted. We took 2 sticks with us and an iron wheel and made a rude pulley. The Arabs were using a similar arrangement with a wooden wheel. They were Awaji; we had seen their camp from the Ta's. There was some objection at first to my photographing but the Shammar with me encouraged me to go on. Not far from the wells is an Awaji bury-ing place with a central tomb, with no wasm on it however. It is the tomb of the fa-ther of their chief shaikh, Mish'an. He was killed in a ghazzu. I rode back with Ghadi and his brother. We had a partial washing day. The temp was 68° and a wind but the sand is not dusty and fine and does not blow. There is a leafless green shrub round here called Girdi—reed like green branches without leaves. The camels love it. We are now at the frontiers of the 'Anazeh and the Shammar. From Gulban, before us, on-wards all is Shammar. The 'Anazeh fendehs who drink at Haizan are all friends of the Shammar. The Awaji have no foes but the Hetaim (?) with whom they quarrelled 3 years ago over a question of pasturage. They had a big fight and lost 40 men (all the

'Anazeh united) while the Htaim lost 30. The chief summering water of the Awaji is Baida Nethel. One of the men at the well asked if I was Nasraniyyeh. I said I was Ingliziyyeh. The shaikh camped here is Sulaiman ibn Khalaf, he is cousin to the big shaikh Mesh'an. He has sent a boy to know if we want anything. As we rode back Ghadi praised to me Ibn Rashid—he was a better surak than the Hwaital. They wd now stay with their own people, with Ibn Rashid. They knew of 'Audeh's raid but cd not warn the Shammar. Yet they praised Audeh—he was melih[?]. The brother Mejned had been in the Victoria[?] Hospital at Damas. and spoke well of the Lakun. When we saw the tents this morning, 'Awwad was all impatience to go and get 'ullum. We sat at night drawing wasms in the sand.

Sun Feb 15 [15 February 1914]

We rode off early, but I did not get a bearing back to Zabran till 11—it was 283, therefore our forward bearing must have been about 100. At 11 I took the forward bearing N of J. Misma 87, but we by no means travelled direct, for we had to avoid the great ga'r and tu'us. My other bearings at 11 were 221–231 Helwan, 180–185 Dalma, 180 Abu Mughair, a single point sticking up from behind, 171–176 Haza'il, 148–132 'Irnan, 116 Argub al Misma', 95–97 Misma'. Judging by the tells I had seen when we started at 6.15, our camping place cannot be far off the first line 100° but I shall be able to tell better when I see Misma and Zabran again. At 12.15 we came to ard, ma'sum and Awwad was anxious to camp, saying his camel was broken and he must go back or leave her with Arabs here. We presently met a Sherari with his camels, rahil, who gave us news of Arab ahead. At 1.30 2 of them overtook us and we asked news. They replied that falsehood was not fit for man and that the Kelab (who are of the Awaji) were ahead and the Swaib beyond al Gulban. Also that Abdullah ibn al Jullul had passed by the jellad road and they had not seen him. We camped in abundance of nusi' and the Arabs came to see us. They are only shepherds here, Sa'id knows them. Since 'Awwad could not persuade one of them to go on with us he is obliged to accompany us himself till we meet Shammar. The Nefud was much smoother today, or at least there was always a good path by the bank tops. Some of the ga'r have a whitish salt(?) over the bottom, as I saw at the bir. There was lots of a slender little plant called Umm al Swait which the camels love, but it is not yet green. The Sherarat says M al M never have trustworthy news; they are not well informed. The man we met today was pasturing his camels as he went. His few goods were packed on one or two of them; one carried his baby. The wife was sitting under an 'irta bush, the man walked. The Nefud, said Awwad when he advised us to take this road, was good for those who feared. I asked 'Ali this morning whether all the Arab disputes were over pasturage and camels. Yes he said most of them. And women? said I. Yes he said, the beni adam quarrel most over women, they are the cause of all disputes. A man takes a wife and she leaves him and goes back to her people, or he divorces her and they quarrel over her possessions. But the customs of the Arabs are not good. A man will take a woman whose husband has died or divorced her and marry her the very next day, though she is with child by the first man. Disputes arise over the parentage of the child, but the woman is the only arbiter. The da'a is referred to her and she says He is the child of fulan. Some women they will never let go; one brother will marry her after another till her hair is white, to keep her wealth or because she comes of a good stock and will bear manly sons. She is like a prisoner among them. But some are not worth a nehaseh[?] and their children are no good. Do they take the daughters of a gomani? said I. Yes, he said, and the woman sides with her husband when he raids her family. The wife of Nur Ibn Sha'lan was a daughter of [space left blank]. She was married first to Nuri's brother and he raided her family, killed her brother and brought the mare home. When she saw her she knew her as the mare of her brother. Where is my brother? she said. He is 'and[?] ahlha, saidla. No she said or you wd not lead in his mare—you have killed him. When her husband died Nuri took her that she might remain in the family. The maidens of the Arabs are fair, but their skin is dirty and they are ill fed said Ali. I saw all these Awaji were small and ill favoured (Salan, the neighbouring shaikh had been in our camp this morning) and Ali replied that they were all dying of hunger and began to sing the praises of the Muntefij who were like kings and their food and their customs like those of the Ottomans. M. al M. said that camels sometimes slipped and fell into the deep steep ga'r of the Nefud. He had been on the way to Jof and a camel bearing a load of waterskins pushed against (dafa') a camel bearing a load of dates. The latter fell over into a ga'r and broke her leg. They hallal her and pulled the date load up with ropes. And the Lord was to be thanked that it was not the water camel which had fallen; that wd have been zahnech. There are 6 days from Jubbah across the Nefud to near Jof without water, 5 nights and the 6th at water. He would have 4 herds each with 2 'abid, 12 men and himself 13 and he would take 8 or 9 loads of water. For in the summer a man wd drink a girbeh wahdhu in a day. There was a cold wind all day but the sun was hot, the temp 73° in the shade after we camped. All the Arabs from Hayyil to Taimah pay ziqa to Ibn al Rashid, 1 real for every 10 beasts. But he no longer holds the country quiet as it was in Mohammad's day, when the Hayyil authority stretched up to the Sukhur. At this moment part of the Hetaim are foes with the Annazeh and it is for fear of their raids that we have kept to the Nefud. All the story Ghadi told me about Haizan is untrue. Haizah was open as late as 4 years ago, and its water was better than that of Haizan which is rather brackish. The Swaid and the Awaji quarrelled and the Swaid filled up both Haizan and Haizah, but the former ineffectually so that it could be opened again. The Awaji filled up Awaid and it has not been opened again.

Mon. Feb. 16 [16 February 1914]

We were off at 6.18 and I got a bearing back to our camp at 8.10. It was 305, therefore we must have been going at about 125°. I also saw the big hill which is the E.

end of J. 'Irnan. Its name is Dhurru and its bearing was 141. At 8.40 our forward bearing was 114 and a little to the W. of it was the ta's, Thailah (116°) which, as I afterwards found, lies a little to the S.W. of the Gulban. At 8.50 I saw the whole line of the Misma (except to the N, they may stretch a little further). The point on which I had taken my former bearings a dip between two high flat topped mountains, was now 95. This part of the Misma is called al 'Anjeh. It must be about 93°–97° or 98°. The lower hills, al Argub, stretched on to 125°. 'Irnan was 143–162, the Dhurru being 143°. At 9 we changed our course to 66 and then wound along sand banks till we found ourselves on the edge of a deep ga'r in which we camped at 11.45. At 12.20 the camels went off to water and I with them. We got to the jelib called al Rozah at 1.5. The bar. was 26.6 at the top and 26.8 at the bottom. There is one well here of very good water. Our well rope was 21 paces. Further E. there are 3 more wells, water slightly brackish like Haizan, of the same depth as the Rozah. We had been in some doubt as to whether the camels wd drink as the day was windy and cold (when I got back to camp the ther. was 63). We tried them in camp with water and they drank greedily, therefore we sent them all down to the Jelib. For unless we find khabari we shall get no water till we reach 'Awaiseh. We found at the well some Wadi Sulaiman watering black goats and camels. They said we shd reach Shammar 'uqub bachir. We took near an hour to water and fill our skins and got back to camp at 3. Sa'id was in these parts last year buying camels from the Awaji and 'Aida. He was a fortnight in camp under the Dhurru. He is often 8 or 9 months away and he reckons to make £T200 by the end, £100 for himself and £100 for his partner in Dam. Muhammad's father Sa'id al Ma'rawi was the first to begin this trade with Nejd. He was several years at Jof as a merchant. This was in the time of Met'ab ibn al Rashid. At that time no other Damascenes dared to traffic in this country. M. al M. has been into the Qasun, but not Sa'id, because, he says, the people are wuhush. M al M used to come twice a year to Nejd, selling goods in the spring and buying camels in the summer. But now the country is much less safe and the trade therefore much more risky. He wd not put his son to it, but he trained up Sa'id. Sometimes in the summer Sa'id buys from the Sukhur at and about Ziza. This is much more convenient of course, but not so profitable because of the competition of other Damascene merchants.

Tues Feb 17 [17 February 1914]

The slopes of sand are nazi', nuzu'. The low sand banks khabb, khubab; the paths round the slopes of a ga'r are khall, khulul. We struck camp early and no sooner was the men's tent down than it began to rain. We marched and were presently overtaken by a torrent. The clouds hung low over the sand hills like fog and 'Awwad declared he could not see the alama or know the road. I knew by the compass that we were all right and we went on, skirting round immense ga'rs. Some were whitened at the bottom where rain water had lain. The clouds lifted a little and we went on but at

8.15 it began to rain again and it was clear that more storms were coming up behind us. We pitched the men's tent and lighted a fire by which we dried ourselves. Heavy rain fell. The sun came out but another storm followed and I gave up hopes of further marching. We pitched all the tents. The rain fell in heavy bouts till past 1, with thunder and hail. Said Ghadi This is a feast day 'and al Arab. 'Awwad. The shaikhs sacrifice a camel. The unwedded girl will marry today. After this rain there will be mara' for 3 months. They say that in a week's time the 'aislib will have grown a foot high and all the trees will be green. The leafless white sapped tree is muti' I think I named it wrongly before. (No, right. The small one is muti, the big one girdi, and there is a middle one called 'addam). About 3 the sun came out and it was hot and stuffy. The rain clouds hung close round 'Irnan, but Misma' was clear. The sand smelt delicious after the rain and was hard to walk on. A pool lay in a neighbouring ga'r. At 5 the clouds blew up from the NW I watched the rain storms sweeping over 'Irnan and it fell again on us heavily. Inshallah 'ala kull al dunya! said the dripping men this morning. I read Hamlet which brought the world back into perspective. 'Uqub bachir = day after tomorrow. Neqotar = we journey, walk.

Wed. Feb 18. [18 February 1914]

Rain storms walking across the Nefud and we came in for the tail of one, but by 11 all the rain had cleared away. The great horseshoes still lay across our path, as they have done since Haizan. The depressions run mostly N and S, the horseshoes face both ways, but most have their back to the W. The depression between two high horseshoe backs in a ridge is called felk (fuluk) The pl. of ga'r is gu'urah. We saw another kind of grass today, sahn; also a small plant about the size of Umm al Swait called Zerhah. A small twittering of birds, the black and white sabri and the hammarah. I took my bearing in the morning onto the 'Anjeh pass—it was 82°. We wandered about a good deal round the gu'urah, but the going was goodish since the sand was harder after the rain. At 10.45 we sighted Zuwal and tents. 'Awwad went off to see who they were and reported them to be some of the W. Sulaiman whom M. al M. said were Anjas min ha illy taht al 'ard. One or two of their people rode out to see us and gave us very contradictory news of the Shammar ahead. Later we passed a few tents and the news was all different, but finally Dafi, Ghadi's brother said he had seen the wife of Mhailam, who is one of the Sanad[?], of the Swaid, and that he was camped there with the W. Sulaiman. Dafi went back to fetch him and we came into camp on high ground. The shaikh himself turned up presently with 2 Shammar boys of the Swaid one of them ('Awwad ibn Hamid al Khlaiwi) who had been with 'Abdullah's caravan going to Taimah, and 4 camels strayed, 2 were found at Gulban and 2 at the Dafafiyyat. These 2 boys went to look for them and are now returning to their people in the Nefud. Al Mhailam goes with us to Hayyil for £12 and the hire of a camel (4 or

5 mej). I have also given him 5 mej. the price of a goat he brought me, and some coffee in return for some semneh. I have also to give him some clothes at Hayyil. We have given the Shammar with us meat and flour—they are starving. Much talk and exchange of news as to the places of tribes, the ghazzu of the Ruwalla and Mejwed, Ghadi's brother, asked in return for news of the ghazzu of the Shammar. Ana illi a'allamah, they say. The Shammar youths brought news that the Maahib had raided the 'Anazeh near Haizan since we were there. The Shaikh Mhailam brought his 2 sons with more semneh for which I gave them cotton kerchiefs.

Thurs Feb 19 [19 February 1914]

Mhailam nearly battal last night but was persuaded that it was contrary to honour. I paid 'Awwad ½ a mej. for Ghadi, shusheh for being let pass through the 'Anazeh country. The Shammar have not followed us to our camp, without a farewell they have left us. It was cold with a bitter NW wind which blew up clouds in the afternoon. I decided to take the road through the jellad though there is some danger from Htaim; but I cannot bear any more of the Nefud. This end of the Nefud is called al Satihah. Nevertheless M al M and Mhailam were always heading off into it and I had to turn them back. From 10 AM onwards Mhailan tried to induce me to camp saying there was no pasture below, arfej or anything. As I was walking on to get warm I met a Shammari shepherd. He held up his right arm as I came near and I held up mine and then gave him the salute. Where was I going? Quddam. Who was with me? Shammar of the Sanad[?]. Whence came I? From Dam. Ya walad! said he. I took my first morning bearing onto al Rediffeh, the big N. Dhullah of Misma'. We passed under it at 12.30 and saw Nejd. An awful landscape, terrifying in its look of extinction. The blackened sandstone crags of Misma drop steeply on the E side; at their feet lie a wilderness of dhullan and gharamil, planted in a barren sandy floor. The separate flat topped hills of Friddat stand behind and to the S., and behind them and to the N the broken line of Habran. Over all scudded clouds borne by the bitter wind. Between and across our path occasional lines of fantastic dhullan and gharamil. "Like a city" said Ali "a ruined[?] city." And Salim "It is Jehannum. We come from the jinnet at 'ard and this is Jehannum. We marched straight on till 2.5, then finding the earth ma'kul and wahl[?] (there was nothing but [space left blank] and eaten grasses) we turned up and camped on the edges of the Nefud. Mhailam said there was arfej below and we ought to have gone there but I don't know—I think it wd have been ma'kul. A man by himself and tentless in the khala is called khalawi. M al M once met a khalawi under 'Irnan who had [illegible] for 3 days in search of tuttem. The Shammar have come! Shelweh announced them by [illegible] at my tent door. The Arabs bring stones with them into the Nefud for their fires. They say Bainakawa bainna[?] Allah.

Fri. Feb. 20 [20 February 1914]

Last night Mhailam was agitated because there was a ferij of Shammar tents near us—we had seen the herdsmen and we did not know who they were. He went out into the dark and cried Oh watchers! whoever is hungry let him come to dinner! With us is Mhailam of the Sanad[?]. We go in peace. Whoever is hungry let him come and eat." But none came. In the morning M al M rode up to their tents and brought back butter. The Shammar stayed behind today. I tipped them. But the brother Dafi came on with us, whereat Mhailam and F. were much agitated, said he was khalawi and might rise up in the night, take a camel and some of our goods and be gone. I know not. But I tipped him and sent him back poor soul. We came down into the jellad which was full of shajar, brukkan which is very like arfej, girdi and others. Also of flights of twittering birds like sparrows, Shaiman. On the sandstone floor water pools were lying. We turned down to one at 7.30 and watered the camels. At 7.13 about a mile from us, bearing 130°, is the jelul of 'Awaid, masdud as I related above by the W. Sulaiman. At 9.10 I got the whole of the Friddat. At 10.15 the Habran pass to which we were going was 82. At 10.25 the Habran thulla Umm al Darub was 79° and the Friddat 219–240 S. end of the Habran range 127°. At 12.7 the Friddat were 219–240, the Misma pass from which we had come 266° and the central saddle of Misma 250. At 12.13 Umm al Darub was 64° (we passed under it at 12.45) and our forward bearing 88°. At 12.45 back to Misma pass 266 and forward 82. We climbed up the sand which lies against the blackened sandstone crags and saw at 12.49, a cup between the thullan below us with khabras lying in it. At 1.33 I took a bearing on a big thulla 65°. It is the northernmost of the ridge which lies behind the West ridge of Habran. The bearing of this whole ridge from my camp was 50.118, 50 being the N end of this thulla. We came into camp under the W. ridge at 2 with abundance of ma'ashy[?]. The sun was hot for the last hour but after we camped I found the ther. only 64°. It may be 1–1½ miles from the W. to the E. ridge where we are camped. A ferij of Shammar lies opposite us with 2 tents of Shammar fro [sic]

Sat. Feb 21. [21 February 1914]

We passed under the middle S. point of Habran, the bearing which I took last night as 118, at 6.45. The bearing of the SW end (the western ridge) was 201. At 7 I got J. Mataleh [Jabal Matali'] 131–147 (but I was taking in a thulla which lies to the NW of the ridge, about 5 miles N of it) and J. Rakham 98–105. I took our forward bearing a little to the left, 107°, but as a matter of fact we did not quite round the N end and the bearing here should be about 103°. At 7.37 it was 286 back to the middle S. point of 6.45, and 96° on—but this too is too much. The back bearings are the right ones today. At 7.56 I got some Dhullan called Marabib, 44°, standing just within the Nafud, and further away Irus al Ma' where I gather there is a jellib. I got there again, at 8.57, together with Rakham and Matala—the latter still including the outlying dhulla. The

SW point of Habran was 252, the bearing back 282, and the extreme SE point (ie the SE point of the E ridge) 328. Irus al Ma stands above Jubbeh [Jubbah] which lies NE of it. At 11.6 I got Marubib and Irus al Ma' again, Matalah 151–167, and the outlying thulla 174. The S.W. point of Habran was 283 and the S.E. 299. At 11.6 we came to the end of the exceedingly flat jellad and entered sand bands with alanda on them. They gradually grew bigger and more rolling as we approached Rakham. At 1.5 the first rocks of Rakham lay on our right hand. We climbed up sand banks and onto the ridge leaving the left hand point, on which my bearings were taken, a mile or so to the left. On top we found a charming place to camp but no water and we had brought only a girbeh. There was khabra about an hour away on the other side in the plain, but we determined to risk it and camp here. Al Hailam ibn Khlaif finally found some water in the rocks. Somewhere in the sand we passed the frontier[?] of the sandstone district. These rocks are granite, very coarse and lava-like. Beyond the wide plain to the S is the long ridge of J. 'Ajjah. There is plenty of 'arfej and Shittad for the camels. I climbed onto a high point above the camp. The recent rains had left deep channels in the sand between the rocks. The shrubs were green and the plants flowering. A sort of berberis with yellow berries and green leaves, a small asphodel which I have seen before, various yellow and purple flowers which I do not know. The thistles had sent up long stalks on which the thorny buds were already swelling. Not a great bounty but in this pitiless land it feasted the eyes. Also the rounded shapes of the granite hills look familiar after the devilish tables and pinnacles of the sandstone. I saw a very long snake which whipped away hastily into the rocks. Hot sun today. We saw gazelles and several ferijs of Shammar—camels pasturing. We blew an ostrich egg and had ostrich omelette for dinner. We gave Hailam a pair of red boots; he is resplendent in his rags. A delicious mountain feeling tonight. M al M told the tale of Muham's succession after killing Bunder. He killed all the sons of Tellal and 2, killed the following day, were thrown into a well. 'Abd ul Aziz succeeded him and was succeeded by his son Mit'ab who was killed by Sultan ibn Hamud. He slew at the same time Muhammad, Mit'ab's brother, and Tallal ibn Na'if ibn Tellal. Mit'ab only reigned a few months and Sultan under a year when he was killed by his brother.

Then Sa'ads uncle, Hamud, brother of his mother Mudi brought back Sa'ad from Medina where he had been sent for safety, and installed him. Sultan had been about to kill him but the child cried and begged him for his life and he was spared. Hamud, the uncle, died in 1907, when Carruthers was in Taimah, and his cousin, Zamil, took his place. Ibrahim, Zamil's brother, is now wakil at Hayyil. M. al M. was in Hayyil when Bunder slew Mit'ab but there was no alarm in the town. All 'Abeyd's descendants are now killed, murdered or in battle, and none are left in Hayyil. There are still 2 living somewhere on the Gulf or at Ghiyath. [Family tree for 'Abdallah and Abayd; 4 generations. See Appendix 2.]

Sun Feb 22 [22 February 1914]

Off at 6. I took a forward bearing onto the Khabra, 76°, and to the right onto
Dulu 81–82, Khashab 88–90, the E point of 'Ajja 91, Saq 100, and the triple peak of
Htalah 148–149, this I never saw again. At 6.10 I got the Marabib 349–357, and Irus al
Ma' 9–11. At 6.40 we came to the khabra and found a good jubb, but there is only water after rain. I went a little out of the way to see Twaiyyah which has some 6 or 7
houses, a plot or two of corn and some tall ithl trees. Some of the inhabitants have
palm trees at Mogug [Mawquq] and go there after the corn is ripe. The Shammar
Ghitheh camp round here in the summer for the sake of the wells and go as far off as
Habran but there is danger in summer of Htaim raids. The people came out with
guns—5 men—thinking we were raiders. They pressed us to stay and drink coffee and
gave us a skin of leben. I got bearings back to the point of Rakham above our camp.
Twaiyyeh [al-Atwa] is in a hollow bottom of the Nefud and we rode first over low
sand banks and then over regular Nefud ground by a hollow way from which we saw
nothing. I got Saq at 8.50 (117) and at 10.40 Dulu' 86–96. At 11 immediately in the right
hand was a deep hollow in which is water, Shbaikah. It is extremely salt [*sic*], but permanent. In the summer the Shammar mix leben with it and drink it. Some way (perhaps a mile) to the left is Shbaikan also permanent water and sweet. At 12.50 we
passed under the spurs of Dulu' perhaps 2 miles from the high point I had taken as the
E. bearing and at 1.14 I saw the high cliff I had taken as the E. end of 'Ajja (106) I cd no
longer see Rakham as there were high sand banks in the way. I took the bearing onto
Dubi' 78°. Before we came into camp we saw some regular Nefud horseshoes, but this
part is not good mara. We got, however, nusi', 'adair and firewood. Several times we
met herdsmen, all of the Ghitheh. They came to us for news and were usually told we
came from the Nefud or from Habran or from Muaddam. Ibrahim, brother of Zamil,
is wakil at Hayyil. Sa'ud is north of Haiyaniyyeh raiding some of the Ruwalla. It was
lovely at dawn in Rakham, the sunrise flushing the granite ["basalt?" written above]
rocks. Near the jubb the rocks looked hard and close woven like basalt or real granite
and 'Ali observed that it was the mill stone rock. Al Hailam is the most charming of
rafiqs. He is not very fond of 'Ali whom he addresses as Ya Agaili. He rebukes him for
sleeping in camp Qum, gum, ghabut al shems! He makes funny swimming[?] movements with his hands as he talks. The granite grit floor is the same as the sandstone
with perhaps one or two plants added—but it all grows in sand filled places so it can't
be much different. Very hot sun today but cool wind and the temp only 66 when we
camped.

Mon. Feb 23. [23 February 1914]

The Nefud was very big till we got near to Dubi'. I went on my old bearing,
78°, till 7.30, for I could not see Dubi ahead. When I got it, it was 80 and we passed under it, leaving to the left about a mile away, at 10.5. At 9.30 I took our forward bearing

as 90, Dubi' as 84, Umm al Gulban [Umm al-Qulban] (a village which I did not see but only the point over it) as 66 and the middle point of al Twal, very far away as 63. At 10.5 I got the E cliff of 'Ajja (which I believe Awjeh) as 126. At 10.20 I got Khashab as 207–208 and Dulu' as 217–220. There were two outstanding rocks to the right, Rock 1 I took as 109 and we passed under it at 10.47 when it was 143—I daresay less than a mile from it. At 11.35 we joined the Jubbah road. For nearly all the morning we had been following a very distinct track through the Nefud, but this way a real hollow road through the sand. Umm al Gulban is a village of the Amir's. He sends his horses to pasture there. It is only some 10 houses. At 11.40 we saw the palms and ethl of Gna' and reached it at 12.5. It pays no ziqat and belongs to a man who is noted for his hospitality. It stands at the junction of 7 roads ["7 khulul" written above], Hayyil, Jubbah, Twaiyyah, Mujay, Umm al Gulban, al Htair al Hafar. Ayyadeh ibn Abicheh is its owner and has a few palm gardens, corn plots, about 20 houses, Indian corn durra, jet, and plum trees khokh which were in flower. The men went to him to buy some tobacco but came back with stuff not fit to smoke. I had made them laugh in their despair by telling them they were like Umm Salim. Dughaz, dughaz! said Ali Hatha mithl al sitt. But just out of Gna' we met 2 tajirs who had come from Hayyil that morning and bought some sweet Baghdad tobacco from them. We followed the road till 1.20 and camped on the very edge of the Nefud. We clothed al Hailam with a Qumbaz an ab-bayya and a kerchief. He put them on over his filthy old tob and kerchief and is as proud as Punch. Horrible strong W wind and stuffy hot. Ther. 74 when we came into camp. There was thunder and rain over 'Ajja but only the very skirts of the rain reached us. There is not more that ½ an hour between Umm al Gulban and Gna'. On this side of Ajja there is a low and broken parallel ridge called al Nahaib pl of al Nahadeh.

Tues Feb 24. [24 February 1914]

M al M and 'Ali rode off at 6 to Hayyil. We got off 10 minutes later. We had had violent rain in the night and the morning was deliciously sweet and fresh. The road led into the hills and we were soon in the granite thullan of the Naha'id. I got Twal Subruwah[?] Jelf (a tell) and Ja'id at 8.45. We passed through the thullan and behind the point which may or may not be Mdeyriyyeh (I think it is not) At 8.55 we stopped till 9.30 to fill some skins at a good pool in the rocks. A mountain feeling in these granite gorges full of green bushes and small flowers. Big tolh trees everywhere and the plain smelling sweet of be'aitheran which was in ineffective yellow flower. I got a bearing on Loqitah at 11 but I think it was only Muham. Ibn al R's. qasr which I got again at 11.45. He used to come out and examine his horses here. It stands in a big palm garden. At 12.35 I saw the village of Loqitah about 2 miles away at a bearing of 85. At 12.45 we came through the hills into the Samra Hayyil, so called from the low tells between us and Hayyil. It is a plain of granite and basalt grit. The NE end of 'Ajja goes trending away on our right hand. We camped at 1 below a tell a little off the road, whence we can see Hayyil. Very still and pleasant. Sa'id told me of his traffickings. He has been at it since the age of 15 and is now 40. His partner, whoever it may happen to be, provides the money and he has half profits for the ta'b and the buying. If he has half profits he shares the possible loss; if he takes a third only he does not suffer. The trade is not what it was for camels sheep and semneh have risen in price in Nejd owing to the competition of Agaili buyers who work merely for hire. If the Egyptian market is good they count to clear £200 to £300 profit on every £1000. The Ra'iyyeh of camels is 71 or 81, of sheep 500. For every Ra'iyyeh of camels they take two herdsmen of the Arabs. A Shammari herd will earn 20 to 30 mej. for travelling with them to Damascus. The sheep are far greater trouble and anxiety. They die or stray, once near Mosul [al-Mawsil] Sa'id lost his whole herd of lambs. "My legs trembled when I heard" he said. But after 2 days' search he recovered them. He never brings in more than 100 or 150 camels at a time because to flood the market spoils it, but M. al Bassam used to bring in 150 ra'iyyehs. The Ma'rawis are the best known and most trusted at this trade. S. once bought in 500 lambs and sold them in the suk of Dam. to a man who did not even to trouble to look at them—"Only give me your hand" he said and paid the price. He once asked a Ruwaili "When the 2 angels come to your grave and ask you of your deeds what will you answer?" He said "I shall say I am a Ruwaili mayyit the Qaul and the hachi is to Ibn Sha'lan, our shaikh; go and ask him."

Wed Feb 25. [25 February 1914]

We got off about 6.30 and rode towards Hayyil. The men were visibly anxious. After we had ridden about ¾ of an hour we saw a company approaching, 3 men on a camel and presently Ali emerged from them (he was the camel rider) came hurrying up to us and said "Kulshi ala kaifna." They had seen Ibrahim who had been most gracious and had said I was welcome. The 2 faris who had dismounted behind, now got onto their horses and came to us. They were 'abid and one carried a lance. They greeted me with much friendliness. Later we were joined by another faris who proved to be Hasan el Da'aifi. We had now passed through the outlying mounds of the Samra, we climbed up between the low hills and saw Hayyil before us, its low mud walls, lately built, set with machicolated towers and tall towers rising from the houses of the town. Palm trees waved green over the walls. A very flat reddish granite grit plain stretches round it. There is a white washed masalla to the S of the town. We skirted round the walls and came in by the Gofar or Medinah gate. Within the gate stretched before us a wide empty street. Immediately to the left I found M al M waiting before the door of a house. I dismounted and was led in by a long passage, sloping up to a roof court and so to a large hall, the palm wood roof carried on whitewashed palm trunks, the walls whitewashed and decorated with pious sayings set in a band of red and blue painted entrelacs; round the walls were carpets and divan cushions.

There are very small windows, in 2 rows one above the other. Here I sat down in a corner on the cushions. It is the outer palace of Muhammad ibn al Rashid, where he used to come and watch the Hajj gathered in the plain outside. In it are lodged important persons who come on a visit. When the men went out to see to the pitching of our tents in the big sammah I climbed up a wooden ladder to the roof and looked over Hayyil. I was called down by a slave boy, Atullah, and there came to me in the roshan an old woman, dressed in a red cotton under robe with a black abbaya over her head. She was followed by another, gaily clad in red and purple cotton under robes an Egyptian gold embroidered scarf over her head, strings and strings of rough pearls with a few emeralds and rubies round her neck; the same strings fell perpendicularly from the neck collar down onto her breast. Her hands were covered with heavy gold rings, some having diamonds set in them. She was Turkiyyeh a Circassian, (so called because of her Turkish origin, her real name is [space left blank]) She lived in C'ple in her childhood, was sent to the Sherif and lived at Mecca for 2 years, in what capacity I do not know, possibly to learn Arabic, and so came here to 'Abd al Aziz. She had forgotten nearly all her Turkish but she told me that Ibrahim sent her to welcome me in case I did not know Arabic. She showed me all the house. The women were sitting in a court which had an inner and outer coffee room. It was formerly used for the reception of Arab shaikhs of importance. Within was another court with small rooms round it wherein were lodged Muhammad's women when he came here, each in a room to herself. Beyond is another small open court, the hosh, in which are planted a sweet lemon, a quince and an apple tree. In the walls of the big roshan are niches, in one of them a telescope, in another a tattered qur'an. The rising passage is open on one side and the roof carried on that side by palm trunk columns. Turkiyyeh talked much of C'ple, the tramvai, the faitunat[?], the arabanat, the food. Here however al hamdalillah the meat was good and cheap and the dates! of them she said Ya hatha al Stambul! if only there were the dates of Hayyil there. And the semneh was cheap here. But look she had grown like an Arab, dressed like an Arab, bare foot and her hair parted in long plats. And she eat with her fingers, handfuls of meat and rice and drank leben and look at her batu! But here was her home and she wished to die here and never go back. Later she asked me to take her with me to Stambul and she wd look after herself there. Abd al Hamid sent 4 Circassians to Muhammad. 2 returned after his death, one besides Turkiyyeh is still here and one is married to [space left blank] and lives at Samawa [al-Samawah]. As soon as the coast was clear of Hayyil people, Salim came and told me and Turkiyyeh and Lu.lu.a came down to see my tents. A lot of slender Abd girls followed. Turkiyyeh showed them all the t[illegible], table and chairs and cooking utensils, and explained their uses, fingering them delicately. She has a merry tongue if sometimes less than honest. "I came here all the way from Stambul to find a rijl" said she "and you have none." Lu.lu.a is caretaker here—she and her husband were here in the time of Muhammad and have stayed on. He husband was killed with Abd al Aziz. With her is a slave woman and her son Atullah the boy. We have a slave door keeper Sa'id. He was taken kesb from the 'Ataiba. They take the slaves like the mares and camels, put the ill favoured ones to the hewing of wood and drawing of water and the well favoured they arm and take into their houses. They have also eunuchs brought from Stambul or Mecca—Tawashi. There is also a citizen of Hayyil, Salih, as watchman. After lunch Turkiyyeh sent for me and I went and sat with her. The harem never go outside the qasr. She was here when Abd al Aziz was killed and spoke of the wailing that followed. An'abdah came and sat with us. Said she "I have not prayed the d[illegible]" "Go and pray, go and pray" said T. It was then more than an hour after noon. Ibrahim was then announced—he did not let me go to him because of the murmuring of the 'ulama. I went to the Roshan and sat down. A tall slave came before Ibrahim and stood in the door, then he entered. He wore on his head a purple and red khuffa with a gold bound agal, was wrapped in a gold embroidered abba and carried a silver mounted sword. Heavily scented with attar of roses. His face is long and thin with a scanty beard and imperial; discoloured teeth and kohl blackened shifting eyes. We talked of the Blunts, Enting[?] and Doughty. Then of affairs to the S. Boraida [Buraydah] now belongs to Ibn al Sa'ud; Anayza ['Unayzah] is under her independent amir and Ibn al S. does not take zaqat from her. The 'Ataiba are partly with the Rashids and partly with the Sa'uds but some of them are gomani to both. Turkiyyeh and Lu.lu.a came to me while I was having tea and T. chatted much as before. She calls the Amir, al Sultan, Allah yasa'idhu. Ali and Sa'ud, sons of Hamud and Salih ibn Subhan, sent us 4 big black Nejd sheep and a bag of rice. Turkiyyeh went back to the qasr with her slave girl at dusk. The slave girl always answered Lubbaiki when she spoke to her. T. said she had not walked so far for years and her legs ached. I walked in the dusk through the wide empty enclosures of our dir. Long mud wall beyond long mud wall with an occasional ruined room or two and the immensely deep sinking of a well—but all the wells are madfun and there is no cultivation in the courts. The long mud walls sometimes run parallel to one another with only a few yards between—great waste of building.

Thurs Feb 26. [26 February 1914]

We sold 6 camels for £T36, with a loss of £T15 on their cost. The one that died had cost us £T8½ so that we have lost in all £T23½. The other 13 camels we sent back to the Nefud with Sayyif and a couple of men to be cured of jerrab. I wrote in the roshan while Lu.lu.a and a little Abdah[?] visitor sat and talked. Before noon came 'Abdullah ibn Tellal with an 'abd, a princely boy, long delicate features, big kohl blackened eyes, gold bound agal and a grave and sorrowful look. In the afternoon came his younger brother Muhammad, also grave and shy, holding by the hand another little boy, of the Jabr house [space left blank] (many of them were slain by Muhammad because they plotted against his life) I took them to my tents and showed them everything. They sat and eat biscuits and apples till Salih fetched them and we sat again in the men's tent. I asked Muhammad whether he cd read and write. Yes, he went to the school. But Abdullah had finished with schooling. "He knows how to read and write?" "Yarif kullesh" with a sweeping of palm over palm. They had 2 slave boys with them. Presently Salih said "They have called the 'asr, will you not pray Muhammad?" And they rose and walked solemnly away hand in hand, looking like little men in their long robes. Muhammad had very long plaits hanging down on either side of his head—a gentle, sad expression. These 2, Sa'ud [the *amir*] and his 2 baby sons (he has 4 wives though he is only about 20) and a small son of Mit'ab ibn Abd al Aziz are all that remain of Abdallah ibn Rashid's descendants. After tea I went with Salim and Sa'id the slave outside the town and sat on a rock scored with modern graffiti, Khatt Abdullah ibn Salih etc. Within the walls the green corn fields shone like jewels. The middle quarter is called Lubbeh, its gate to the S.E. the Lubbeh Gate. There are 5 gates in all. There is some empty space within the walls but most is gardens. To the S. are some large detached garden grounds, walled and towered. Pink almonds flowered in them, or plums. The tall tower in the midst was that of the Barzan. Sa'ud set off 2 months ago, the early rains being good—they raid in the rains. He will perhaps be back in a month. He has 800 men with him; he does not take the villagers but levies a service indemnity from them. When he goes out on such expeditions he takes one or two extra ra'iyyehs of camels with him to replace the slain. And they had some mares with them. He gives to each man provisions and arms according to the number of men he is called upon to bring with him. He is now raiding the Ruwalla; last year it was the Sherarat. He does not raid in the summer except it be very close at hand. Salih has drawn out a masalla beside the men's tents with a rounded mihrab having a few stones set upright to outline its tip, and 2 suffa for the men to stand along. Ibrahim sent his 'abd to enquire after my health. At night I sat in the men's tent. M al M was gone to take a gift to Ibrahim, khaffa, Abba and kumbaj[?] of silk, with 2 boxes of sweetmeats. Also two khaffas and some sweetmeats to the senders of the sheep and rice. Salih spoke of the Rashid tragedies. Sa'ud when he came back from Medina had all the children of the Abeyd house put to death. They were I think Majids. His uncle Hamud dissuaded him saying he should have no blood on his hands. He replied that there should be no blood and had them strangled. He is faris and ghazzai. Mit'ab was killed by Sultan near Gofar; he brought his body back and buried him in a well in the Barzam. The little son of Abd al Aziz, Muhammad, he killed with his own hand, the child praying for mercy. Hamud saved Sa'ud. Mudi was wife of Muhammad; when he died Abd al Aziz took her. Subhan was wazir to Muhammad and so was Hamud brother of Mudi.

Fri. Feb 27 [27 February 1914]

Wrote my diary and took a bad latitude in the morning. Sat a little with old Lu.lu.a and photographed the house. In the evening after dark Ibrahim sent a mare and a couple of slaves—Hasan and 'Id. I rode through the pitch dark streets, very clean and almost empty—sometimes the black figure of a woman creeping along the wall. One of the men carried a lantern. We passed through a big wooden gate into the Suq, locked doors with a low step before them, and so by the colonnaded façade of the mosque to the wooden gate of the qasr. Clay seats in the outer wall of the qasr. I rode along a narrow open way between walls to a second gate which was opened by another slave. There I dismounted and went through a big antechamber divided from the roshan by a clay battlemented screen-wall. This roshan was a very spacious and lofty room, the roof supported by great stone columns covered with jiss—square capitals. The floor of hand beaten jiss almost like marble. Round the wall carpets and cushions. Ibrahim sat before a great oblong m[illegible] in which burned a fire. They all rose and I sat down beside them. The talk followed the safe paths of history. He produced from under the cushions a daftar in which he had written the principal events with their dates in the history of the Reshid. The qasr was begun by the Ibn Ali with whom the Reshids disputed, the shikhah Abdullah father of Muhammad completed the outer wall. The interior was built bit by bit. The Shammar are not of one jidd but the Ja'far, to whom the Rashid belong come from the Qahtan from near Yemen. They took their Nejd dirah kesb. He spoke of an old masalla with hills about 4 hours from the town. They say they found small round stones munaqqash about 4 days from here on the Derb Zubaidah and from the description they sound like cuneiform. Meantime, slave boys brought us glasses of tea and sweet lemons to squeeze into them—then most excellent coffee. Ibrahim said Bander had no son he had a daughter—but 7 brothers in all. Naif only left a son. Finally the slaves brought censors [sic] with burning 'ud and swung them 3 times in the face of each of the company. With this I rose and went back through the dark streets. I tipped each of the doorkeepers 2 reals and Hasan, 'Id and another who was with me 4 reals. Hasan and 'Id were also mulabbis. They sat for a little in F's tent drinking coffee and so to bed.

Sat Feb 28 [28 February 1914]

Turkiyyeh came again. I sat with her in the morning and she told me all her history. She was the daughter of a Circassian soldier who divorced her mother. They went back to the mother's home, but the grandmother—God send her to the fire—hated the mother and drove her out or else made their life a burden. Turkiyyeh strayed away with a little brother on her shoulder and was picked up by some people she didn't know who they were, who carried them to "Brussa" and sold them. She never saw the brother again. His name was Mustafa and on his right foot he had one toe twisted over another—she twisted her own beautiful toes to show me—and she was always looking for one called Mustafa with toes like that. She was sold to C'ple and travelled 6 days to get there. They landed at night and she was put onto a mule and taken to the house of an old woman. There she remained till she was nearly of marriagable [sic] age and was then sold again. She was taken down to a ship and told it was merely to see the sight and then left there and carried off by Arab men whose speech she did not understand. She slept on deck—al 'odab[?] ghali—and knew not a soul. They were quarantined 25 days somewhere in a quarantine station and the people who died on the ship were taken up and pitched into the sea. They arrived at Jedda [Jiddah] and she was taken to a house for the night and then sent up to Medina. There she was 2 years in the Sherif's house as serving maid to one of his daughters—her mother was a Circassian and they all employed Circassian maids as being more trustworthy. She never went out and never saw bait al rasul, sall allahu 'alaihi wa salam. But in the summer they went up to Tayyif [al-Taif]. She then passed into the hands of an old woman whom she called al Haidiyyeh, very rich and important, and went with her to Mecca. The Haidiyyeh told her that she wished to marry her to her adopted son, a Persian boy who was with them and would load her with jewels. She always eat with the Haidiyyeh and was made much of. With him T. fell in love at first sight and kayyift at the prospect. They then travelled on to Nejd and when they got there they all lodged in a sawah[?] on the outskirts of the town and an agent of the Amir came down to see the Haidiyyeh. T. did not know if there was a previous arrangement between them but when she saw the man she began to suspect something. She was taken away screaming and wailed all the way through the suq. "Oh wah wah these Arabs! they are all Arabs with lay qurun and bare feet, wah wah." And the Persian boy ran after her wailing. When she reached the qasr she refused to enter and for the first few days she refused to eat (with her fingers). She said well she wd stay a week. Then she was told that the Amir wanted her and she wd stay with them and become a Mashmeh and remain always and go out into the gardens and eat of the best. Finally Muhammad came to her and told her she was his daughter and he wd take care of her. She loved him and said there was none like him. No other has ever had her. She said that in his day they were all at rest but now when the Amir was away raiding they all feared attack. Each of the women has a jariyyah, but the shaikhat have 10 and 15. They have quantities of jewels—the necklace she wore when she first came to see me belongs to them. Fatima rules them all—she is very clever and can read and write. Mudi is ghashimeh taht ammha. They do absolutely nothing all day. She was made a wahabiyyeh and she can read and write. She prays the 5 prayers. In Ramazan the night prayer begins at 5 Arabic ["10 or so" written above] and goes on in summer till 10 and in winter till 11—however tired you may be and if your head aches and your body aches and your legs ache, pray you must. They then eat before dawn, sing the dawn prayers and sleep. In the afternoon I photographed her and the roshan and told her things of Europe which she eagerly repeated to Lu.lu.a. She asked me what was the difference between Xians and Moslems—I said the second half of the confession of faith. They begged me to pronounce it and I said the first half. Would I not say the second? I said you could say anything with your lips but not with your heart. I was going out for a walk when I was told that some of the Suhban women were coming to see me. I stayed but they did not come. They sent to say that Sulaiman had said it was past the gharbat al shems. Ibrahim sent 'Id to see me in the evening with a present of [illegible] T. says the people here think of women as dogs and so treat them—not like the Inglis and the Turks. The day that Abd al Aziz fell he was raiding against Ibn Sa'ud and near his country. When he camped his men warned him to set guards and not to sleep or light fires and he refused to listen saying that Ibn S. dared not attack him. They came into camp and killed sheep, feasted and slept. In the middle of the night the enemy appeared. When they saw Ibn S. upon them they still dared not wake the Amir. At last one went and touched his foot, he woke and still refused to believe. Then when the foe was actually among them he leapt to his horse, rode to a standard which he thought was his own, but it was Ibn Sa'ud's. His voice was recognized and he was slain[?].

MARCH 1914

Sun March 1. [1 March 1914]

Ibrahim sent me a mare today and at the same time returned my present to him and Zamil. He sent the khazneh dar to ask if they were from me or from Alu Qasim; a few moments later a woman appeared with them in a basket. I rode out to his garden which was full of flowering plums, almonds and apples, and then round the walls of the town. Only the Luddeh and Samah quarters are walled. When I came in discussed the situation with Abu Q. lunched and sat for a time with Lu.lu.ah. All the men were invited to dinner by Ali's relations—by special consent of Ibrahim! They came back about 5.30. It was very hot and stuffy, thundery—and by dinner time I had a headache and went to bed early, but not to sleep. Turkiyyeh sent her 'abdeh with some naranj and a citron. I read the whole of Acts in the afternoon and felt at home with the sensible Romans confronted by Paul and at home with him too.

Mon. March 2. [2 March 1914]

Wind and dust, a little rain. I discussed plans with the men then went to the Roshan and wrote out my road. The slave women came in by ones and twos and chattered softly, finally I sent them away. They went with many a ba'd hayyeh! Ravens fly about on samah[?] and great rakhihams which have a cry like a kite. At night a little owl cries softly. Yesterday I was wakened by a cock crowing near my tent—a very feeble crow of a very small cock we had bought. I subsequently eat him and he was very tough. His crow was the best part of him—it sounded so homelike in this savage place. Before sunrise and at night I hear Salih chanting the prayers—with a very beautiful soft and sweet voice. Salim wonders at the devout manner of their praying and says that in Dam. many a man will interrupt his prayers to answer a question and go on Bisinellah al rahman [illegible] But if you make so much as a gesture out of place the whole prayer is nought. Abu Q. came in having seen Ibrahim and talked to Fatima, she veiled. They both say they have no knowledge of my money and it is clear they won't give it up. I have just £T40, enough if Ibrahim lets us go. I am to see him tonight. An anxious day—khair inshallah! ma gesir illa khair. Salim thinks our marriage customs hard—if the woman has no children or inkaseraf that the man may not take another wife. But he looks upon the Nejd seclusion as barbarous and thinks death were better. Fattuh made answer "You think only of the men in this matter. Divorce is hard on the woman." "Eh wallah" said Salim. Fatima seems to be the power behind the throne here but I don't suppose she will see me. At 5.30 came 'Ali with good help. His uncles here are from 'Anezah and the Rashids are in great need of their assistance. For Ibn Sa'ud has sent word to Boraidah and 'Anezah that he intends to go raiding—when [where?] not mentioned—and wants their aid. The arms from C'ple are to be entrusted to 'Ali's uncles who are to lead an expedition against 'Anezah. The doors will be opened to them and they will slay the Slaim Abd al Aziz ibn al Slaim— the Amirs of 'Anezeh. 'Ali's uncles are very indignant at the treatment which has been accorded to me and have already spoken to Ibrahim. All is, they say, from the hand of the kelbeh Fatima. 'Ali suggests that one or more of his uncles should come to the Barzan tonight when I interview Ibrahim and I have jumped at the idea. [line of Arabic characters] Ali's uncles are called Salih al Haiya ["Ihaya" written above] and Hamad from 'Anezah. I need not say that they did not come but Ibrahim was very civil. We went past the Meshab—they sit under the mosque gallery in the morning and in the shadow of the wall in the afternoon—and after we had passed through the inner door we went upstairs to a small roshan with 2 columns, square capitals with dog tooth. Here we sat and Ibrahim came presently. We talked first of rumours from the Amir, that he is E. of Jof. Then I discussed the matter of the presents—which we brought back with us—and the money. Concerning which I. said he had no information. Subsequently when I told him I intended to go, he said the rafiq would be ready. Then we talked of other matters. He said the Shammar have been here more than 200 years and less than 500. They find no old birs round about Hayyil. Before the Shammar were established here there was no govt of any kind. I tipped the doorkeepers of the outer gate, the gate in the suq. The building stone is brought from under Samra.

Tues. March 3. [3 March 1914]

Ali went early into the town and reported that his uncle had seen Ibrahim this morning and had sent him to Fatima. I sent him and F. and M. al M. into the town to see about calling in the camels. I sat with the men and made Salih tell me the story of the defeat of Abd al Aziz. It was somewhere wara al Qasun, 8 days they took to return walking; it is 5 days on the dulul. They had raided and spoiled the Mtair who sent to Riyad and suggested to Ibn Sa'ud that they should combine against Ibn Rashid. He accordingly marched out with them and Ibn Rashid did not believe that he wd come against him. They camped, as I said before, and he insisted against all counsel in resting that night—in the jellad near the Nefud. They killed and eat and slept. In the night they heard the sound of people, horses. They rose and told Abd al Aziz who refused to believe. Katbthab he said. "Shubb al nar." They made up the fires and this was their undoing for the foe saw them and shot at them. A. al A. then jumped up and cried them to horse. With a handful of slaves he rode forward against the enemy crying Ana akhu Nara—this is the battle cry of the Rashid and is also used by the slaves of their house. (The Shammar cry Khail al Rahman San'us. The Twail: Khail wa hadla Tawaili.) They heard his voice and knew him. He was pierced by a spear and fell from his horse. They brought the news to Ibn Sa'ud who was himself some hours behind. He refused to believe till they showed him A. al A.'s ring. The Qusman cut off his head and carried it round the Qasim to show that he was really dead. They knew it for his face was fair and he had a long beard and moustaches. Ibn Sa'ud buried his body. His men had been surrounded—they took us from behind—and in the night they cd not see. It was the will of God said Salih. As soon as the Arabs heard that A. al A. was dead they broke and dispersed and the Hayyil men left everything and fled mostly on foot. Rain today and thunder. The wife of Sa'id, a slave of Muhammad, came to see me, a pretty graceful negress with a soft sweet voice. She and Sa'id were with Saud in Medina 6 or 7 years, some say 6 years, and some 7 she said. She wore European clothes then. Here she returned to the dark purple green hehmeed[?] women's robe and the orange inner robe. Abdallah ibn al Jullul asked for 1000 camels to fetch the stuff from Medain Salih and got only 400. A camel carries 50 rifles without ammunition. But all the 1000 loads may not be arms. They say he is going to carry the stuff to Taimah by relays and subsequently in the summer, when the Arabs are in their summer places, bring it to Hayyil. Sa'id told a [illegible] story last night. He was going into the Great Mosque at Dam. and at the gate he met a woman with a baby. She begged him to hold it while she went in to fetch her husband. He took it and wrapped it in his abba. She did not return. Then came one of the mosque people, very angry and said every day he brought a baby to the mosque and this was the third and now he shd take it away with the two others which were accordingly handed over to him. And off he went with the 3 in his abba. He went back to his father and related the tale. "You are in bad luck," said Faris "what do you intend to [illegible]?" "We belong to God and to him we return" said S. "I must go and find a woman who will nurse them." So he went down to the suq and sought out a friend who told him of a woman. He fetched the babies—and whether bint or walad he did not know—and went off to the woman, hiding them in his cloak like rabbits. He knocked at the door but fearing to show them all at once he did not open his cloak. Then he went in and explained the matter—there was a woman who had died in their house and this was the baby, wd she nurse it? And with that he opened his cloak and there they were like rabbits. But the other 2 he said wd she take for only one day till he found somewhere to place them. She agreed and they fixed on a price and he went out to buy her semneh and meat so that she might eat and have milk. When he returned he was sitting in the house and there was a knock at the door. She said it was her husband who wd kill and murder her if he found Sa'id there. So they wrapped the babies in a qatifa and him she bade to sit upon the bed and hung a sadajeh in front of him. It was not the husband, but a neighbour and another and another followed Said sitting there from the duhr till the 'asr. Then at last came the husband and said he was tired and had fever and bade her prepare the farsheh. She said she had washed it and hung it up to dry on the roof. But he strode across the room pulled down the sadajeh and found Said wrapped in his abba and holding it before his eyes. The man stood amazed and S. cried out "Not I only! there is another in that sauduq[?] and another wrapped in the Qatifa. The man turned round to look and S. jumped up and ran out of the house. "And afterwards?" said I. "Wallah ya sitt the rest of the tale is unknown to me. They constantly bring children and leave them in the mosques where they are brought up and taught trades."

Wed. March 4 [4 March 1914]

News has come through Arabs that Ibn Sha'lan retreated east before Ibn Rashid and the latter took Jof without a shot fired. 'Ali says that the Ruwalla did not wish Ibn Sha'lan to hold Jof as it is a constant source of dispute. At 11 came Sa'id al Muhammad the 'abd and Muhammad [space left blank] and said I could not go till news came from the Amir. I replied that I was sated with Hayyil and wished for the road. That I asked of Ibrahim nothing but a rafiq. Said said Ma yesir. I then went down and called up M al M and 'Ali and the conversation was repeated. I reiterated my request for a rafiq and they their refusal. They then left and I sent 'Ali to his uncles to find out what was in their mind. He returned with his cousin 'Abdallah ibn Muhammad (Muhammad was killed by the Sa'ud faction in 'Anezeh.) Ali came to F.'s tent and said his uncles were of opinion that the talk meant nothing but politeness. I hope it may be so. I then went and talked to Abdallah. He said 'Anezeh was founded in his grandfather's time. Some shepherds were pasturing their flocks there and a goat scratched up the soil and water was found. The town is called after the 'anz. At 6 came a man and an invitation from the Harem. I dined and went through the moonlit streets. We turned to the left from the qasr gate and I was greeted by Turkiyyeh, who took me into a big roshan where I found the mother of Sa'ud, Mudi who was married to Muhammad before she married Abd al Aziz. A very pretty woman, in a gown of

Indian brocade and a black scarf over her head. Sa'ud's two boys, much bejewelled, dressed in Indian brocades, with wondering big kohl blackened eyes, were brought to see me. Also a small sister with ropes of uneven pearls hanging from her cap. A very pretty girl, one of Sa'ud's wives, very shy; dressed in brilliant brocades with a gold embroidered scarf over her head. An old sister of Abd al Aziz also and the other Circassian, younger and prettier than Tukiyyeh. Lots of other women, one very elaborately dressed and jewelled may have been another wife of Sa'ud's. Turkiyyeh, sitting before me, was Tarjman. We had tea and coffee, sweetmeats—those I bought!—with sweet lemons and citrons and pomegranates. Then more coffee. They asked me to repeat some of the Injil in English and I recited Blessed are the pure in heart and translated. Then Turkiyyeh took me into a little inner garden, with a citron and lemons hanging over a tank. So back and took my leave after the 'ad. I was then taken into the roshan of Sa'ud where I found M al M and Sa'id the eunuch. There is a band of entrelac and inscriptions high up on the wall, worked in juss and painted brown and white. So through a court where there were 4 small cannon to see Muirah, widow of Hamud and wife of Sa'ud. She has a small son and there was with her the small son of Mit'ab. Turkiyyeh came here too. Muirah is also pretty, round faced. So home. The whole scene was exactly like the Arabian Nights. The big roshans all carpeted, the women in their brilliant clothes, the slave girls and a few slave boys. The great columned rooms have a considerable splendour of size and space.

Thurs. March 5. [5 March 1914]

Negotiations as to my departure continue. M. al M. went to Hamud this morning and he is to see Ibrahim. Meantime the camels have not yet come. Mudi sent a jariyyub with apologies and excuses and hopes that when the Amir returned I wd visit them by day. I replied with salaams that I was leaving. Fellah suggested that if I wanted money I should sell him! The supply of slaves is small nowadays. They come from Mecca and Jeddah [Jiddah, Jedda]. A good slave girl used to be bought for 200 reals, now you cannot buy a bad one for 500 says Lu.lu.ah. A slave boy, his mother and small sister fetched a thousand reals. After dinner came Turkiyyeh and I told her of all my difficulties. She is married to 'Ubaid al Gharamil who is brother to the standard bearer of the Hajj. M. al Rashid gave her a house and married her to 'Ubaid 2 years before his death. 'Ubaid divorced his wife and has not taken another except when he was 6 years away with Abd al Aziz in Qasim he married a woman there and divorced her before he left and Turkiyyeh never saw her. She and the daughter by the first wife and a slave girl live alone in the house. She is very happy except that of the 7 children she has had 6 died at birth and one a year after. She has been 19 years married and boasts of its being a long time, whereas other women have been married and divorced many times. There was a rumour that Fatima wd send for me, but T. said it was untrue.

Fri. March 6 [6 March 1914]

She sent her 'abdeh in the morning with a gift of leben and a warning not to speak too much of my departure. Ali al Hamud sent word as T. [Turkiyyeh] had told me, to invite me to a garden at an hour after noon. I went and found him and his elder brother M. or rather I found first a number of small boys, sons of various Suhhans, and also Mit'ab's son, all dressed in Indian brocades (the Zabun), and gold embroidered farmaliyyehs and white khaffas woven with many colours. Next came the two Hamud boys with Sa'id al Muhammad the euneuch and Muhammad ibn Shomar[?] who was once wahil in Dam. and a party who afterwards proved to be the Hayyil doctor (he said he wd like to go to Beyrout to study). The boys hung up their abbas and swords and we all sat on carpets in the garden house and drank tea and coffee and eat fruits and sweets. I then expressed my wishes with regard to the money and my journey and was met with polite refusals until the arrival of the bashir. We then all walked about the garden, the small children walking solemnly in their long brilliant robes. The two elder boys talked a little; the younger 'Ali has a merry boyish face unlike all the other solemn countenances. I asked them what they did and one of the abds replied that they sat in state reception all the morning as became shaikhs. We then sat down again and drank more tea and coffee till near the 'asr, when I rose and went. Sa'id al M. came with me and I again expressed my wishes. He and Muham. ibn Shomar came to us after prayers and I talked to them again. When they left they told M. al M. that I would not leave till the bashir arrived. The camels came in with Sayyif and the old 'Abdullah who had been pasturing them. After dinner Sa'id and Muhammad came back with the money and full permission to go when I liked. So all had ended well!

Sat. March 7 [7 March 1914]

Took an azimuth and made preparations for departure. At 11 came a man and permission to see the qasr. I lunched and went off with F., M. al M, Salim, Fellah and Mustafa. Much excitement in the streets but so far as I cd see no ill will. In the little market place the Beduin women were selling milk and butter and semneh. I was received at the qasr by Sa'id, who did not look pleased and a pale faced man with sore eyes whose name I do not know. He it was who took me round the Modif and allowed me (even encouraged me) to photograph. We went through the great gate into a little court with inscrips and entrelac, columned on 3 sides, and the walls with a rude band of frescoes, ships[?], 4 or 5 very antiquated pieces of artillery in it (before the time of Mohammad they said) into the kahwah columned too, where were the largest dallals I ever saw. The kahwaji has a little enclosed place to himself, against the wall, where he made us coffee, for the big hearth was cold. Then we went down a long passage to the left of the gate, between high walls but not roofed into another court with

3 or 4 more cannon, and so into the Modif court, in 2 storeys, columned all round. Below and above rooms for guests and the great dishes for meat and rice hung on the walls. At the farther end was the kitchen, its columns and roof black with smoke. The huge cooking pots, 2 of them big enough to boil a camel, stood raised on stones against the wall and along 2 sides the Saj for bread making. There is a slave to each saj. At one end the women were pounding taman[?] and singing as they worked. The dull reds or oranges of their robes splendid against the smoke black columns. Beyond the kitchen is a tiny open court with a water basin in it. The water is pumped in by a suwani outside. So back to the Modif court where I photographed and upstairs where we were brought dates and fresh butter. The balustrade of the gallery and also the roof are garnished with the usual battlement motive. Here the Arab shaikhs are lodged. Then back to the gate. The extraordinary beauty of the gate doorway with the slaves in their richly coloured cotton robes standing in it. I photographed outside, the Mashab and the mosque colonnade and then came in and had coffee in the Modif. The little Muhammad son of Tellal sat by me. As I walked away there came an invitation from Turkiyyeh. I went to her house with F. and M. al M. and 'Atullah and was received with enthusiasm. She apologized for the smallness of her house after the qasr. I said it was the house of my sister. Inside the door was a tiny kahwa (she said it was the house of a woman—her husband receives his friends in the kahwah of his family's house—and then a court with a naranj and a citron growing in it—the fruit hung like big jewels. Out of this opened the room in which we sat. The bedroom to one side. Above this room was an upper roshan opening onto an open court and we went upstairs onto its roof and looked over Hayyil. The women sitting on their roofs came in to see me and little Muhammad whom I photographed. Ya ba'd haiyyu[?]! said T. why do you come in clothes like a bedawi. You should wear shaikhs' clothes and a sword. She said she had gone to Mudi and Fatima and told all my tale and they said was that all? To which she replied that there was nothing else in my mind. Thereupon they let me go. When I got back to my house I went outside the town and photographed from the inscribed rock. A crowd of little boys, all very friendly. Singular beauty of Hayyil in the afternoon light, standing in the flat plain of clean grit, with the gardens about it and the rocky peaks of 'Ajah beyond. At night I paid off my men and then sat with Lu.lu.ah Mabrukah and 'Atullah and drank tea in the dim kahwah, the columns lost in blackness.

Sun. March 8. [8 March 1914]

Off at 9. As soon as I was up came 'Uthman (the slave with henna dyed beard and heavily painted furtive eyes—a sinister looking man.) I found him in the roshan with my rafiq Mashkhur ibn Ghazi of the 'Abdeh, the tribe to which the Rashid belong, and Ali. He brought a message to say I was not to go by Dubaib on account of danger but by Haiyyaniyyeh [al-Hayyaniyah] and Gaitanah. I replied that all roads

Qasr Azraq. Rebuilt entrance to second-century A.D. *Roman fort with twelfth-century Arabic inscription above doorway. Photograph by Gertrude Bell.* Courtesy of the University of Newcastle upon Tyne.

were the same and when he had gone told Ali that the road was biyaq[?] as soon as we got out of Hayyil. 'Uthman came back on a mare to see me out of the town. Ali has gone away to buy tobacco and take leave of his uncles. I left his dulul for him and went taking an affectionate farewell of M al M, Salim, Sa'id and Mustafa—they had all begged from me this morning but Salim to whom I had already given a revolver. It was a shining morning. A wonderful mirage hung over the palm gardens and the gorge of 'Ajah wherein lies 'Uqbeh. The air light and clear. In spite of the imprisonment I carry away a deep impression of the beauty and charm of it all—the dustlessness, the silence, with no wheeled vehicles, only the pad of the camels in the soft grit, or of donkeys. Yesterday a caravan came from Medina—I saw the camels straggling in through the town gate. So off with F., Fellah and Sayyif—8 camels in all. Rode round the walls of the town, along the narrow gorge between the two samras—here the gardens are unwalled and passed Swaifly which is now ruined and uninhabited. Nothing but ithl trees. N. of the ruins are two new walled-in jellibs which the Amir has given to some Meshhadi but no cultivation. Before Swaifly we turned aside from the Buq'a [Baq'a] road which was my true way. At Swaifly 'Uthman left us and we rode on over the plain. 'Ali did not appear and at 12 I began to grow anxious and Mashkhur opined that he did not know the way. Also I found we were not making for [space left blank] which was our trysting place. We rode on till we saw its palms and then searched all round for Ali through my glasses. Under 'Ajah the sarrah made it difficult to see clearly. Mashkhur got onto F's camel and rode back to Hayyil! F. walked to a tell whence he saw 'Ali and fired a rifle shot. We sat still, now knowing. At length I went to the tell and saw F in his white robes walking to the village. There he found Ali who rode out to us. We camped about a mile from the village and 2 hours later Mashkhur came back from the Shuyukh. He is a native of the village and went to see his family. He returned after dark with a little daughter whom he frequently embraced, a lamb and some butter and leben. A slave also brought us some fodder for the tired camel. Our tents are under a low sandstone rock. Delicious soft fresh night. Mashkhur is cousin on the mother's side to al Hailam and very like him. All the Sanad[?] are like that said M al M—lightheaded.

Mon. March 9. [9 March 1914]

Maskhur came back from the village with the new loads. Another shining morning. 'Ajah looking at dawn but we did not get off till 6, the men being unskilful wonderful with the low sun on its back rocks. The plain covered with thin grass, looking quite green in front. The camels went pretty well. The lamb walked for a bit and then rode in Sayyif's arms and slept. My bearing was between Humaimi and Jelf. At about 10 we met 3 camel riders, one clothed in scarlet. They were the bashirs from the Amir. He has taken Jof and Shkaka [Sakakah] without a shot fired. Some friendly Shammari warned the Dughmi (W. Ali) who was camped near and he fled off to

Nawwaf who also fled, he and Nuri N and E towards Palmyra [Tadmur]. Jof was left empty except for the town folk and Sa'ud walked in. He has now gone E and lies between Haizal and Haiyyaniyyeh—on the road they mean me to take. The messengers bore salutations to me and one wanted to turn back with us—to show me the road and the water, but Ali dissuaded him since his camel was worn out. Near the hills there were some Meshhed Arabs camped—B. Hasan. Jelf and Humaimi are a continuous line of low sandstone rocks; we rode through them in about ¼ of an hour. On the further side were some Shammar encamped, to whom we gave the news from the Amir which they had not heard. We dropped down into a dry khabra and camped in the higher ground on the opposite side. Enough 'aishb for the camels. On the way we broke to Mashkhur my intention to go to Dubaib. He was much agitated, fearing to disobey the direct order of the Shuyukh. I said I had told Ibrahim. He said the order was not from him but from Fatima. Ali then spoke with a silken tongue. Arabs all the way, the world rabi', no khauf inshallah, my bounty wd be increased. Finally Mashkhur was persuaded. And I tonight have the true freedom of the desert and rejoice therein. The lamb was killed. F. took what we wanted and 'Ali broke up the rest, and boiled it, innards and all, in our biggest tanjarah[?]. So we are all mabsutin bil hail! Mashkhur relates when 'Abd al Aziz was killed Sultan was at Jof. He returned (and married Mudi bil gharb) He, Sa'ud and Faysal plotted against Mit'ab. They all rode out to Fitiq (eh) to hunt. The Amir and his brothers and Tellal rode on with 3 sons of Hamud (at their suggestion) to look for a good camping ground. The 3 rode behind and with them one more. Each picked his man and shot. They then brought the slaves and slew the living over the bodies of the dead. Sa'ud (the present Amir) was spared for his mother Mudi's sake (bint Subhan). Mudi bint Hamud, mother of the 3 sons of Abd al Aziz who were killed, was on pilgrimage at Medina and died of grief. Sultan and Sa'ud his brother presently fell out. Sultan was of a bad and unpopular nature. They agreed that he should go to Taimah and be wahil there leaving Sa'ud as shah. He went and with him a company of 800. As soon as he was gone the khazneh dar informed Sa'ud that he had taken all the treasure. Sa'ud summoned the townspeople to the number of 2000 (this must be an exaggeration) rode after him, caught him at Mogug and slew him. Then Hamud al Subhan slew Sa'ud, entering the palace and taking him there. Whereat he brought back the little Sa'ud from Medina. Al Bariyyeh mulkna said 'Ali today.

Tues March 10 [10 March 1914]

I gave up the idea of Dubaib having come to the conclusion that the stones were fossils! We were off early, just after sunrise and watered at a khabra. We put the Gulban of Taiyim a little to the right. Flocks of black sheep and Shammari shepherds. On the farther side of the level bottom in which are the gulban we entered the Nefud and travelled along a well marked khall which we only left once when we missed our way. The Nefud a garden of flowering weeds, often white with daisies. Nothing else but 'irta (not yet green) and 'adir. Where we camped there was a little dry subat and hammat. Towards midday the gu'urah became rather large and in the afternoon there were a few tu's. 'Ali was 18 years with the post, taking jobs with merchants when they presented themselves. At first the postman was paid 28 mej a month but as the road became more known the pay lessened. For caravans from Baghdad to Dam. he would get from £10 to £20, varying with the size of the caravan. Every tent paying so much. Twaiyyeh ('Atwa on the map) is now they say to the S.E. of us and Hamatiyyeh to the NE. The Shammar call Sirius al Sha'ri, the name I have heard before; but the Harb call him al Mirzim. Al Miyazin is the t[illegible] name for Orion: the Arabs call him al Jozeh. Mashkhur knew also Ṣhail or Sḥail—Canopus or Jupiter? and Aldebaran as [space left blank].

Wed. March 11. [11 March 1914]

We got off very early, before sunrise and went on our way by the khall. Innumerable tu'us to the right called the Mejlis and in the middle of the morning the Nefud rather big, but nothing like the deep gu'urah of the W. side. The horseshoes here point S. We saw locusts flyings and hawks (bashiq (eh)) eating them. 'Ali much wanted to hunt some for roasting. He says they are like prawns. At 10.45 the Nefud grew much smaller, with patches of jelad between the sand banks. Also the pasturage better; hammat and sabat greening and plenty of white and yellow daisies besides the purple silih. We caught sight of the Um[?] dulla al Jibelli which lies E. of Haiyaniyyeh before we camped. Marched well today. Mashkhur has been to Mashhad with the bairek of the Hajj. He and 'Ali talked today of the Amir's bairek and Mashkhur declared that the Amir's followers round it reached for a day's journey before and behind. Last night we talked of express trains and how they passed through mts. Mashkhur opined that they must be better than the babord of the Sultan and asked why we did not give him such. We talked also of aeroplanes and wireless telegraphy and Mashkhur called upon his God at my reports. Fellah. Tel and telephones I believe for I have seen them with my eyes, but the tel without khait that I cannot believe. I said messages might be passing over our heads at that moment. 2 Sinjara passed the night with us coming from the Amir and going to fetch kiswa from Hayyil. They talked of the taking of Jof and of the Ruwalla. "I take refuge in God" said the elder man, lifting up his hand. "They are our enemies. They took 20 of our maidens." I subsequently asked 'Ali what he meant. He said when Nuri took Jof he slew a number of the inhabitants and destroyed their houses and carried off some of their daughters. The Amir has this time slain noone but his people have eaten their crops and plundered a good deal. I observed that the Jofiyyin have no fun either way. "They are between the devil and the jinn" said Ali. Mashkhur calls to prayer every sunset and

Fellah gets up and joins him. I hear his call to prayer at dawn. They kneel down first and wash their hands in sand but he does not take off his abba.

Thurs March 12 [12 March 1914]

Grey today and pleasantly chilly. We rode through smallish Nefud till we got to Hayaniyyeh where there is a qasr over the well. It was built by 'Abdullah, Muhammad's father. It is rectangular with 2 towers, the higher over the well. One of the battlements of this tower was wrapped round with rags to make it look like a head keeping guard. There are 2 heavy wooden doors faced with iron. In each tower there is a ground floor room where the well keeper lives with his family. If he sees a gomani of Ibn Rashid he shoots and prevents his drawing water. The well is 25 ba' (50 paces) deep. We had seen locusts in the morning; Sayyif and Mashkhur had caught and roasted them. The well keeper brought out 3 large dishes full of locusts fried in semneh and my men carried off great handfuls. He gave us also leben. Mashkhur Ahubb al jarrad. Ahubb hal tuyur. We had met a camel rider in the morning who told us the Amir had rahal eastwards. We crossed a wide strip of jalad and came again into very shallow Nefud, through which we rode for an hour. Then another strip of jalad and then more shallow Nefud. Plentiful 'aishb and 'arfej. Three swallows flew with us—I saw one 2 days ago. Ali and Mashkhur gave me some more battle cries. The slaves of Ibn Rashid: Khayyal al Khail! wa ana 'abd al Shuyukh! Or those not slaves: Wa ana fada'wi al Shuyukh. Ibn Sa'ud: Khayyal al khail! wa ana Ibn Mijled. The universal Shammar cry is Khayyal al Rahundu w'al San'asi. Al Sana'is! The Tuman: Al gala'i ya Tuman. Ibn Sha'lan: Khayyal al 'alya wa ibn Naif (and those upon [illegible]?) Ibn Smair: ('Anazeh) Fahad al zeraq wa ana akhu 'Adrah. Muhtefig: al mansha'[?] (i.e. Mecca) walad al Sherif. Because they are Ashraf. Agail (i.e. Qusman): Wahad[?] 'Ali! Hasan al Muhanna, shaikh of Boraida: Khayyal al khail wa ana akhu Khussa. Ibn Hadhdhal: Ana akhu Batla. Said 'Ali, [illegible] Sayyif, what is the cry of the Sherarat? Sayyif: Yakhtaru kul wahid 'ala ukhthu.

Friday March 13 [13 March 1914]

We continued our extremely boring way across the low sandhills of the Dehannah [al-Dahna]. Although it is not called Nefud the flora is that of the Nefud and not of the Hamad. Lots of 'alga with their black flowers. We passed a small jubb with a rijm over it and came down a slope called al Rabdeh into the open sandy flats of the Dechach (Deqaa'). Here we saw some flocks and were told by the herdsman that we were going too much N. Finally we got out of the sand into the jalad of the Hejarrah. Stock, mignonette, several kind of dandelions and many other small unknown flowers. The ground was rolling here and gathering into shallow wadis full of 'arfej. We saw some tents and herds of the Abdeh (Ibn 'Ajel, who is khal of Abd al Aziz al Rashid) and camped in the rising ground beyond. A boy came to us and gave us news that the Amir had had a message from Ajemi ibn Sa'dun asking him to help him in raiding the Mtair and the Duffir and has gone off east to the burak of the derb Zubaideh and probably further east. The men who camped with us were very likely being sent to Hayyil to gather forces for this raid. We marched 9¼ hours today. A little rain last night and a few drops this morning but the clouds luckily held up. It's still cloudy tonight.

Sat. March 14 [14 March 1914]

Went on over the rolling ground seeing camels and herdsmen at long intervals. Our course was W. of N. on account of water. At 9.10 the ground was sandy. They call this Nefud though it is quite hard, the Aqrab is its name. There are 2 nazis (nazitani) explained Mashkhur called the Ajarib. We must have been in this ground for about 2 hours. Then we came out into Hamad again, the Dehannah which reaches up to the Batn. At 12.20 we reached 2 Abdeh tents where a shaikh called Khanus gave us milk and was very anxious that we should stay to dine, our camels should rest and feed and ghabab[?] ash Shems. We gave him tobacco. He walked on with us some way directing us to the Jelta water in the W. al Khadd [Wadi al-Khadd]. He wanted to go back, get his mare (rachib hal faras) and bring us a dabihah. He had been with the Amir at Jof. There was some resistance for the Shammar lost 5 men. They took kiswa of dates, 'aish etc. We came into camp at 3.15 in a tributary valley of the Khabb, full of grass and flowering weeds, daisies etc. Also gaisum and ghutba—the flora of the Hamad as 'Ali pointed at. Near us is a favourite camping ground of Muhammad's with a mesjid laid out in big stones, the S side and the mihrab. Hard by the rectangle of the coffee fire. Mashkhur was with 'Abd al Aziz when he was killed. When he rushed out against the enemy he cried Al bariah, jib al bariah wa ana akhu Nura. And some say that the 'abaid of Sultan killed him as he stood in the light of the fire, for they say that when Mit'ab was killed the 'abaid said We slew thy father and now we slay them. Sultan shot Mit'ab, Sa'ud Tallal and Faysal Mish'al. Sultan was unwilling to undertake the shooting of the Amir but Sa'ud said whoever kills Mit'ab, he will be Amir. Muhammad was at Hayyil. He took refuge with Hamud (ana dakhilak). Then Sultan said "What do the people say? And they answered "That Muhammad is shaikh. They do not want the sons of 'Abaid." Thereupon he slew him. He had been in the Jebel Druze [Jabal al-Duruz] fleeing from Abd al Aziz who wd have killed him. A al A was mazyun and mahbib, but the 8 years war in the Qasim ruined everyone. The camels had jarrab and the men were kept away from their tents and their families. Mashkhur was 10 days getting back to Hayyil. The battle field was to the left of the Qasim, i.e. W. He was with Muhammad when he raided Riyad. It is much bigger than Hayyil and the castle of the shaikhs splendid. Allah mabarak[?] fik. But the hills round are quite low like the hills here—no thullyan. He was rather anxious when he found that the Amir was really behind us and kept repeating what he would say to the shuyukh. He talked of my dirah, of our mines of gold "and we have nothing but this earth and if there is rain we eat and if there is drought we dry up and starve." He caught a hedgehog today, gunfid.

Sun. March 15. [15 March 1914]

Off at 5.40 and got into the W. al Khadd at 6. We marched down it past a marah of Ibn Rashid with the brush wood filed round the place of the tents, there must have been 50 of them, and a mihrab marked out with stones. Just below, at 7.50, we reached the Jeltah, where the valley drew together in a little drop and narrowed between low rocky banks. But we found no water—we marched on down it, by patches of sidr thorns and thick grass till at 9.25 we found a big pool where we watered. We went on by the valley till 10.30 and shortly after we left it, it lost itself in a low bottom and that was the end of it. At 10.35 the jelib of al Raq'ah lay to the right. There are several other gulban here to the right, exactly where I do not know. They are all called generally[?] al Hazlan. We went on over flat and rather stony ground with occasional patches of grass and shih (I saw an iris) till at 12.50 we reached Loqah [Lawqah]. Here there are 3 or 4 wells in use from 15 to 25 ba' deep, the shallowest being in the low ground to the S. There are a great number of other wells madfun. It is a summering place of the Shammar. A masjid marked out by the wells. Beyond it we came into a land of very low banks and at 3.15 camped near some Sinjara. It was hot in the afternoon; a tedious day but we covered a good deal of ground. Last night Mashkhur observed that he had been to Medinah and he had been with the shuyukh but no one had ever informed him that there existed anyone like has sitt. He wd return to the shuyukh and he wd have a great deal to say. He wd say Oh Shuyukh you cook your burghul with water but 'and has sitt the burghul is cooked with semen.

Mon. March 16. [16 March 1914]

I paid off Mashkhur giving him 5 mej for camel hire and 5 mej bakhshish over and above the 10 reals which was the shart at Hayyil—these he had received there. The old man, Salim, who had agree to come with me, battal this morning. We engaged a young man called Zaid who went off to get his dulul and never turned up. The Sinjara were rahilin and we all rode off together, horsemen and camels and flocks. One man with a lance. We went off on our way and 2 hours later one of the old men who had sat round our campfire and brought us milk turned up with his brother behind him on the dulul. The brother he deposited with us as rafiq. We rode all day over broken ground, broad flat bottoms separated by low banks. Patches of green grass and yellow flowering weeds of dandelion kind, and the blue grey ajram which has not greened yet, and the blue grey shih. Cold and windy. About 2 we saw tareh[?] ahead and sheered off a little to the left, coming into camp under some banks.

The 'aishb fairly good. The men brought in kamr (chamr) which they toasted over the fire. Our rafiq has innocently told us the true story of Ibn Rashids raid. They reached Skakah [Sakakah]; the people abandoned their houses and took refuge in the qasr. The Shammar pillaged the houses—provisions were all they found for the valuables and the women were in the castle. Did you not take Jof? said I. No he said wa ash shuf ma shufna. Sahih? said I. Egh Wallah. Wallah? said I. Egh Billah. Ali says that Mashkhur was strictly charged to convey me to the Amir. I asked him whether he thought that when in our rafiq's tales "Ibn Rashid" said Ya Shammar—so and so—it was Sa'ud or Zamil? Ali said Zamil, Sa'ud was only the resm[?]. He says his uncles have been offered blood money by Ibn Sa'ud if they will come back to 'Anezeh but they have refused, saying they must have life for life. Their idea is to profit by the Rashid help and arms, to take 'Anezah, and their revenge, send away the Slaim—and then hold 'Anezah under the protection of Ibn Sa'ud. The Rashids have been ruined by their family quarrels says Ali and are on the decline. If it had not been for the support of the Ott. govt. they wd have gone long ago. He told the tale of Ibn Sa'ud's recapture of Riyad. Ibn Sabah offered him 500 men but he asked for 14 only, 2 being his own cousins. They rode out and alighted at Der'aya [al-Diriyah]. Abd al A. and his 2 cousins went alone at night to the town. He climbed on the back of the other 2 who hoisted him over the wall of the qasr into the haram. He knocked at the door. A slave girl sleeping at the door woke and answered. He said "Go fetch 'ammatik." She brought A. al A's wife, Umm Nirah, saying "One knocks at the door." Umm N. came and said Ent min. She feared it might be Ibn Rashid's rajajil. He answered Wa min enti? She said again Ent min? He said None other than Halalik. She opened and fell on his neck. He said this is not the time for kisses and for love, ba'd ain inshallah. Then he called the women and asked them where Ibn Rashid's rajajil lodged and who slept in the qasr. He hauled in his 2 cousins by rope and they crept over the roofs, found the rajajil sleeping, killed the chief man and the others threw up the game. He sent for the remaining jaish, the rest of the 14 and brought them into the qasr. Next morning the town was apprized of the fact that Abd al A had come back and held the qasr and acquiesced in the accomplished fact bit ghasb[?], whether they liked it or not. Ibn Rashid's rajajil, to the number of some 50 were sent away and it was only when all this was done that Ibn Sabah's jaish appeared.

Tues March 17. [17 March 1914]

It froze hard in the night. We rode down into the Batn which is a belt of low ground, but not very low, broken into banks and basms and stretching a great distance. Here we presently were approached by 3 camel riders of the 'Abdeh who came out to know our business. We saw some white Slubbah donkeys in the distance. We were now near the limits of the Shammar and 'Ali was anxious as to our relations with the Ri'u, the Meshhed tribes, who he said, are much worse than the Bedu. Our rafiq

Sa'aiyid ran out and questioned some women who said they were Bedu camping with some of the Ri'u behind us. We rode on and presently dropped into our encampment of Ri'u. At the first tent we passed some women were wailing the dead, their their [sic] arms thrown up to heaven. We met 2 more women who were coming down to the washing. 'Ali stopped and asked whether it were man or woman. A man. Shab or shaiyid. La allah yusallimah, walad tayyib. A man came out of one of the tents towards us. 'Ali greeted him and he returned the greeting, but took 'Ali's gun and bade us come to his tent. Asked what dauleh we belonged to. To the dauleh of M. Rashid said 'Ali. 'Ali said that that was where we were coming. We dismounted and they nowwakhed[?] the camels and while we sat in the tent a man proceeded to rifle my saddle bags. 'Ali protested that that was not zain and he was told to desist. The conversation was at first very uphill. 'Ali said we had come from Hayyil where we had stayed 16 days and had met the Amir in the W. al Khadd and were going on to Meshhed. We wanted a rafiq. The ferij behind us had told us to come on to him and he would give us a rafiq. And why do you not camp in their menzel[?] where the aishb is zain and the fug'u wajid? (Fuqu are kamr) It was the order of the govt. that I shd take a rafiq from every tribe. When he said he came from Baghdad a man replied that the people of Baghdad were gom to them. 'Ali replied rather angrily that if they wanted our loads they had better say so and shalah us. No said the man there has been no rifling[?] yet and Fellah intervened with a word while I said No all we wanted was a rafiq from them upon our road. They then went and talked outside. A green turbaned Sayyid came in and sat by me—he was quite friendly. Finally the atmosphere cleared, but they declare that they daren't go by the straight road because they fear people whom they do not know and could only take us to Sbitza. I tried to get off that moment but 'Ali thought it better to camp with them, which we did after eating dates and semen with the shaikh. They then all repaired to our camp fire and talked. I heard Ali giving them all sorts of false news about the taking of Jof. Ali sang to me the praises of the Muntefiq. They are far more generous than the Rashid. What they undertake always is to pay the price of blood to any man of their people who has had the misfortune to murder someone, and the price of a bride to any who is not rich enough to buy one— shughl muluk, added 'Ali. The Beni Hassan—for that is what they are—sat round my camp fire at night and waited till the lamb was cooked. I made great friends with them, especially with the blue eyed shaikh Jadu'. They gaith round Samawa and they told me of the Warkah [Erech, Uruk] diggings. Jadu' knows Muham. Daghestani and wondered at my intimate acquaintance with men and things.

Wed March 18. [18 March 1914]

Took affectionate leave of Jadu to whom we gave boots and 2 mej with which he was well pleased. Sa'aiyid returned to his people with 4 mej and many mutual blessings and I took as rafiq Mazhir. Another Hassani from the ferik behind joined us on the way out. We went by the derb al 'adleh without a word said of Shbilza! 'Ali observed that his dulul was unable to march today and when I asked why, replied that it was because of the thiql of kithib which she carried! It grew heavier as we went, for the tale of our doings, with still more embroideries (photographs of the Amir and his harem and the Jof story) were told to the other Hasani. Towards the end of the Batn the ground was sandy and the vegetation that of the Nefud—hammat, with pink flowers, alanda, nusi'. Then we crossed a flint strewn ridge at 8.50 and came out onto downs, covered in places with shijar and flowering weeds and grasses. Small red poppies and the little purple horned poppy, stock, daisies etc. At 11 we left to the left a low ridge, the J. Shaikhal, which ran away from us to the SW. Then long stretches of the cup[?] like downs[?]. At 2.30 we came to good 'aishb but rather mistakenly pushed on and fared worse. S. wind and cloud, a heavy scud of rain in the morning. After we came into camp the wind rose and brought the rain with it. Very refreshing. I spent the day in dreams and the evening in anxious thought as to the news which awaits me in Baghdad—good please God. And this rain will probably put an end to our anxieties about water.

Thurs March 19. [19 March 1914]

The rain blew over east and did us no good. When we had been gone an hour we sighted tents and our two rafiqs were in a great perturbation. We stopped and sent one off to see what Arabs they were and he presently returned with 2 horsemen. They were the Beni Salamah, closely akin to the B. Hassan. Our 2 Hasan now left us and we took on the Salamat. We rode by the wide and shallow W. al Hisb [Hasb, Sha'ib] from 9.25 till 11.22 when it went off to the right. It goes they say to the Bahr. The Salamah summer east of Meshhed. In the afternoon the rafiqs began to grow alarmed at the thought of people they did not know and talked of turning back, they said they cd not spend the night with us. Ali answered with soft words—we wd drink coffee and eat together and tomorrow please God they would Gotar[?] in safety on their way and we on ours. At about 2 we sighted sheep and their alarm increased. We debated whether we should camp or look for the tents but shortly after we saw the tents quite near and sent on a khayyal to them while we followed. As soon as we saw him dismount ["howwal" written above] at the tent door and enter into conversation we howwakhed and proceeded to pitch tents. They were the Ghazalat who are the most powerful of the Ri'u and with a rafiq from them I hope we may be in safety. They all came and drank coffee with us including a consumptive Sayyid who wd not turn his eyes on me. F. has prescribed figs, bameh and milk for his complaint, and has provided the figs and bameh. Small blue irises today and flocks of qata'. It was deliciously cold this morning after the rain. These are some of the Ri'u tribes: B. Hasan, B. Salamah, Ghazalat, Da'wa, Zubaid, Buhlail, Lam, Imarah, 'Afej, Bdur, Isar, Ba'amir. One of our rafiqs wore a yellow over a scarlet qumbaz. They all wear white 'ugl, the women and children have silver collars round their necks. When I asked my rafiq whether they had had snow Dennet al thalj he did not know what thalj was. He swore bil Sayyid that Ruhbeh was 3 days off. Much intrigued by my compass which I exhibited to him in camp. He was encouraged by one of the ghazalat to put it to his eye, and when he hesitatingly did so the ghazalah jumped on him to frighten him and all the company laughed.

Fri. 20. [20 March 1914]

Our rafiq is a grave grey bearded man of consideration. His name is Dawi. He has been rafiq to Ibn Rashid's tamman caravans and has been to Hayyil in the dor of Abd al Aziz in a matter of camels. He was, said he, mazyun. Settling matters with him delayed us and we did not get off till 6. I gave my 2 rafiqs 1½ mej. apiece and they complained to 'Ali that I had only given them one. At some outlying tents of the ferih we stopped and Dawi asked news of water. The sleepiest boy in the world was dragged out of slumber—he had been keeping guard over the sheep all night and was sleeping in the sun under his abba. He came up rubbing his eyes and murmuring "Ma ta howwalim? Qahweh." We came to the water at 8.40, al Jawarid, the channels and a shallow bottom with a muddy ghadir which has no outlet. Here we found a member of the Ma'dan filling skins and watering sheep and donkeys, a wild looking lot. Dawi explained our presence and they were very friendly. One said to Dawi Shu isur[?] al rafieh ma'ak? He said Isur ha sittah. If he had not been with us, said 'Ali, we should have had trouble—dabahana. But they stand in awe of the Ghazalat and wd not dare to come out so far camping but for the fact that they are under their wing. The Bedu wd fall upon them. They wore the usual red and yellow qamabiz[?]. The water was muddy and stagnant, with green slime on it. So we rode on over an endless flat country, not quite flat. We crossed another hollow bottom, a sort of wadi, full of trees and good 'aishb. Then we must very gradually have risen to a very small extent, for at 3 we had a low low ridge of banks in front of us. No mar'a. We tried to get across it into the sha'ib, but it was too wide and we came into camp with bad mar'a at 3.45. Al ba'arus nasibhum 'atil says Fattuh. There is a big sort of hemlock leaved plant called Khaishun which they like and a little 'arfej and sparse flowering weeds. And here we are on the 13th day from Hayyil still hanging loose in the desert! Our course was very much east today. The camels smell strongly of green fodder—not nice. We sat round the fire under the stars, Dawi's grave and splendid face in profile as he looked into the embers. I said Al lailahsan min al nahar[?]. He. Wallah ahsan, argah. Faqt al nahar ilhu asbab lil beni adam. Al rahah bit lail said I. Wal safar said he. Remember Khair allah wajid. Alhamdulillah. One of the Duhlail at the water this morning—he had an evil squinting face—offered Dawi 30 liras if he wd leave us. I said some of the Beni Adam were created by Satan not by God. Ai billah said he.

Sat. 21. [21 March 1914]

Off at 5.25 and in an hour came to valleys with good grass and trees—going down to al Hisb. We touched al Hisb at 6.25 and left it at 6.43. It was about ¼ of a mile from us at 7.18 and went off to the right. We crossed it at 10.5, touched it again at 11.55, left it at 12.7. (At 2.5 we were in a side valley going down to Hisb; where it comes in and the road crosses Hisb) We got onto the Qasr al Rubaimi[?] road at 6.25 and followed it till 2.30. Where we left it, it goes on at 58° to the W. al Hisb and crosses it at Hafneh where there were tents and flocks, we learnt. Just before we left the road we met a large qaffl[?] of Ri'u coming from Meshhed. The men surrounded us, coming up from all sides and wd have stripped us of everything. They laid hands on our camels. But Dawi addressed them and one of them knew him. Is that a Sayyid, said he, who has taken hold of the camels rasan? And the man dropped it. We rode on and they asked him where he had brought us from and why he let all that mal pass through. Riding away on the Sayyid road we looked back and saw a large caravan crossing the Hisb. 2 men were observed following us, on donkeys, galloping. We hurried on, crossed a side valley with a horrible water pool, but the bank blue with irises and still hurried on. One man on a donkey still followed us. Finally Dawi was given a rifle and sent back to parley with him. I fear lest he shd fire at me he said. He turned out to be an Arab from the tents at Hafneh who feared we might be a ghazzu. He was much afraid that Dawi wd shoot him. Dawi explained and he turned back. He said to Dawi Ana min ahlah, ana min al Ruwaitat [remainder of sentence largely illegible]. With all this we only came into camp at 4.15 in a shallow sha'ib with a fair amount of 'aishb. When we had left the Ma'dan today Dawi said to 'Ali They wd not have let you pass—wala'in 'Audi khabar said 'A Ana ibn[?] al 'Iraq. It for [illegible] as we sat round the fire. 'Ali: Waish 'ilmah? ju'an? We saw a nest with 3 eggs in a shijan today—like the eggs in the hole near our tents when we camped with the Ghazalat. 'Ali covered them up with a tree that our camels might not tread on them.

Sun 22 [22 March 1914]

We found as usual beautiful 'aishb soon after we had left camp and a clear water pool under some chalk rocks. Here we filled and washed our water skins and set off across the plain to 'Ain al Sayyid. As we rode a shepherd sent a rifle bullet between our camels' legs—we heard the whizz of it. Dawi bade his camel kneel, took a rifle and went off to expostulate—they were 5 or 6 men with flocks. 'Ali when he drew near rebuked him loudly—Wd a gomani come over the open desert in broad day ala kaifhu with hamilat? And if he was afraid the qa'ideh was to send a bullet over the riders' heads till he found out who they were. A horseman came up joined in this scene and the man admitted he was wrong. The horseman rode on with us. Presently we sighted another making for us across the plain. Ali waved his abba—useless! he shot at us too, but from far off. Our horseman went out and explained. We crossed a dry irrigation canal and near it a bit of a large stone column with a square base attached. The qasr looked big and I thought it really might be something, but when we came near it it was clear that it was not very old. Brick facing and rough stone and mortar [illegible] the walls. No decoration over the gate but a little spare[?] panelling on the sides of the double tower in which the door is set. Inside in the gate chamber roof like those in the Qumreh at Baghdad. The interior is full of houses all of which seemed to be modern. There is a small village outside built mostly of old bricks which they dig out of the ground. The inhabitants are mainly Arabs who grow corn on the abundant water of the 'ain, but some are Meshahadeh. They were all very civil. A foreigner has been there this winter related an old man. I rode to the mazar which is modern, bought a cast brick tile and so away on the high road to Meshhed of which we cd see the shining dome on the tar. We met a party of Arab zawwar who asked for news and a party of the qasr people who knew Dawi. Otherwise they wd probably have robbed us. We camed [camped?] in some sand hills with handh and gadhgab for the camels and an amazing swarm of sandflies. We stayed from 1 till 3 and it then ocurred to me to ask 'Ali if we were safe. He said we were not—too near the road, his mind not at rest. So we broke up camp in ½ an hour, carried the dinner in saucepans and marched off till at sunset we saw a village of wattle huts to the right of the road. There was corn in front of us and we feared water channels and mud—we had already passed through one patch—so we turned off and camped there, the villagers being most civil. They did not seem surprised at our having a hot dinner with us! They are Meshahadeh.

Mon. 23. *[23 March 1914]*

F. went off in the night to get a cart and we at dawn. We had some difficulty with a tottering bridge and a muddy path between water fields but we got through—into gardens and palms and beautiful green and up the steep bare banks to the wall. No F! I got off, the people stared so, and walked into the crowded bazaar where I found, with kind help, the man he had taken the cart from and heard he had gone off northwards. We took the camels all round the town—cemetaries [sic] onto the Husain road and I sent 'Ali to look for F. on the other road coming up from the Bahr. He went to the wrong place and came back very cross. It was hot. I sat in the shade of a tomb. Then I went with him—no F.—and sent him back to the carriage man whom he did not find. Finally I went back—the clock striking was very civilized!—found the man again, sat in his shop and heard F. had gone to Masalla! All mighty polite. We bought oranges, mounted the camels and rode off. An hour later we met F. walking. He had left the post cart at Masalla whether it wd wait he did not know. We had wasted 3 hours at Nejef. He rode on and we followed. The cart waited. I was greeted by many friends as we bundled into it and went off at a gallop with 4 horses. At Khan Hamad [Khan al-Hammad] the gendarmes came to talk while I drank tea, the good jondurma; at the next khan the same and some soldiers. You Arab are wala'in[?] al walidani said I. They burst out. The rifle the khife [*sic*] the revolver—nothing else, and dib dib dib! Wain ayyam Nazim Pasha! it is the same cry everywhere. Near Husain the road was broken by a broken bridge. We drove over the country and forded a canal where we nearly spent the night. Into Husain in the dark—street lamps and open shops and musty smell of town after desert. I went straight to M. Husain Khan ["Khan Bahadur" written above] and he kept me to dinner. He said the govt was Kharban, he did not think Jawid wd do much. He had brought a reputation for great cruelty in Albania in the war—but with Albanians! He had not made a good impression in Kerbela, lodged on the wrong people, called on the wrong people. From Nejef he had sent £4000 odd govt. money back to Baghdad by the post and it had been robbed on the way to Kerbela a thing which had not happened for a long time. All the reins fell loose during the war; they were so anxious not to have disturbances. And then there is Sayyid Talib of Basrah who was working for independence. They have sent 800 troops there—they said it was to be 2000 but it worked out at less. But he is Sunni and all the Arabs round about Shi'a so that he had not much influence, except what his wealth gives him. He was going to England. What shall you do with your family said[?]? Leave them here said he, I shall probably divorce my wife before I go. I . !!! "She is not a pleasant wife" said he "I have borne with her 15 years. And she quarrels with my mother who is very kind to her. A man's duty is to obey his mother. She may take my 2 little girls or I may take them, just as she likes. I should like to have them—I don't mind." He thought the Islamic law of divorce best, marriage a partnership like a business partnership. The Prophet had said divorce was to be regarded as one of the gravest matters. He did not think there were more than 15% divorces among respectable people. A man knew his wife wd marry another and he did not like the idea of his companion going to another. The custom of female seclusion was not the law of the Quran. It was said that a woman was to be clad up to the neck and down to the hands and feet, no more. But the custom had grown up and even the great mullah at Nejef admitted it wrong but said they did not dare to tell the people so lest they should say it was against the law of Islam. Complained that our consuls won't listen to advice and go wrong because they do not know the custom and thought of the people. He set right a carriage difficulty—there were no post carriages because of the crowd of pilgrims returning after the No Raz. He bought off a Kurdish family for me with 1£T. Excellent Persian dinner. So home to sleep at the posting merkez. Hot and stuffy. To bed after 11.

Tues 24. [24 March 1914]

And up at 2 very sleepy and cross. Drove out of Kerbela by night. The huge Babylonian landscape looked very desolate and dreary, all the wealth and life gone, when the sun came. We stopped at Musayyib [al-Musayyib], bought bread, eggs, and cream and eat. The river very full. Then a wind and dust. The peasants plodding along the road in wind and dust and sun—so it must have been in the oldest days, except that the silted up canals then flowed and the land was green. To Baghdad at 1.30. Went to Abd al Ahad's inn in a shahtur and dropped down the river to the Residency. (The first thing I saw when I arrived was the rly works—and the only thing going forward and not round and round—but slowly). Col. Erskine gave me my letters. She is ill. I went back to the inn and spent the night reading and writing.

Wed 25 [25 March 1914]

Wrote to D. Sent telegrams. Went to the Residency at 12 stayed to lunch and sat with Mrs E. [Erskine]. Came back and wrote. Very hot.

Thurs 26. [26 March 1914]

Read and wrote all morning. Went to the Residency at 4, took their motor boat and called on the Meissners. He told me that the rly construction was hung up for badness of transport, quarrels with Lynch, the boats he had sent out not suitable, draught too large for water, or engines too small for current. He says the new company is still born. When they saw Erskine they were much rassurés. If we had meant a forward policy here we wd not have sent a man who knew no language and nothing of the country. M. Meissner very beautiful. Coffee beer and tea! Lovely carpets and he has a wonderful pot of brownish gold glaze with legless phoenixes and flowers on it in lighter relief. So back and sat with Mrs E. where I found Mrs Todd [Tod] who asked me to stay. Then to the Hesses, where I found [space left blank]. He took me home and told me I was quite right about Nazim and that Jemal had done nothing but Hesse disliked the one and liked the second and talks according to sentiment. An Indian boy here in the new Inchcape[?] Co. had been at Bahrain. Ther 140, sinks to 110 at 7 PM. No water, no vegetation.

27. [27 March 1914]

Musa Patchachi and the Nawabs came to see me. He now regrets Nazim. Says everything is kharban, trade suffers, nothing doing. Partly because of the war. Discussed Germany, Russia and Anatolia as though partition were inevitable. A Syrian in this hotel who is a friend of Sayyid Talib's says he has great influence, just as much with Shi'as as with Sunnis. His friend is Khazal of Muhammurah a Shi'a. He never wanted independence for Basrah but only reforms—Arab officials, Arab nationality to the fore[?] etc. Tea with the Tods and Mr Wills. They say the Turks have tried to persuade Ibn Sabbah to help them to drive out Ibn Sa'ud but of course he won't. He took Hofuf and Ogair without a shot, having a large party in both towns, turned out the troops, about 500 in all, and seized all arms and provisions. Then he did the same by Qatif—not more than 600 soldiers in all. They tried to recapture Qatif and were unsuccessful—perhaps this is the origin of the tale of English landing or arms?—driven back to the sea with loss. Probably it's a put up job with Ibn Sabah—Ibn Saud will hand over to him part of the Hasa which will thus automatically pass under our[?] protection. It wd have been difficult for him to take it himself—and for us! The Sh. of Muhammerah is under the influence of a dancing girl. Impayable story of Hajji Rayis al Tujar, a rich merchant, who travelled to Europe and brought back to the Sh. as a present 2 life size wax figures of ladies completely attired in evening dress. They had wooden hands but he had them replaced by wax hands at a cost of 250 francs a hand to make them complete. You ought to have put a gramaphone in each said Mr Wills. Khush fikr said he. Live women he said wd have been too expensive. Dined with the Meissners—the Tods and I went together. Meissner took me in and M. Sevian, Regir[?], on my other hand. He had been at Adana during the massacres. Talked afterwards to Subhi Bey head of 2nd Army Corps, just arrived, whom I told about the Rashid and Jof. Also to M. Aublé whom I had seen near Nisibin in 1911. He fully confirmed my impression of the kharban state of the country, said the Mosul road not safe. Then to M [space left blank] Italian consul. Left at 1 AM.

Sat 28 [28 March 1914]

Breakfasted with the Naqib at 8. He was deeply interested in my stories of Hayyil. His wife is a Ja'far by origin like the Rashid and many of the Shammar. They are of various Jidda but the Abdeh are 'Araba—the northern Arabs Must'ariba (he is one) from Ishmael ibn Ibrahim. He questioned me as to Shakespeare's visit to Ibn Sa'ud wanting to know whether the taking of the Hasa had been arranged with us. Asked had we permitted arms to go through Kwait and what was our arrangement with Muscat [Masqat] and the French. He talked much of Europe and was well informed as to European relations. He said the word Nejd meant hill country, Tahama plain and Hajaz what lies between. Then to Musa Patchaji. Saw his wife and daughter Zekkiyyeh who is married and has a daughter. He also says things have gone to ruin, regrets Nazim—King Stork! No one here will take any part in politics because they can do nothing against the Committee. So to the Tods. Bought abas and izars and lunched with them. At 3 went with Mrs Tod and Meissner to see the rly works. The debarquement in a palm garden, cranes working, engines being put together in open air. The line laid to the station will probably become a high road—they are aligning their official houses along it. Great sheds for stones—they have neither stone, nor sand, nor wood nor water. They make concrete, grind up pebbles to sand and the water is too much impregnated with salts. The station fittings of teak because of white ants. Saw the hospital, the sisters' lodgings, drank soda water at the little factory. They treat all illnesses, not only accidents and women and children too. Walked out to the great [illegible] which digs up the earth with which they make the embankment on which the station is built. A crowd of people always looking on—it seemed alive!

Then to station—it is only a goods shed fitted up for station till they see how big a station they will need. If they get permission for Basrah the station will have to be bigger. In one of the sheds we saw the bells for the station—great bells stamped Bagdad [*sic*]. He hauled some men over the coals for using rails to hammer on. So walked back, drank beer at the Hotel Bagdadbahn. The town will be built on that side and when the rly embankment provides against floods all the land will be building land. Members of the staff are buying it in their own names, but I gather in the interests of the company. Hauptmann Weid a very pleasant head of a section walked with us. Dined with the Hesses, where I met Mr Whitley (Jackson's head man) and the Italian Consul. Acrimonious discussion with Hesse about Nazim Pasha.

Sun. 29. [29 March 1914]

Very hot. Wrote in morning and packed with F. Lunched with the Tods. Wrote after lunch. Mr Whitley came to see me at 5 and told me that Jackson and Pearson are in competition for the Habbaniyyeh which I regret. We went to tea with the Tods. After I had dressed I went back and discussed with Mr Tod the steamboat question. He read me his despatches home. Mr Whitley dined. We talked afterwards of archaeology and of the value of learning in itself. Also of the basis of morality!

Mon. 30. [30 March 1914]

Off at 5 across the river, the early light touching[?] it and the guffas full of workmen. The 2 bridges broken by the wind. Sayyif crossed with us, going over to the canals. We sat in a kahwah for an hour waiting for the Victoria which at last turned up. 4 horses, a driver and a little boy clinging behind—shaitan. I slept a little and thought a great deal. The horses went well. Lots of pilgrims and tahtirahwans. Hot—blazing. Just before Haswah the road was cut by a canal, bridge unfinished. Falalih came up and piled brushwood on the quntarah and dragged over the carriage. We lunched at Haswa I sitting in my niche of 5 years ago—as hot, and oh the flies! So on. At Mahawil [Khan al-Mahawil] I walked out and looked at the palm trees by the nahr—I had lunched there 5 years ago. Opposite the Hommera tell the arabaji said he cd not cross the Nahr and must go back to a quntarah. I got out, leapt the nahr, walked over Hommera and the qasr where the Natur wanted bahkshish and another with a gun looked at me doubtfully, and so through the village to the Expeditions haus. Koldewey received me with open arms.[1] Buddensieg appeared. Wachsmuth and [space left blank] are the other 2. At dinner I told tales and K. talked of the people. Land questions will be very difficult. No one knows to whom the land belongs. At Quairish the villagers give ¼ of the harvest to men of Hilleh and elsewhere, but say the land belongs to them. Why do you pay ¼? says K. We have always done it they

1. Robert Koldewey, pioneering German archaeologist.

reply. K. regrets the ancient east passing, with the rly etc. Baghdad is no more the same.

Tues 31 [31 March 1914]

Breakfasted at 6.30 with K [Koldewey] and we walked out to the diggings. They are excavating the NE corner of the qasr. We walked along the Via Sacra to the Merkes where we looked at the temple of Ishtar and the old old houses to the E. of it. So across the Sahn to the Tower of Babel. We sat on the edge of the pit, looked at it— Etiwananki[?]. The outer brick is all gone—some robbed by Alexander who piled up Hommera with it. They have found half a cylinder here and the other half in Hommera. The sundried brick core is there in part. Within it a core not yet of bricks. I call that old said K. How old? said I? 10000, 20000 years how can I tell. It is one of the oldest temples in Babylonia. It was a great square block with 3 stairs and a temple on the top, to Marduk, like the Esagila temple of Marduk below. Its great size impressed it on the imagination of the world. He thinks the ziggurat were all so—an upper temple corresponding to the temple below; the upper temple very little if at all smaller. On all there is space for the upper temple. At Ann Adad one of the temples on each of the zigurrats [*sic*]. No trace anywhere of winding stair. There must be a prehistoric civilization of which we know nothing. He wants some of the very old houses—they wd be best found in one of the very old tells which had not been reinhabited—Fara for instance. At Fara below all the houses they found a great depth of soil not virgin; occasional sherds or beads in it. The houses left no trace, b[illegible] wood or tents. But the sherds and beads meant an immensely long Kultur. He thinks the uralt population was certainly Semitic. The Sumerians came onto the top of it, absorbed it and were influenced by it. So we went to Esagila. The outer lines of the temple have been found by subterranean diggings. They have left the inner cella which K wants to dig out completely. So down to the Parthian houses which he wd very much like to dig. The very long colonnade is possibly an agora. The Hanging Gardens were built by Nebuch. for a Sasan. wife to remind her of her mountains! But the gardens were not planted high up. They were low down beneath the vaulted substructures. It is still possible that they may be found in the Babil [Babel] mound. So back to the house where we looked at plans, the qasr and Boghaz Keui [Bogazkale, Hattusas]. K. sees the primitive liwan in the qasr. Many of the big rooms on the courts have wide openings. This must have been the parent of Hatra [al-Hadr] and Ctesiphon. The Hittite liwan with its columned front is different—another type of liwan. The B. Keui plans are quite fremd [*sic*]. But there is something of the khilani—double faced in the big temple and the rooms tend to be latitudinal. The jutting out cella here with its involved[?] entrance and windows must be foreign. Later? Puchstein says it was all of one date. Borrowed from where? K. thinks the Syrian-Hittite idea possible. The Niffe [Nippur?] Parthian house he thinks quite Greek, the similarities with the big Babylon house fortuitous. Nonsense about its likeness to the Troy house. Badri Bey lunched and we talked of Hayyil. Photographed K and then walked out again with him to the Via Sacra and so along the Tigris to Babil. Here Alexander died. The river then flowed between Babil and the qasr and returned between the qasr and Esagila. When the fever burnt in him they carried him to the palace across the river, Babil. He had been living in the qasr which had perhaps been patched up for him. Babylon was to be the capital of his empire. The generals slept that night in the baths at hand—we saw the [illegible] heaps. Next day the fever burnt higher. They lay that night in Esagila, waiting for a vision from the god telling them how to heal him. Next morning he was dead. He was 32 said K. At 32 I had barely left school and he had conquered the world. Then came death, unfortunately and it all fell to pieces. We cfed [compared] him with Napoleon and the Romans—the Romans good honest unimaginative people, Alexander the romance of the world. I said Nap. never loved. K. Yes Alex. loved—Roxana and others. He was mad in Babylon—the perpetual drunkenness, then the story of his killing his friend. Drunk night and day. I said You must be mad to conquer the world. We talked of the Acts and of the good Romans standing perplexed before Paul. Pleasant evening. My launch arrived.

APRIL 1914

Wed. Ap. 1. [1 April 1914]

Breakfasted with K. One of the cats is called after me. Walked out onto the diggings where I found Wachsmuth who told me of his Braut and of how amazingly clever she is! He showed me the earth corners marking the edges of wall holes where from the bricks have been taken. All that they are digging are substructures. What look like chambers are the holes of the brick robbers. They left little walls between lest the earth should slide in on them. You know them from chambers by the fact that the walls are not of faced brick but of broken brick. So back and before 9 onto my launch. Steamed up to the Hindiyyeh [Shatt al-Hindiyah] till 1.30. Heavenly, the land all green—mud built villages with heaps of brushwood round for coffee fires, palm surrounded. People and cattle ruminating on the bank. Corn fields in the ear. Some of the villages look as if they wd fall immediately, those built of burnt brick, big farms[?] I suppose. Pomegranates in flower. Children run along the bank to watch and ford side canals. Jirds under old mulberry trees. This ancient song of their river will soon cease; Lynch and Blockey Crea are selling them pumps as fast as they can. It has ceased on the Tigris. Jays flitting in the brushwood, swallows dipping their wings in Euphrates. I found Mr Warbrick and Mrs Whitley, Mlle Sevian and Mlle Mugelle daughter of the French govt engineer. Her mother is an Arab. We lunched and afterwards I walked for 2 hrs with Mr Warbrick. We looked at the old dam. It was never filled up in the centre and the stream hollowed the narrow channel till at last it was over 30 ft deep. The Hindiyyeh flood which turned the main river into this bed happened some 20 years ago. Since then the dam has been patched twice but they cd not fill up the centre. There is a fine brick pyramid recording its building—the inscrip. is in Turkish which no one can read, it tells of a monument which was never finished and is now almost swept away—this year's floods it is hoped will destroy the revetments of the banks. The new dam records itself. We had passed through the little Hilleh regulator coming from Babylon. In the deep water under the barrage there is now a wonderful fishing ground, because the fish from the sea (and lakes?) cannot get up over the barrage. The lock is on the left bank. We crossed by the footbridge. The rail still lies over the main part; when it is taken away that will be the bridge. It will probably become the main road from Baghdad to Kufa and Nejef. Sefinehs with lateen sails coming down the river. They are horribly daring, load the sefinehs to the gunwhales.

Thurs Ap 2. [2 April 1914]

Off at 9 and in ¾ of an hour or an hour up to Musayyib where I found my victoria. Horrible wind and dust storms. Lunched at Mahmudiyyeh [al-Mahmudiyah] where the little boy dropped off and was no where to be found, much to my agitation. He turned up before we left—he had been paying off an old score on gomani! Got in to Baghdad at 5. Found Mr Tod's kavass and ballam and came straight to them—delicious[?] welcome. Mr Wills still here the negotiations with the Turks about their boats being still in air—a difference of 47% between them! They think they gain about £6000 in every afternoon's discussion. Talked again of shipping and then of trade in general—Mr Wills says the Germans have taken the trade in small objects which the English cd not bother with but says Mr Tod they have grown very wealthy over it. They import not much of their own; Austrian sugar and d[illegible] German ships. They get as much work out of the native as the Englishmen but they are less well liked because they are [illegible] But Mr Tod thinks they are less trouble to deal with than the English. They ask for less writing. Only you must see them yourself; they like to see the head man. The people won't use cube sugar being accustomed to loaf and English firms won't make loaf. They ought to sell cube sugar for 6 months at a proportionately low price and get it established. They showed me a tiny Quran in a box made in Germany—the people think they come from the Hejaz and bay! Slade well satisfied with the Persian oil fields. The headquarters for the Indian navy is to be Muhammarah, 18 miles from the rail head at Basrah where troops cd be poured down. Mr Wills thinks that the Shaikh of Muhammarah must be used to guard the oil fields and the Persian frontier where the oil passes. Kwait is allowed to import arms only for his own defence. For the last 2 years the Contraband trade in arms is all stopped in Kwait. It is now stopped in Mascat [Muscat]—we have bought off a French firm for £40000. Rifles very difficult to obtain in Baghdad. Only the best are to be had and they are very dear. German firms employ about half the European clerks we do and pay them not near so well. But they have one or two able men among their employés—the rest are of a lower order. The Jews are the real competitors. They have taken the piece goods trade and they are beginning to attack the machinery trade.

Fri. Ap. 3. [3 April 1914]

Began my articles for the *Times* and wrote most of the day. The Meissners came to tea and we dined at the Erskines which was very dull.

Sat. Ap 4 [4 April 1914]

Wrote. Post came in with a short letter from D. We called on Mme Meissner where we found a Mme Kalisch whom I had seen with her husband at Eregli [Cybistra Heraclea] 3 years ago. A Frenchman, agent for Hennessey's brandy, has arrived in Baghdad, Count Costa de Beauregard is his name, deaf but gay. He lunched here today.

Sun. Ap 5. [5 April 1914]

Wrote. Mr Wills went to the barrage.

Mon. Ap 6. [6 April 1914]

Wrote. Went on the river and photographed. Went to rose garden.

Tues Ap 7 [7 April 1914]

Wrote till I felt quite ill. Walked out into the desert with Selman to Nazim Pasha's barracks and was picked up by Mr Tod. We drove together round the walls and so in. No, all this happened on Wed. On Tuesday I had tea with Mme Kalisch. Mr Wills came back and M. de Beauregard and the French Consul, M. Guy, dined.

Wed. Ap. 8 [8 April 1914]

See above. Wrote all day. 'Ali brought his uncle, [space left blank] al Kenning[?] to see me. They all say that Ibn Sa'ud is the stronger. 'Ali reports that the Hejaz rows are real—Sherif against Vali. This may be very serious. Pleasant bridge in evening.

Thurs. Ap 9. [9 April 1914]

Finished my articles before breakfast. They are now being typewritten with great labour. Shopped in the bazaar with Mr Tod and walked in it with Mr Wills in the afternoon. Called on Mrs Erskine and then Mrs Tod and I drove out to the golf course. Family bridge.

Fri. Ap. 10. [10 April 1914]

Wrote letters. M. de Beauregard came in and out. Then Mr Tod brought in

'Abd al Qader Kadairi who has Baghdad in his hands. He had come in 2 days earlier also. Charming man. After lunch Mr Wills and I walked and drove out to Gararah where we sat in a garden of the Nawab's with the Lynch employés who were Easter picknicking [sic] there. The garden a tangle of weeds, orange trees, myrtle, moulting roses all fallen into decay since the old Naqib's death. But very lovely. Mr Wills thinks there will be Indian immigration when the irrigation begins—at any rate Muhammadan Indian. Already Gray MacKenzie employ Indians almost wholly for [illegible] etc—only labourers are Arab. Dined with Mr Richarz—the guests were M. de Beauregard and Mr Whitley. Exquisite night—full moon on Tigris. Richarz played the Char Freitag music—Du weinst, siche! es lacht die Ane. Mr Whitley says Meissner pays 3 times in wages what they pay but the money does not go to the workmen. It goes into the pocket of Greek contractors. All his contracts immensely dear. Mr Tod saw one for bricks today, bricks at Samarra. He was paying double their cost; here the contractor was an Arab, the Firman Firma's agent. Yet they don't like the Germans and come back to Jacksons for a lower wage. Muqawilah is contract. As regards the Habaniyyeh, Jackson have the contract for it, provisionally—if other terms are not made with someone else. Also for the next job, which wd probably be the Feluja barrage. No talk of Tigris work yet. The first there wd be on the Diyalah [Diyala, Sirwan]. The effect of the Hindiyyeh barrage is felt 80 kils up the river—the water has risen which has of course improved all the canals out of the Euphrates to that point.

Sat. Ap 11 [11 April 1914]

Went at 8 to the Naqib; we talked of the Indian situation. He said Moslem estrangement was due entirely to the Balkan war. I pointed out that we had helped Turkey for 60 years and no improvement had been made; he had himself said it went back rather than forward. Were we to go on for ever? He wd not tell me anything about the Hejaz. Gave him some free trade principles with regard to British and German competition here. When we parted he said we might never meet again, and he looks very old. Wrote letters. At 5 we went out with the Meissners on the river and got home at 8—champagne and beer! the river very mysterious at night, with the dark jungle at the edge and the lights of the houses. I talked to Meissner of Turkish political men. He thinks Izzet Pasha (of Yemen) the best; he is absolutely honest. Ahmed Izzet is the cleverest. Jemal is the best of the Committee men without doubt. He has no opinion at all of Enver. Talked this morning with the Naqib of irrigation and asked him about the population. He said without doubt they were not enough. From Samarra to Nejd he reckoned not more than 5 million. The old population of Baghdad was once a million—but he reckoned Baghdad from Samarra to Musayyib. What about Indian Moslem immigration? He said there wd be no objection, even to the immigration of but parast [sic], but they wd only be allowed to occupy lands which were wholly without owners. I doubt whether there wd be much land of that sort or whether it would be of much value.

Mon. 13. [13 April 1914]

Off at 5.30, Mr Wills up not the Tods. When we got outside the town or rather in the suburbs across the river the poll[?] of the carriage broke and we had to fetch another. It was Hassun's carriage and we had the same driver as before and the little shaitan of a boy. While we waited F. told me the story of 'Ali. He, angry at my refusing to take ibn 'ammhu with me—he wished to escape his military service—and at my refusing to pay for his [illegible] for going out with the camels which I had not ordered, refused to leave and called back the camels. F. going down in the afternoon found them. He called in Ali's uncle who remonstrated and produced Salih, Leachman's man. He asked £T15, and F. came to tell me and did not find me. F. went back made it up with Ali and paid the brother 3 or 4 mej. Thereat he thought they left, but they did not; they waited till dawn and left then taking the ibn 'amm with them whom 'Ali hoped to palm off on me as a stranger. The result was that then we got to Feluja at about 2—we had waited an hour at the halfway khan where I lunched in my £T2 carriage—no camels and no 'Ali. They came in after 4. Ali in the devil's own temper and I dismissed him at once and told him he might walk back to Baghdad. I did not know then of the ibn 'amm. We picked up a Dulaimi, Zobah and rode out; 'Ali walked a little way and asked for wages. I said God was between him and me and I wd put the whole matter in the hands of M. al Bassam. We rode out ½ an hour—the camels tired having come the whole way from Baghdad, they are moulting horribly—and camped near Zobah's tents. 'Ali then appeared and I demanded a full apology which he refused. He got 1½ mej. out of F. for his expenses back at which I was indignant. I wanted him to come to me for them. Hot still night. The stars came out, Sirius first, then the Bear, Leo's sicle [sic], Capella in haze, Aldebaran, Procyon above me. I went to bed on the hard ground and did not sleep. A ¾ moon rose in the middle of the night and looked me in the eye. It was deformed and huge and red on the horizon. Dogs barked and prowled round.

Tues 14. [14 April 1914]

We got off at 5.15—'Ali did not return. Rode by the big Euphrates and through much corn land; then out into barer country with the barren earth hills coming down to the river. Not really hot till we got to or near Ramadi which we did at 1.30. A good march. Went to Shaikh 'Ali Sulaiman—he was gone to Baghdad but his brothers received me and lodged me in a garden. We sat in an open tent and drank coffee, then went to my tent, drank tea with orange flower water in it and discussed the question of the rafiq. Many tales now of 'Ali's iniquities—how he pocketed 1 lira minus ¼ of a mej. of the lira and 2 mej. I gave him at Nejef; took all our provisions and eat them in his house, never invited the men to eat with him, kept various of our goods and has not returned them, pocketed the money F. gave him to buy food for the 2 who went out with the camels and left them to starve etc. I have got a rafiq called 'Adwan for £17 to go with me to Ga'rah and sallim me into the hands of the 'Anazeh. [line of Arabic characters] The temp. at 4 was just under 80. The day we picknicked [sic] Mr Tod said that the important point about the transport was that he who controlled it controlled the trade of the 'Iraq. They now come to him for pumps and things; if the rly people take the transport they will go to them. And just at the moment when the trade is developing. He told me that the Germans were making a determined attempt to conquer the trade on the Karun. A Turkish shipping Co. was started—it could not have been started without substantial aid from the Germans, which was given. Then Meissner had the right to run 2 steamboats at Basrah for the rly transport. Lynch had started a post boat on the Karun by which they made a little money but their shipping there never paid until the oil Co began. They have a small subsidy. Meissner's two boats had very little to do—one was hired out to the Turkish Co. to run the post between Basrah and Muhammerah. Mr Tod complained to Meissner who said he did not know of the business and at once stopped it. But Mr Tod says why do they want the Karun trade, out of which Lynch can scarcely make money, if not for a political end?

Wed. 15. [15 April 1914]

Off at 5.10 and crossed the bridge over the canal at 5.20. Very hot; I was very sleepy and it was bitter dull. Fortunately I shortly got a bearing on a great smoke giant from Abu Jir [Abu el-Jir]. 'Adwan said the Arabs lighted the wells for winnis[?]—they yatawannasun. The desert is already seeding and withering. From 3 to 4 after we got into camp the shade temperature was 91. Then came a dust and thunder storm. Much anxiety as to the stability of our tents. It blew like mad and rained a little. The Arab tents came down, but ours stood, to the surprise of 'Adwan. He told me today the traditional origin of the Dulaim. There came out of Nejd bil awwal, Thamir and his brother Jabbar, the former jid of the Dulaim and the latter of the Jebur. Guided by a Slubby they reached Muhaiwir [Muhaywir]. That was not its name in the old days; he did not know its name. It was called Muhaiwir because the Arabs wandered round and about it. There they found Arab and these hid the well under a farash, for they said these be janabin, strangers and we will not let them drink our well; we will keep the water for ourselves. But really there is enough water at Muhaiwir for all the 'Arab to drink. And the Slubbi sought for the well and could not find it. At last he said Seek under that bait, and they pulled down the bait and found the water under the farash. Then came gomani and Thamir and Jabbar being such a small company were afraid.

And Thamir's daughter took the dulul, al Ihnai's, and put written tidings into her shedad and all alone the dulul returned to Nejd. Now when she reached Nejd she found men watering the camels at a well, and being athirst she drew near and drank. She drank and drank until the girth broke and the shedad fell to the ground. Out dropped the letters, and 2 of the waterers picked them up and read and went to the help of the two brothers. Since then the Dulaim have held the dirah. Al dunya 'atij said 'Adwan.

Thurs. 16. [16 April 1914]

Off at 5.10. It was still very hot but there were thunder storms about and the sun was sometimes clouded over, when it felt quite cool. The temp was 89° when we came into camp at Wizeh. The desert burnt, but still full of safarah, and the mignonette plant grown very big and brilliant red and orange horned poppies, and the lavender blue flowered plant. We reached Wizeh in 6½ hours, pitched tents and in half an hour I went out to plan the qasr in the burning sun. There was a little breeze—it was not so bad. It is almost exactly the same as Khubbaz but more ruined. Also I think less carefully built. Uncut stones and mortar and the walls have all been plastered. The towers have fallen; the gate towers were not rounded. Outside the gate was covered by a calotte set over a horizontal squinch and outset twice from the wall. But the vaults of the rooms had no outset. In the SE chamber the well which is said to have gone down to the underground water. The jorah by which you descend to the water is some 110 paces away, an immense hole about 100 ft deep with a passage in the rock opening from it. The man we had taken from Abu Jir insisted on carrying two rifles. Al silah zain he said. We brought the matarat and a girbeh. The passage was sometimes a mere crack through the rock, sometimes it opened out into great halls. There was one biggish chamber; then we dropped down into a huge hall, when from the passage was so low that we cd just creep through on our stomachs. It lifted again and we came to the water, cold and very clear. We waded in and filled our waterskin which we had great labour in carrying out. The 'Anazeh sometimes in summer water their sheep from here! We had left 3 lights burning at various twists in the path and found our way back easily. We were glad to see the light of day. Dan al dunya said Fattuh. They all declare they wd not go in alone, not if they were dying of thirst, for fear of losing themselves along the many passages which open in all directions. It is called Wizeh because the Arab yatawaz'an in getting water from it. We filled some skins in the morning at al Jelta in the Wadi Abu Jir—it is a jelta, a dry waterfall with a pool below. 'Adwan collects the sheep tax for the Govt. It has been raised this year from 3 piastres to over 4. But the shaikhs eat more than the Govt. he says. They eat the cultivators who can't escape from them. Ali Sulaiman is responsible for all the road from 'Anah to Feluja; in the Jezireh roads the Shammar 'Asi shaikhs are mas'ul.

Fri. 17. [17 April 1914]

Off at 4.50, cool and pleasant, a wind and the temp never higher than 85. We made a long march over dull ground, low steps up which we passed. Plenty of grass and weeds but mostly withered or seeding. The Dulaim summer mostly on the Shatt but some stay by the wells, Abu Jir, Themail, Asileh, 'Ain al Arnab and others. Ali Sulaiman used to raid while his father was alive; now he does not any more. 'Adwan has raided the Jezireh Shammar with whom they were at feud. Did you enjoy it? I asked. We do it for tuma' he said. Don't you enjoy falling on the foe? "Eh wallah!" We saw fresh footprints of horsemen. Adwan said Shammar of the Jezireh yudowwarun 'ala 'Anazeh. Abdallah al Rashid was once in 'Anah and married a woman who bore him a child. Their descendants are still living in 'Anah. Bad night.

Sat. 18 [18 April 1914]

And consequently tired today. Relentless Hamad as flat as possible with 5 ft rises swimming over the mirage miles away, descending as we approached and sitting down on the Hamad. Lots of 'aishb. Cool west wind. We saw the ruined gate of 'Amej [Qasr 'Amij] to the right, after we had crossed the Sha'ib 'Amej which is nothing of a valley but remarkable for its abundance of daisies, 18 in high, regular hay. It loses itself in the ga'. Then we fell into the Derb Zubaideh and shortly after sighted camels grazing. 'Adwan went for the news. They were Amarat and the shaikh was a nephew of Fahd Beg. The latter has probably left Ga'rah. The ghazzu of which we saw tracks yesterday were Shammar; they lifted 40 camels this morning. We camped near the road and a man came to us who told us the Fahd Beg had been raiding the Wulud 'Ali. Ibn Sha'lan has been raiding the Sba', but got nothing. He has now returned to near Jof. The Ruwalla have raided the Shammar of Nejd and taken large chesb. We tried to get this man as a rafiq but he refused to come on our terms and 'Adwan has gone off to see Jad'an, the nephew of Fahd. Not the Jad'an I saw 5 years ago in the Jezireh. He is dead. He was a cousin of Fahd's I think. Slept for ½ an hour on my camel today. Rather saddle sore and an ankle rubbed, bother it.

Sun 19. [19 April 1914]

Off at 5 with 'Adwan and F, to Jad'an's big camp, a good 5 miles off. We trotted. The tents all huddled together through fear of yesterday's raid. A man ran by us and told us of it. They had pursued, taken 10 mares and killed 2, also a man. "Did his comrades wait to bury him?" I said. "No wallah, they left him to be eaten by the dogs." So he lies on the wide Hamad till the dogs come to finish the business. Jad'an was rahil— all the tents coming down, hawdaj and chitb on the lovely camels. Heaps of nagas and foals. We sat in his tent while coffee was made and the women loaded. I was tired and afraid of the long day before us and rather inclined to cry! However Jad'an was very kind. La tiftikeri he said, "you shall have all you wish. We are at your service and honoured." I got a rafiq, 'Asaf, the man we saw yesterday, for 3 mej. a day and he is to take us to Buharra if I like. Second fence behind us. We trotted back an hour and picked up the camels (Jad'an followed F. and asked him to tell me to send him a rifle!) Then I parted sorrowfully from 'Adwan who kissed my hand and went on his way. Long dull ride. When we were in the W. Mu'aidin[?] 2 camel riders bore down on us. F. and 'Asaf whipped out their rifles and loaded. The men shouted angry questions. But it was all right; they were men of Ibn Mijlad's and friends as soon as they knew we were not to be feared. We came down a side valley into the Hauran and camped near Muhaiwir. A guest came in, old, deaf and lame; he had been looking for a strayed mare—near Homs!—and was now looking for his people, the Swailmat (Swailmeh) Rain. 'Adwan prayed in camp. He and F. spoke very disparagingly of the Bedu and the miserable life they led—fear and hunger. "Now they are mabsutin" said 'Adwan. "You should see them in the gaith. Hunger." They agreed that the best thing was to be like 'Ali Beg, live in a house and take tribute from his Arab. We asked one of the Anazeh why they did not go to the fine pasture of the Sha'ib 'Amej. "Al thumma" he said. There was a gazelle fawn in Jad'an's tent. It slept on my knee through the long talk, curled up like a Mycaenean ivory with a pointed hoof sticking up over its ear. It was the only creature in the company wholly devoid of apprehension. Scarlet horned poppies. They call gazelle dabi'.

Mon. Ap 20. [20 April 1914]

Heavy rain in the night—winter rain. The men trenched my tent and it held good with swelled canvass [sic]. When we came down to Muhaiwir (in a temp. dropped 20°) the clear pool was dry—it was only a water hole. In the ghadir a large pool but matrub. We dug holes in the sandy bank and got water, but little better. I have enough Wizeh water. All the bank was fouled. Tents of the Swailmat (Ibn Bekr) in the valley and lots of camels going up to pasture. On the flat Hamad above 1000s of them. They drifted across the post road like a wide slow river. The 'Anazeh being muhakkanun[?] wd not despoil caravans in a ghazzu like the Shammar or the Daffir. The herdsmen walked or rode with us for half hours and Asaf was careful to say that I came from Hayil which caused much admiration. One of the men came on with us and is our guest. He is going to Ibn Hadhdhal. (Ibn Mijlad is shaikh of the Sulatin.) He asked why I had not horses and carriages. "Kafi" said I. "Ana arid ahsan lakum" said he. Asaf told me they raided the Wulud Sulaiman last year and took much chesb. He said they were the Wulud al Shaitan. I said I was glad and we spoke of Saiyah. "Afrak al sinain wa azrak al 'ainair la takhowwi" said he. Azrak: 'awi, one eyed. We saw a pair of big duck like birds, shhaibi. Asaf talked of tais, a sort of dur. We killed a snake— hamash, hamish. Also an aqrab in camp. Fellah said a propos of our camp last night "La tinzil bil faid (slope) wa lan bil qaid[?]." We crossed the W. al Za'i and stopped for 20 min. for the camels to graze. I fell asleep at once with my arm for a pillow. At 1.47

we sighted the first tells of the Ga'rah and dropped into it at 2.10 when we came into camp near the derb. I registered no higher temp than 67. Cloudy. They say to one another Ya bedowwi with a strong accent on the second syllable.

Tues Ap 21 [21 April 1914]

Asaf was in rather a state of mind last night because a man he did not know, probably a Ruwaili, had alighted at our tents and then gone on. He feared he might return and lift camels, but he did not. Cloudy morning. Off at 5.25 and marched in the Derb till 7.20 when we turned off towards Helgum. We met a man of Fahd Beg's looking out for Agail to take the khuyyi from them; he turned back with us. Note that Afaif, Agharri, Melussa, Hedir and the qasr of Helgum are all on the edges of the Ga'rah. It stretches on for about an hour beyond Bir Melussa [Bir al-Mulusi] where there is a qasr. As we came down to Helgum the world was full of Amarat tents, I counted 150 in Fahd Beg's camp. He had a mudif and a big haram tent and 4 smaller tents. I alighted at the mudif where I found him, a very pleasant old man who made me welcome. I got in at 10.5. We sat and talked. He asked if the 'Iraq was quiet, I said no. We talked of Basrah and Sayyid Talib. went to my tent and lunched after which I drank coffee with Fahd. He talked of the Hindiyyeh, asked if there were a bridge there and wd the road to Nejef run that way. He said the Hindiyyeh did him good but he feared the Habbaniyyeh wd injure him. I said the increase in water wd do him good. He questioned me closely as to why I travelled. "There is lying among Islam but not among the English—tell me the truth. Why do so many travellers come into the desert. Is it for profit or for industries?" I said no it was for whims and for ma'rafah. He said he cd not believe it. The traveller might die, it was dangerous, it was toilsome. But I insisted, said the English had no profit to make out of the desert. They did not sit at home much but saw the world. Sadaqt? [I] said. Sadaqt he answered. Then I photographed him and his wife and rode off to the qasr which was a good 4 miles off. Most curious place on a sort of peninsular above the Ga'rah. A wall with towers guards the only approach from the Hamad. Very rough building, uncut stones laid dry; the towers slightly rounded but I think more from [illegible] [accident?] than from design. Chambers in them, with rounded outer end. They must have been covered by a rude vault. A large sticking out bastion was so much ruined that I have possibly not got its form right. The gate seemed to be at the opposite end of the wall. Behind, the whole area of the peninsular was covered with ruins, rude heaps of stones, some a hollow circle. No sign of water storage but the valley below full of birs. Somewhere on the E. side there is a path with steps leading down said Asaf. I did not go as a storm was blowing up. We got back to the tents just before heavy rain and hail. Last night we had two guests, Salatin. They rode in, nowwakhed the dulul, took off the Khurj, let her go and walked into the men's tent, to dine and sleep. It is deliciously simple and Arcadian. Here at sunset the camel herds come in, gambolling, the nagas and the calves, with great hoyyo calling and grunting. The beg came to my tent and we talked of the Iraq and the future of Turkey and of our friends in Baghdad. They brought dinner to us—roast lamb, stuffed with curried rice and resting on a pile of rice, bread, leben and patties, very good. Then we sat on, the dusk fell and the rain and it was near 8 when Fahd Beg left. They say they find bones and sheep's horns and pot sherds, coloured, in Helgum. At Malussa town of the same kind, only ruin heaps, alamat, high up on the hill top, higher and bigger than Helgum, with a stair leading down to the wells. Pot sherds there too and pot handles. We took a man of the Ruwalla as rafiq, his name 'Ubaid.

Wed. Ap 22. [22 April 1914]

Cold. Had coffee with Fahd and Mit'ab, his eldest son. The latter showed me a revolver which Musil had sent him and spoke well of him, sadiqna. Then off with my 2 rafiqs. The bearings I took to points on the edge of the Ga'rah so that they mark its limits. We met 2 Amarat who told us they had seen the fire of a ghazzu last night, people coming from the N, they didn't know where. They had probably returned to Homs. Two Slubba with donkeys and sheep travel with us. Wild wind in our teeth, rainstorms marching over the world and occasionally catching us in their skirts. We got out of the Ga'rah at 11.10 and marched on over desolate country with very low rocky tells and rocky ridges. We got into camp in rather too open ground, but found no better near 'aishb and it was too far to go on to the the [sic] Swab [Wadi al-Sawab]. The camels did not eat much because of the cold. The Ruwaili tried to go back in the middle of the morning, he said he feared the long road and desired to return to his people. F. represented to him that it wd be 'aib and he came on after changing his camel—he said he did not like his mount. Cold, wind, dust and rain. Very tired. Slept for an hour when I came in and a great many hours at night.

Thurs. 23 [23 April 1914]

Cold and grey but the weather cleared and warmed after 10 AM. We crossed the W. al 'Awaj at 6.30. Assaf called it first W. al Herri and then said it was 'Awaj min al Herryan. It goes on its own account to the Shatt. At 7.40 the W. al Waiziyyeh, so called from the green waizeh shijar[?] which was also plentiful in the Swab. I found coarse blue glazed sherds and sherds unglazed. We got to the Swab at 9, half an hour below the qasr. It is the biggest of these valleys. It comes from three heads said Assaf which join just above the qasr. Only one gate of the qasr is standing. The stones uncut, the mortar mud. A big sort of caravanserai near it, of which only foundations remain. Wells madfun in the valley and ruins on the opposite side of the wadi, but indistinguishable. Built, these, without mortar of any kind. Stayed till 11.5. Across the valley we crossed a very flat piece of country in which as Assaf observed the Bedouin fears[?]. At 11.42 clear trace of road—big stones heaped on either side. It is say the

Slubba, the road from Helgum to W. Swab, W. al Miyya and Bukharra. At 1.40 we
came to a pool in a bit of sloping rock. It is called Howwiyyat al Rtaimiyyeh and is
marked by a rijm. It dries of course later. From the Swab this country is the head water shed of small valleys almost indistinguishable here, the Rtaimiyyeh. They go to
the Swab. At 3.48 we entered a tributary of the W. al Ruthiyyeh and followed it down
till it joined the main ghadir of the Ruthiyyeh where we camped. A pool of bad water
in the ghadir. The Slubba still with us, their sheep very tired with our long marches.
They left last night in the middle of the night and we caught them up at the qasr.
Pleasant evening at last. No wind, light airs, warm and nice. The Slubba are going to
W. al Miyya where they left their people 8 days ago to go to Fahd "on account of the
dawwab" said they—the two donkeys?

Fri. 24. [24 April 1914]

It blew and rained a little in the night but I did not wake. We rode over high
plains in gray rainyish weather and presently saw something lying on the ground. It
was 3 dead mares and 2 dead zilim said Assaf. A Fed'an ghazzu had met a Ruwalla
ghazzu 10 nights ago. The Ruwalla were manteli[?], but not the Fed'an. They took the
Fed'an mares, killing 3. Then the Fed'an attacked them with their spears as they rode
away, killed 2 men and took back the mares. F. went off to see if he could pick up an
asa'i, but I edged away—why should I be haunted by their bloody ghosts? There was
no asa'i—the Slubba must have gathered up everything. An hour later F. said he saw
zuwal—I said it must be rabbuna the Slubba but Assaf declared he had seen 2 camel
riders making for the valley ahead. He unslung and loaded his rifle. I[t] was the
Slubba. Assaf said "Gomna beni Kubais!" And the camel riders were one solitary
camel whom we found in the wadi going down to the Miya. Muhammad the Slubba
came up and said ahalham[?] were near the W. al Butm and wd we not camp with
them that night. We reached the W. al Miya at 10.30 and 10 minutes lower down came
to the qasr, al Tayyar: It was nothing but a rudely built wall, 10 paces square, enclosing
graves. It is a ziyyarat of the Slubba. But near by there were foundations of house
walls on the ground. On the opposite bank heaps of stones—I went up to look at
them. They may have been only rijm or they may have been remains of houses. We
crossed the valley, bearing 260, and at 11.20 came to 2 birs, hayyat, living. The water is
6 ba' deep in spring and 10 in summer, always there. Then we followed down the valley and at 12 came to a mound round which there were foundations of square rooms
arranged apparantly [sic] on the caravanserai plan—at any rate I saw an angle thus:
[sketch of ground plan]. Here the W. al Butm joins the Miya—I did not take the bearing but we fell into the Butm later. Higher up the Miya is Umm al Salabiq with the
same sort of foundations. At 12.10 we left the main valley going 120 and followed up a
side valley, 2.10. A tributary came in, 185, and at 12.17 we left our tributary going 240
and crossed over to the Butm which we reached at 12.40. It flowed down at 65 and we

followed it till 2.10 and left it going 265. It was full of water pools. At 2.5 there was a ruin heap with a bir in the valley and at 2.10 another. The valley was extremely rich in grass[?]. In all these ruin heaps the Slubba dig and find antiqat, ibriq, said Assaf. At 2.10 we turned up a shallow side valley and came out at 2.35 onto an extraordinarily flat barren plain. At 2.46 we saw far away the long line of the J. al 'Ulub, too far off to get a bearing on the whole length of them—I took what I could. We hurried in order to get to a nugrah and ma'asha and finally found a very shallow valley with naitun in it where we camped at 3.28. Windy but bright and sunny. Not hot. Terrible plague of s[and?] flies.

Sat 25. [25 April 1914]

Off at 5.25—mist hanging all over the desert but it blew off at 8 and the sun came out. We marched till 7.45 over the great flat. F. gave an alarm of zol but it was nothing. At 7.45 we were in the very shallow Wadi al Uwairid. We then crossed 5 Salahib, and in a tributary of one of them stopped to let the camels eat the beautiful grass. Be hal rantha[?] khallihum yu dahhin said Assaf. At 10.30 I saw the mountains, so faint, such children of the mist that I could not believe in them. But an hour later on top of another ridge they were clear, the Palmyrene hills. At 11.15 we crossed the first of the Jiffah tributaries and at 12.40 came to another Jiffah valley where we found Slubba with sheep. We alighted at their tents and bought some dehin[?]—semen. They were very friendly, pressed us to stay saying they had never seen a khatun before. One man was dressed in gazelle skin robe. The desert is quiet; an encampment of Fed'an somewhere to the right. At 2.40 we reached the main Jiffah valley and camped with the mountains in full view of my open tent. The ther. was 70. [written at top of page:] Great bargaining with the Slubba. God between us and you and the price of a Homs ratl is 1¼ mej but that of a Damascus ratl 1½. We call God to witness.

Sun. 26. [26 April 1914]

Off before dawn, clear and still. Crossed 2 Halba valleys which go into the Milh of Tudmor [Tadmur, Palmyra]. A mighty storm crossed our path in front of us, thunder, flickering lightning and bent hail clouds following behind, scourged by a wind we could not feel. It all passed over into the hills but afterwards malicious scuds of rain troubled us, after all the splendour and the pageant had passed. What with the weather and with his anxiety at seeing tracks of a big ghazzu—so he thought them—Assaf went too much to the N. We hove up against tents and flocks of the Sba', Ibn Sa'aiyid and Masraf, and their herdmen put us straight. We were in sight of Tudmor lying in a bay of the hills and facing the desert. Seen thus it looked indeed like the Arab city, the desert city, not the Roman. The ground sandy with shih and sand plants I had not seen since the Nefud—particularly the tree with whip like green streamers for leaves. Seeing that Buharra was too far off we camped in a wadi in these sand hills with good 'aishb after 9½ hrs march. Very tired and perplexed because my rafiqs cannot guide me to the ruined khans. Have sent Assaf off to Masruf's tents to see if he can get a man. He came back with a man. Thunder and rain. Sayyif brought in a lot of qata[?] eggs. [written at top of page:] Assaf found some fledgling khabbara

Mon 27. [27 April 1914]

But the man demanded too high a fee and I dismissed him. He returned and asked me to take him but we could come to no terms and finally he went off for good. Light rain in the morning, but later a wind and clear. We saw the Palmyra temple and columned street clearly. After the sand the earth was rather mahl, flehfleh and mlaih[?] but occasional patches of flowers, poppies (dedekhan) yellow daisies etc. The Palmyra milh lay between us and the town. So we came to Buharra which is separated from the desert by low hills. Saw and photographed some outlying buildings, then rode on to the town ruins and joined my camels at the high tower and house and gate of Sakkariyyeh where there is an excellent well, the best water in the place. Here we filled our skins and went on 3 hours to Khan al Hallabat. No work there. Rough mediaeval work; thick walls frequently added to by laying the new wall against the old; corner towers which have been 3 storeys high, and traces of interior buildings but I could not see that these were bound in to the outer walls. Outside the gate half buried lay a rudely cut engaged column. No other architectural features of any kind. A shallow valley near must have provided the water supply—it gave my camels 'aishb. The khan is between two ranges of hills, the lower separating it from the desert. We passed over much muddy slippery ground this morning, after the heavy rain. Assaf was very anxious about robbers last night. There were men of some of the Raqqah tribes—Umar and others—camped with Masraf and he feared they might steal our camels.

Yesterday morning after the thunderstorm we met a solitary man walking in the desert. We tried him with Arabic, Turkish and Persian but he gave no answer. Assaf said he must be a Persian dervish who had lost his way. We gave him bread which he accepted. Then we rode on into the western rains; he followed us for a little then turned back and walked on into the eastern rains. The desert is full of young birds.

Tues. Ap. 28. [28 April 1914]

We were off at 5. At 6.15 there was an oblong block with a rude moulding at the top along the narrow sides. It was face down and much too big to move but it looked as though it might be inscribed. Near by was a short column—a milestone? At 7.45 were 4 similar columns, two inscribed but I could only read on one TRA and on the other TA. At 8.10 I saw a building in the hills and went to it. It was a rectangular guard house—on the mediaeval or the Roman road?—undatable. A tower apparently with the door high up for I saw no trace of a door in the standing walls. But they were

much ruined. At 10.45 there was a khan under the hills to the right, about 1½ miles away. Through my glasses it looked exactly like Hallabat and I did not go to it—a square wall with corner towers. We were riding all this time up a wadi—we came to the water parting at 11.43 and rode down the tributary of another valley, crossing through the hills at right angles to us. We crossed it at 2.15. At 12.10 there was a bit of column uninscribed. The valley was about a mile wide here but it widened out and at the cross valley it must have been 3 miles wide. I took bearings on two high points on either side of us ahead[?] They were the buttresses of ranges running along side the cross valley. The low hills to the S. of us came to an end at 1.35 when the bearing of the end

Southwest tower, medieval Khan al Hallabat. Photograph by Gertrude Bell. Courtesy of the University of Newcastle upon Tyne.

point 185. This way [sketch of area] The S. point was nearly but not quite so high as the N. point. But the hills dropped rapidly from it whereas from the N point they are the main ridge. We camped at 3.15 in another tributary of the cross valley. Horrible NW wind.

Wed 29. [29 April 1914]

It blew all night and was still blowing this morning. Bitterly cold. I rode till 9 in my fur coat. At 8.30 we crossed a water parting the bar. was 26.5. We rode on over a sort of plateau with hills on both sides, and then down slightly. Sighted a khan at a bearing of 243. F and I hurried on but at 10.15 we saw another, at 362. So we left the others to go on to the first and rode ourselves to the second which we reached at 11.20. It must have been nearly 4 miles away. Beyond it the Qaryatain [al-Qaryatayn] road crossed a low ridge. It was a square of walls, 2 metres thick, with rect. towers ["bastions" written above] at the corners and a rect. bay (mosque? but the plan for the mihrab was ruined) at the S. side. Door in the E. wall, ruined. No interior buildings. Birkeh behind. So we cut across the hills to the original ruin which we reached at 1.10 and found the others there. It was a rect. wall with round towers at the corners and one in the middle of each of 3 sides. In the 4th (W. side) the gate. No interior build- ings. We turned into the hills. The old road very clear by reason of a rock cutting and water storage arrangements. We thougt [sic] to ride 2 hours and camp, but we got onto high ground enclosed by hills and absolutely barren. At 4.4 we crossed a little ridge, between the bounding hills and saw a wide hill enclosed plain below us with a green valley far away. We reached the green, which proved to be good grass, at 5 and camped in the open. There are tents far away in the hills above us, men and cattle— horses or donkeys and 2 donkeys in the sha'ib near. I suppose they are only ri'u and I don't care Hot in the afternoon.

Thurs. 30. [30 April 1914]

They were Bedu. We saw them all moving camp next day. 2 men on a camel came and explored us but were soon satisfied that we were harmless. When we got over a ridge we saw Hermon [Jebel el-Sheikh] and a village clinging to a hillside. Sparse cultivation and stocks—barley about 5 in high. Presently peasants pulling it up. So we rode down to Dumair by a wadi with traces of an old bridge near the village and I took my last bearing on the pediment of the temple. All the village threshing floors piled high with grass. The gardens behind their mud walls in summer leaf. We rode on through the village and could find nothing for the camels. Finally we went on to Adra and camped beside a pool almost exactly on the spot where I mounted my camel on Dec 15. Bought grass for the camels. The sun set and all the bare hills blue purple with Hermon in shadow.

Fri. May 1 [1 May 1914]

F. Muhammad al M. and Selim came in the morning. Did nothing all day but lie about and read papers. Mr Devey came in the afternoon and stayed 2 hours. Told me of the motor sent to Ibn Rashid and of the row between the Vali and the Sherif.

Sun 3. [3 May 1914]

M. al M. and Muhiyy ud Din came in the morning. Lay about all day too tired to do anything.

Mon 4. [4 May 1914]

M al M came to do accounts. Rows about payment. Muhammad al Bassam came and paid for my camels which he bought at £19 a piece—very cheap. Drove after tea with the Mackinnons. Damascus all in summer.

Tues 5. [5 May 1914]

Mashaka came down from the Consulate and we compromised with M al M for a payment of £120—I was done! Came to tea a certain Mr Gillan and Mr Aostrad a Swede. Miss Johnson, nice missionary woman arrived in the afternoon. Better.

Wed.6 [6 May 1914]

Packed. Canon Hananer came to say goodbye and Mr Gilan to play tennis.

Thurs 7. [7 May 1914]

Off to Damascus, Mr Devey and M al M to see me off. Parted with F. at Rayyaq [Rayak] whence he went to Aleppo. Very lovely over the Lebanon, high snow and spring green. Mr Cumberbatch met me and took me to the Consulate. Mr Grain, judge from Alexandria, and Mr Honey dined.

Fri. 8. [8 May 1914]

Went to see Father Rouzevalle who showed me my book. Then to Cook's and so to the College where I found Dr Bliss. Mary Dodge came in with a Mr Sayer whose brother married President Wilson's daughter. Dr Bliss talked about Bryce who had just been there. Bryce thought that France with her present colonial obligations and internal conditions wd be unable to absorb Syria in any political sense[?]. So back to a long slow evening.

Sat. 9. [9 May 1914]

Mrs C.'s [Cumberbatch's] brother, Mr Rees, arrived with his wife and little boy. Mr C. saw me off. My boat the Equateur, singularly ruinous. Doors won't shut and windows won't open. Mr C. introduced me to the Vali, Bekir Sami Pasha, a Circassian, going up on leave to C'ple. Also to an Englishman called Andrews, out here on business. Mr Gillan and Mr Sayer on board, and a dull English woman Miss Harris. Very crowded. I have a small dark cabin to myself.

Sun. 10. [10 May 1914]

Lovely weather. The admirable Anatolian coast, snow crowned, drifted before us all the afternoon. We passed Rhodes [Rodhos] just after dark.

Mon. 11 [11 May 1914]

Reached Samos in the morning and stayed all day. Very hot. After lunch Mr Sayer and I went on shore taking an American girl, Miss Smith who has been studying archaeology at Jerusalem. We annexed an English speaking Greek from Smyrna [Izmir]. He deserted from the Turkish army and fought on his own through the 2 wars. He said the Bulgarians much the worst foes, more cruel, killed more women and children. Tried to see the museum but it was shut and the key in the possession of the Commandant. All official buildings occupied by the Greek garrison. Went off to find the Director but in his rose garlanded court heard he was away. So to the Director of the Gymnasium, a courteous gentleman, M[onsieur] Georges Sotziou, who came with us. He showed us the old Govt. house where the Xian prince, nominated in C'ple, held his councils since the Treaty of Berlin. Also here the minute Chamber where sat 19[?] deputies from different parts of the island. Now they are to send 3 deputies to the Athens chamber and are waiting for the Greek officials from Athens. I wonder whether they will like it better. The Council Chamber hung with the portraits of Samian worthies, all except Pythagaoras who was born here. He was however represented in a relief, philosopher's scroll in hand, over one of the schools. In a building occupied by soldiers we discovered an archaic statue, rude local work draped like the Parthenon Athenas, but the museum was shut. We took leave of the Director and went on up the hill, past the old Turkish barracks. The little fort above had been bombarded by the Italian fleet and the garrison evicted. The old Samos town was at the other side of the island, facing Priene and greedy Miletus. Ephesus too was quite near. Wiegand has excavated the temple. We climbed into the upper town, enchanting. Winding steep streets with white houses set corner wise and frothing over with tiny rose garlanded gardens. Carnations hanging from the hite balconies. We had sirop in a tiny café. Admirable views over the blue wonder of the bay and the steep coasts. Girls at their lacemaking, one ran after me and gave me a cluster of roses and carnations. All the inhabitants Greek, and the place quite Greek, not Turkish at all. So down and another attempt at the museum. The Commandant—we tried to get at him but the sentry "guessed he aint awake yet" and his conjecture was confirmed in equally good Yankee by the sentry opposite. They had returned from Wisconsin at the time of the war. We gave up the museum and walked to the extreme end of the town where we had sirop, baklawa and coffee in a tiny café. So back after buying loquats[?] in the market. As we steamed out of Samos the 2 mountain heads of the interior rose up over the little white town.

Tues 12. [12 May 1914]

Reached Smyrna early. Mr Sayer and I went on shore, drove round about and called on Edward Whittall. He said that things were very bad here. They have an infamous Vali, strong Committee man. Policy of intolerable pinpricks against the Greeks, seemingly in the hope that they will be forced to leave and the Turks step into their place as merchants. The Whittalls have tried taking Turkish clerks but have been obliged to abandon the attempt, they are so hopelessly stupid. The Vali and authorities are inciting the Mohammadan population against the Xians and Mr Whittall fears a massacre. The Vali is also most insolent to foreigners. A few days ago he told a British firm of fig buyers that he had issued orders that figs were not to be sold to them. This has been reported to the Consulate at C'ple. Terrible plague of locusts, things very black. Constant reports that the Greeks are going to make war with Turkey for the islands which the Turks won't give up. Mr W. says he does not see how they can give up Chios [Khios] and Mytelene [Mitilini] guarding the great port of Smyrna. They are strengthening the garrisons—200 officers passed through yesterday. The great talk about the Turkish navy and the buying of new Dreadnoughts make the Greeks feel they must hurry. My guide yesterday said they were bound to fight Turkey on the sea. They were not afraid of Bulgaria because Roumania stands behind her. The Captain of this ship took out Mark Kerr and his officers. He says he hears they are making little head way with the Greeks. The latter are so puffed up that it is impossible to teach them anything.

Wed. 13 [13 May 1914]

Passed through the Dardanelles [Canakkale Bogazi] at dawn.

Appendix B: Ibrahim's Daftar

[A.H.] 1250 [A.D. 1834] accession of Abdallah ibn al Rashid

1258 [1842] he put to death (dhabhat) the people of Qasim in Baqa

1261 [1845] he raided 'Anezah with horsemen

1263 [1846] he died

1271 [1854] raid on Jof murder of Khlaif hakim in Jof one of the [illegible] people

1272 [1855] (war) [Arabic characters] Shammar and Ruwalla raid one another

1276 [1859] murder of 'Abdallah ibn Salim Slaim brother of Zamir[?] and the people of 'Anazeh in al Wadi ["al Rummeh" written above] (Abd al Aziz ibn Abdallah is now Emir)

1279 [1862] slaughter of the people of Anezeh by the hand of 'Ubaid ibn al Rashid and Muhammad ibn Faisal ibn Saud

1284 [1867] Tallal ibn al Rashid died God have mercy on him

1285 [1868] Mit'ab ibn al R. died

1286 [1869] 'Ubaid ibn al R. died

1289 [1872] Bunder died

1291 [1874] Hamad and Ibn 'Abaid ibn R. hajjed

1300 [1882] M. ibn Rashid [Muhammad ibn Rashid, M. ibn R] raided 'Ataiba and took M. ibn Sa'ud and their taking of 'Arwa gulban water

1301 [1883] M ibn Rashid raided Abdallah ibn Sa'ud and 'Ataibah in the Hamadeh warad Qasim

1305 [1887] the children of Sa'ud attacked their uncle Abdallah ibn Faisal and M. al R. brought him out of al Riyad [Ar Riyad, Riyadh] [Arabic characters] he sent a private letter to M. al R. who came and raided Riyad and brought him to Hayyil where he stayed 2 years. Sent him back with gifts he reached[?] 'Ared al Imam and then died and M. al R. was ruler over all

1307 [1889] 'Abd al Rahman al Faisal attacked Salim al Sabhan and M. ibn R. brought him out of Riyad

1308 [1890] M ibn R raided and took from 'Abd al Rahman al Haraimla between Riyad and al Hauta [al-Hawtah] and Hariq [al-Hariq]

1309 [1891] M ibn R Allah have mercy on him and his coming to the Murrah in the sand south of Qasim

1310 [1892] M ibn R. God's mercy upon him raided and took Ibn Hamaid Shaikh of 'Ataiba first in Shabairek and second in al Rahawi, SE of Riyad

1311 [1893] M ibn R. God have mercy on him raided the Howaitat and the Beni Sakhr in the Tubaiq and his last raid was upon the 'Ataibah in his mountain[?]

1312 [1894] Raid of M ibn R and his taking from the 'Alman near Qwait

1315 [1897] M. ibn R did God have mercy on him (The first raid of Abd al Aziz God have mercy on him was upon the Hamanud[?] of 'Ataibah and the second on the Ruwalla.) (correction of following entry)

1316 [1898] Abd al Aziz Allah yerhamu raided first Akhidh ibn Shaqir and second he took the 'Anazeh in the Widyan

1317 [1899] Raid of A. al A Allah yerhamhu and first his taking of 'Ataibah and second of Wadi Sabi' [Arabic characters] [illegible] and third his coming against the Dawasir and fourth against the 'Ataibah [illegible] Sama of Wafat [Arabic characters]

1318 [1900] Raid of A al A Allah yerhamhu and first his coming against Sa'dun and the Dafir and his taking the mulaqat Sa'dun and Ibn Sabah and 'Abd al Rahman al Faisal in al Tarfiyyeh Qasim

1319 [1901] Abd al Aziz ibn Sa'ud's slaughter [Arabic characters]

1322 [1904] Appearance of soldiers with A al A ibn R God yerhamhu and kon al Bakairiyyeh this side of Rass

1324 [1906] death of A al A ibn R Allah yerhamha in Safar[1]

1324 [1906] slaughter of Mit'ab Allah yerhama and his brothers in Dhilqa'deh

1325 [1907] Sa'ud b. A. al A. ibn R Allah yusallimhu went to Mecca in the end of Dhilhajeh

1326 [1908] Sa'ud b. A. al A. ibn R Allah yusallimhu came to the throne (julus)

1327 [1909] Going of Sa'ud to A al A al Rashid against A al A ibn Sa'ud at Jabariyyeh E of Riyad in the spring

1328 [1910] Going of Sa'ud ibn R. against 'Anazeh and Ruwallah and his taking of them at Jamaima in Safar

1329 [1911] Raid of Sa'ud Allah yusallimhu first madajhu (road) Sa'dun and Dafir and afterwards his going against the Suqur Arabs of the Hadhdhal and second his going against the Ghadawirah 'Iraq and third his going against the Nawamseh and the slaughter of a ghazu, first of Sha'ban

1331 [1912] Raid of Sa'ud Allah yusallimhu and his victory over Dafir and the people of the Shatt the day he sought refuge on account of Sa'dun yefza' al 'Ajmi son of Sa'dun

1. In December 1906, Mi'tab, the ruler of Hayyil, was killed by three of his nephews. In 1908, his surviving brother, Saud ibn 'Abd al-Aziz al-Rashid, became *amir*. He was away during Bell's captivity at Hayyil (see Vassiliev 1998, 211).

1331 [1912] Saud Ibn A al A went against the Sherarat and secondly against 'Ataibah

1200 [1785] Thuwaini al Sa'dun goes against ([Arabic characters]) Boraidah [Buraydah]

1201 [1786] Hjailan goes against the Jebel

1212 [1797] Raid of al 'Adwah slaughter of Mutloq al A[illegible] Jeraba

1217 [1802] Raid of Sa'ud ibn Sa'ud on Fazbat ([Arabic characters]) al Husaini

1218 [1803] death of Abd al Aziz b. Muham. b. Sa'ud

1225 [1810] Sa'ud raided al Sham

1226 [1811] slaughter of al Klhaif

1228 [1813] slaughter of Sa'ud ibn Abd al Aziz

1231 [1815] expedition of Talman Pasha against Nejd

1233 [1817] Ibrahim Pasha

1234 [1818] beginning of the reign of Turki ibn 'Abdallah

1250 [1834] slaughter of the soldiers of Isma'il

1254 [1838] appearance [Arabic characters] of Khurshah Pasha

1259 [1843] " of Abdallah ibn Thinyan

1263 [1847] appearance of the Sheri Muhammad ibn 'Awn

1282 [1865] death of Faisal ibn Turki

1288 [1871] Saud ibn Faisal took his brother Muhammad and [unclear] [line of Arabic above]

1292 [1875] Sa'ud ibn Faisal died and 'Abdallah returned to Riyad

1328 [1910] Visit of the Sherif Husain Pasha to Nejd in Sha'ban

1329 [1911] the Sherif Husain set forth to the war against Yemen and the opposition [Arabic characters] of al Idrisi in Jamada

1329 [1911] al mukawinat [Arabic characters] which took place between Sa'dun and the Dufir [Arabic characters] Hamud ibn Darit [left unfinished]

    1 Turki ibn Sa'ud [died A.D. 1834][2]

    _____|_____

    2 Faisal [died 1837] 'Abd al-Rahman [died 1891] 3

    _____|_____ 'Abd al-Aziz 5 [Ibn Saud died 1953]

    4 Abdallah Muhammad Abdalaziz[illegible]

    Ghazalan[illegible]

2. It appears that Bell intended to chart a brief genealogy of the House of Saud but left it unfinished.

Glossary

abba: flowing robe

'abd (pl. *'abid*): slave

'abdah: slave woman

abu naum: "Mr. Sleepy" (literally, father of sleep)

(ya) agail: hurry up

'agal: rope

ahubb al bint: I love the girl

'ajin: dough

'ajist: I aged

ajnabi: foreigner

akhu: brother

al: the

aliq: dried grass

allaha akbar: God is greatest

allah yasa'idhu: God help him

'amenti: my aunt

ana: I

ana nashud or unshud billah: God be my witness

arabhanat: carts

'araq: arrack (a strong alcoholic drink)

asa'i: stick

ashab al nar: friends of the devil

'asr: afternoon prayer

attar: perfume

badhtha tayyib: she has good luck

baida': desert, wilderness

bait al rasul, sall allahu 'alaihi wa salam: house of Prophet, peace be upon him

bakhshish: tip, gratuity

battal ghazzus: quit raiding

bedu, bedawi: bedouin

beg: bey (Ottoman title)

beni adam: mankind

billah: by God

bint: girl

birkeh: pool

bismillah: in the name of God

buyut: homes

chowwish: staff sergeant

daftar: notebook

daif: guest

dallal: type of pot for making coffee

dhabanaha: we slew it

dira, dirah (pl. *dir*): bedouin land, homeland, region

dulul: female riding camel

(ya) dunya: (oh) world

egh billah sahih—wa'l shof ma shufna: yes, by God, it is true—and we did not even set eyes on it

egh wallah: yes, really

faitunat: carriages

faris: rider

farsheh: bedding

felalih: cultivation

fellah (pl. *fellahin*): farmer, peasant

fitr: mushrooms

fizz u alaina: jump at us

ga'r, ga'rah: pit, cavity

ghadir: stream

ghashimeh taht ammha: innocent like an infant

ghazzai: raider

ghazzu: raid, attack

gom, gomani: people, folk (used here to mean enemy)

guffa: round boat

hajj: pilgrimage

(ya) hajjaj yusikum bi khair: Hajjaj, we bid you a good evening

(al) hamdalillah, hamdu lillah: thanks to God

haram: women

haram: it is forbidden

(ya) hatha al stamboul: give me Istanbul

hawa: at a breath

hosh: small open court

hukm allah: (such is) the command of God

ibn al halal: good fellow

injil: the New Testament

inshallah: God willing

ishtaghalthu be idi: I made it with my hand

jariyyah: slave girl

jedid: fresh, new

jehannum: Hell

jellad: leather merchant; executioner

jerab: scabies

jidd: grandfather, ancestor

jiss: gypsum

jiss: square capitals

jof: cavity, depression

kahwah: café, coffeehouse

kahwaji: coffee seller

kayyift: was delighted

keffiyeh: headdress

kelbeh: dog, bitch

kelek: raft of inflated skins

kesb: attack

khabra: bedouin dwelling

khaffa: headdress

khair: (with) goodness, happiness

khala, khall: empty

khalawi: in emptiness

khan: inn

kharban: ruined (adj.)

kharrabat: I ruined

khatt: handwriting

khurj: saddlebag

khurz: saddle

khush fikr: a sweet thought

kull hu tayyib: it is all good

kulshi ala kaifna: everything is as we wish

kumbaj: men's long garment

laban, leben: yogurt

la billah: no, by God

la hayyatak wa hayyat allah: not on your life or the life of God

la tifkikeri: do not be anxious

ma'al wad: to the valley

madafi: hostel, inn

madfun: buried

ma istahait al rigil: I did not desire (literally, have an appetite for) men

ma'rafah: knowledge

masalla: place for prayer

mej.: Mecidiye, an Ottoman silver coin worth twenty piasters

menzil: stopping place, campsite

meskin: miserable fellow

mihrab: prayer niche

miri: fee for using state land

modif, mudif: host

mu'allim: teacher

Mughrebi: North African

munaqqash: engraved

naga: female camel

naqib: head of the descendants of the Prophet

nar: fire, Hell

naranj: bitter orange

narghileh: water pipe, hookah

nasallim 'aly al khteyyal: (we want) to greet the old man

nasib: fate

nowwakh: make (a camel) kneel

nuqtah: post, point

(al) 'odab [odah] ghali: the cabin is expensive

qabb hu nadif: he is clean

qaimmaqam: district governor

qasr: palace

qatifa: velvet, plush

qirbeh: water skin

quran: Koran

qurun: horns

rafiq: guide; companion (used here for safe crossing)

rahalin: traveling

rais al tujar: chief of the merchants

ra'iyyeh: flock, herd

rajajil: men

rajl: man

rebaba: stringed instrument like the fiddle

rijm: mound

roshan: hall

sabkha: salt marsh, salt swamp

sadaqt? . . . sadaqt: Do you believe (me)? . . . I believe (you)

sagh: entire, full

sahih?: is it true?

saj: round brass plate

samneh, semneh, semen: clarified butter

sawah: inn

sayyid: chief, lord, title of descendant of Muhammad

sennet al thalj: the year of snow

sept (sibt): branch of a tribe

shaikha, shikha (pl. *shaikhat*): old women

shaikh al dowleh: government sheikh

shajar: trees

shayyatin al 'arab: they are devils, the Arabs

shedad: riding saddle (of a camel)

shih: a variety of wormwood

shuft al mant [maut] wa battalt: I saw death and I quit

subhan allah: praise be to God

suffa: molding, ledge

sug: market

suq: ride on

suwani: metal serving plates

t'ab: fatigue

(ya) tabb [rabb]: (oh) Lord

tawakkil allah: trust in God

tell: hill

tramvai: tramway

tu's, tu'us: sand dunes

'ud: wood, stick

ulema: religious leadership

wadi: valley; dried river bed

wa kasarna yaum: and we have broken a day

wakil: deputy, representative

(ya) walad: fellow, boy

walad 'adil: a just boy

wallah, wallahi: really, by God

wa'r: rock debris; rugged terrain

wasm: tribal mark; tribal band

wazir: deputy, minister

ya: oh

yarif kullesh: he knows everything

yuth bahuna: they will slay us

yuzbashi: captain

zain: nice, pretty

zaqat: alms tax

zelameh: manservant

zol: shadow, shade

Works Cited

PRIMARY SOURCES

Bell, Gertrude Lowthian. 1911. *Amurath to Amurath.* London: William Heinemann.

———. 1913–1914. *Arabian Diaries.* Gertrude Bell Archive. Robinson Library. University of Newcastle upon Tyne.

———. 1914a. "A Journey in Northern Arabia." *Geographical Journal* 44: 76–77.

———. 1914b. *The Palace and Mosque at Ukhaidir.* Oxford: Clarendon Press.

———. 1928a. *Persian Pictures.* Preface by Sir E. Denison Ross. 1894. Reprint. London: Ernest Benn.

———. 1928b. *Poems from the Divan of Hafiz.* Preface by E. Denison Ross. 1897. Reprint. London: William Heinemann.

———. 1985. *The Desert and the Sown.* 1907. Reprint. London: Virago.

Bell, Lady, ed. 1926. "Private Memoir of Hugo Bell." Special Collections. Robinson Library. University of Newcastle upon Tyne.

———. 1927. *The Letters of Gertrude Bell.* New York: Boni and Liveright.

Correspondence of Gertrude Bell and Charles Doughty-Wylie. Gertrude Bell Archive. Robinson Library. University of Newcastle upon Tyne.

OFFICIAL DOCUMENTS

Government of India Archives. Baghdad High Commission Files. 1921–1926. 19/1 vol. 1. New Delhi.

Public Records Office. Foreign Office. 1916–1917. Political. Baghdad. 882.23. *Arab Bureau.* Her Majesty's Stationery Office. London. Firestone Library. Princeton University. Princeton, N.J. Microfilm no. 06335.

———. L/P&S 10/576, File 4744/1915. Her Majesty's Stationery Office. London.

———. War Department. Secret Series. S.P./16. Vols. 15–17. Her Majesty's Stationery Office. London. Firestone Library. Princeton University. Princeton, N.J. Microfilm extracts from the *Arab Bulletin.*

GENERAL WORKS

Alloula, Malek. 1986. *The Colonial Harem.* Translated by Myrna Godzich and Wlad Godzich. Minneapolis: Univ. of Minnesota Press.

Batatu, Hanna. 1978. *The Old Social Classes and the Revolutionary Movements in Iraq.* Princeton: Princeton Univ. Press.

Blunt, Lady Anne. 1881. *Pilgrimage to Nejd: The Cradle of the Arab Race.* 2 vols. London: John Murray.

Bowersock, G. W. 1983. *Roman Arabia.* Cambridge: Harvard Univ. Press.

Brent, Peter. 1978. *Far Arabia: Explorers of the Myth.* 1977. Reprint. London: Newton Abbot.

Brooks, David. 1995. *The Age of Upheaval: Edwardian Politics, 1898–1914.* Manchester: Manchester Univ. Press.

Burgoyne, Elizabeth. 1958. *Gertrude Bell: From Her Personal Papers, 1889–1914.* 2 vols. London: Ernest Benn.

Cornwallis, Kinahan. *The Arab War.* 1940. Reprint. London: Golden Cockrill Press.

Deardon, Seaton. 1969–1970. "The Doughty-Wylie Letters." *Cornhill Magazine* no. 1062.

Doughty, Charles. 1979. *Travels in Arabia Deserta.* Vol. 1. 1888. Reprint. New York: Dover.

Earle, Edward M. 1923. *The Great Powers and the Baghdad Railway: A Study in Imperialism.* New York: Macmillan.

Facey, William, with William Grant. 1996. *Saudi Arabia: By the First Photographers.* London: Stacey International.

Garnett, David, ed. 1949. *The Letters of T. E. Lawrence.* New York: Doubleday.

Godfrey, Jonathan. 1998. *Gertrude Bell, Photographer: A Preliminary Report into Her Cameras and Methods.* Newcastle: Univ. of Newcastle upon Tyne.

Goodman, Susan. 1985. *Gertrude Bell.* Leamington Spa, England: Berg.

Grant [Harris], Christina Phelps. 1937. *The Syrian Desert: Caravans, Travel and Exploration.* London: A. & C. Black.

Halsband, Robert, ed. 1970. *The Selected Letters of Lady Mary Wortley Montagu.* New York: St. Martin's Press.

Hogarth, David. 1927. "Gertrude Bell's Journey to Hayil." *Geographical Journal* 70, no. 1: 1–27.

Hourani, Albert. 1991. *A History of the Arab Peoples.* Cambridge: Harvard Univ. Press.

Jabbur, Jabrail. 1995. *The Bedouins of the Desert: Aspects of Nomadic Life in the Arab East.* Translated by Lawrence I. Conrad. Albany: State Univ. of New York Press.

Kinross, Lord. 1979. *The Ottoman Centuries: The Rise and Fall of the Turkish Empire.* New York: Morrow-Quill.

Mabro, Judy. 1996. *Veiled Half-Truths: Western Travelers' Perceptions of Middle Eastern Women.* London: I. B. Tauris.

Mack, John E. 1976. *A Prince of Our Disorder: The Life of T. E. Lawrence.* Boston: Little, Brown.

Marchand, Susan. 1996. *Down from Olympus: Archaeology and Philhellenism in Germany, 1750–1970*. Princeton: Princeton Univ. Press.

Melman, Billie. 1995. *Women's Orients: English Women and the Middle East, 1718–1918*. Ann Arbor: Univ. of Michigan Press.

Morris, A. S. A. 1977. *C. P. Trevelyan, 1870–1958*. London: Blackstaff Press.

Murray, Janet. 1982. *Strong-Minded Women and Other Lost Voices from Nineteenth-Century England*. New York: Pantheon.

Philby, Harry St. John Bridger. 1948. *Arabian Days*. London: Robert Hale.

Rihani, Ameen. 1930. *Around the Coasts of Arabia*. London: William Heinemann.

Said, Edward W. 1978. *Orientalism*. New York: Pantheon.

Shikara, Ahmad. 1987. *Iraqi Politics, 1921–1941*. London: LAAM.

Sluglett, Peter. 1976. *Britain in Iraq, 1914–1932*. London: Ithaca Press.

Snelling, Stephen. 1999. *Gallipoli*. London: Sutton.

Stubbs, William. 1903. *The Constitutional History of England in Its Origin and Development*. 6th ed. Vol. 1. Oxford: Clarendon Press.

Vassiliev, Alexei. 1998. *The History of Saudi Arabia*. London: Saqi Books.

Waldron, Ann. 1989. "Travels in Syria: Scenes from a Nineteenth-Century Archaeologist's Diary." *Princeton Alumni Weekly* 89, no. 15 (5 Apr.): 15–20.

Wallach, Janet. 1996. *Desert Queen: The Extraordinary Life of Gertrude Bell*. New York: Doubleday.

Ward, Phillip. 1983. *Ha'il: Oasis City of Saudi Arabia*. London: Oleander Press.

Westenfeld, H. Ferdenand. 1859. *Vergleichungs Tabellin der Muhammedanischen und Christlichen Zeitrechtnung*. Leipzig.

Westrate, Bruce. 1992. *The Arab Bureau: British Policy in the Middle East, 1916–1920*. University Park: Pennsylvania State Univ. Press.

Wilson, Jeremy. 1989. *Lawrence of Arabia*. London: William Heinemann.

Winder, R. Bayly. 1980. *Saudi Arabia in the Nineteenth Century*. New York: Farrar, Straus, and Giroux.

Winstone, H. V. F. 1978a. *Captain Shakespear: A Portrait*. London: Quartet Books.

———. 1978b. *Gertrude Bell*. London: Jonathan Cape.

Yapp, M. E. 1987. *The Making of the Modern Middle East, 1792–1923*. Essex: Addison, Wesley, Longman.

Index

Gertrude Bell: The Arabian Diaries, 1913–1914 was designed and composed in 10.75/16 Monotype Dante by Kachergis Book Design of Pittsboro, North Carolina; printed by offset on 80-pound Mohawk Vellum and Smyth-sewn and bound over binder boards in ICG Cialux cloth by Sheridan Books of Ann Arbor, Michigan; published by Syracuse University Press, Syracuse, New York 13244-5160.